The Best
FREE
THINGS
for
SENIORS

by Linda & Bob Kalian

Library of Congress Cataloging-in-Publication Data
Kalian, Robert
Kalian, Linda

The Best Free Things For Seniors

ISBN 0-934968-13-6

1. Consumer Reference   2. Catalog Free Things

This book is intended as general consumer information only and does not contain professional advice. The reader is urged to seek out and consult with a lawyer, financial advisor, health care and other professionals.

Quantity discounts are available. Teachers, fund raisers, premium users, write to us at the address below regarding the quantities needed.

Publisher: Roblin Press, 405 Tarrytown Road Suite 414,White Plains, NY 10607
(914) 347-6671   Fax: (914) 592-1167
Be sure to visit our Web site at: www.freethingsusa.com

Contents

3

A Few Words Before You Start

When 77 year old astronaut John Glenn made his historic return to space it proved once and for all what Satchel Paige said years ago: *"Age is a question of mind over matter...if you don't mind, it doesn't matter."*

This book is dedicated to the concept that your journey through life can be a ball at any age and especially during your senior years if you maintain a positive attitude and keep your mind and body active, healthy and involved.

We've discovered that no matter what your age, no matter what your financial situation, there are all kinds of special government and private programs to help you enjoy all the best life has to offer. And once you become a senior, it gets better...*much better!* It's true...the best is yet to come!

But to take advantage of all the terrific benefits, you must first know about them. That's why we researched and wrote this book. In it you are about to discover that you are floating in an ocean of free things, exciting programs and amazing discounts that you never knew existed. Simply keep your eyes and ears open and follow these few tips:

1. Use this book as your first and most valuable resource. It is chuck full of great stuff of every kind. Some are in this book to save you money, others will solve problems or bring you benefits. But there are also a ton of fascinating freebies that are here mostly for fun.

2. Always ask one simple question... *"do you offer senior citizen discounts?"* You'll be amazed at how often just by saying those 6 words you will save 10%, sometimes

a lot more, on whatever you are buying. But you must ask.

3. If you're not a member already, join AARP. It's called the American Association For Retired Persons but it is open to anyone 50 years of age or older, retired or not. By joining you will immediately qualify for special discounts on everything from prescription drugs to car rentals and hotel reservations. The cost? Just $8.00 a year and that even includes your spouse! For that small amount you will be joining the over 32 million members who get all the special membership benefits including a subscription to their magazine, *Modern Maturity*. To join or to get more information, call them toll-free at: **1-800-424-3410**.

4. Keep it simple. No need to write if you can pick up the phone and call. We've included the phone numbers (many are toll-free) throughout the book along with web sites wherever they're available.

5. If you have a computer, make life even simpler by 'surfing the net'. The number is growing daily but today an estimated 50% of seniors have a computer. But if you don't yet have one, visit your local library which is almost certain to have computers you can use. You'll be amazed at how easy it is to use and just how much valuable information you can get off of the Internet in no time.

6. Near the back of the book (in the sections with shaded page edges) we've included a number of important directories you'll find useful in getting answers, solving problems and getting benefits that are coming to you.

So if you need legal help, or dental care or if you have a consumer complaint, or need medications you can't afford, keep in mind that help is often just a phone call away. And if you need assistance and aren't sure exactly who to call for help, start by checking the directory and calling your local *"Office of The Aging"*. It is a great resource for an instant referral to the right agency or department.

7. If a listing calls for a 'SASE' that means that when you write in for your free item, include a long (#10) Self-Addressed Stamped Envelope that you've written your return address on.

8. While we've done our best to put together the most complete and up-to-date information possible, once the book is in print addresses and phone numbers can and will change. Offers may be withdrawn (although in our experience the offers are generally replaced with a new and often even better one. But if you do come across a change or deletion that should be made in the next edition, we would genuinely appreciate it if you would let us know by writing:

Revisions Editor
Roblin Press
P.O. Box 125
Hartsdale, NY 10530

9. Hope you enjoy the book. If you can think of anything that would make the next edition of the book better for you, please let us know at the address above. We'd love to hear from you. Thank you.

10. Remember, you worked your tail off all your life. Now it's your turn to enjoy all the very best your golden years have in store for you.

An Ocean Of Free Things

Help For Seniors Is Just A Phone Call Away

Imagine how great it would be to be able to pick up the phone and get dozens of services delivered right to your front door! Well guess what? You really can. It's called *Eldercare Locator* and calling this one toll-free phone number will connect you to a wide range of services for seniors no matter where you live in the U.S. These services include Meals-On-Wheels (for home delivered meals), legal assistance, help with housing problems, recreation, adult daycare, home health care services, nursing home ombudsman (to help you get the treatment you deserve) and a whole lot more. Calling this one number allows you to tap into a nationwide network of organizations for seniors in all areas of the country.

Getting the right help at the right time is worth a fortune but it costs you nothing. If you are calling for someone else, just be sure to have the name, address and zip code of the person needing assistance plus a description of the type of service they need. Contact:

ELDERCARE LOCATOR
NATIONAL ASSOCIATION OF AREA
AGENCIES ON AGING
1112 16TH ST., NW
WASHINGTON, DC 20036
Call between 9 am and 5 pm Monday through Friday:
1-800-677-1116

Free For The Asking Right In Your Back Yard

In your search for the best that life has to offer for free or practically free, the first thing to remember is that there are lots of things all around you that are free for the asking that you might never have thought of. All you have to do is be aware of them and to ASK. Here are just a few examples:

Free Long Distance Phone Calls

Because of all the intense competition between phone companies, if you are willing to switch companies they will offer you all kinds of deals from $100.00 checks to several hours of free calls with no obligation to stay with them after you have used up your free long distance calls.

5¢ A Minute On All Long Distance Calls

After you've used your free calls, shop around for the best deal before you sign up with another phone company. Companies like IDT now offer long distance service for as little as 5¢ a minute, 24 hours a day, 7 days a week. Companies like IDT are called 'resellers' since they buy time from long distance companies and resell this time to you at low prices. For more information on their 5¢ a minute plan call IDT at: **1-800-CALL-IDT (THAT'S 1-800-225-5438)**

Free For Using Your Credit Card

The credit card war is heating up...and you stand to benefit. Today more and more banks and companies are offering credit cards that come with added bonuses for using them. For example, some banks offer credit cards that give you one frequent flyer mile for each dollar you charge on their card. You can use the miles to get free airline tickets.

Also, many larger chain stores offer you free dollars to spend in their store just for opening a charge account with them. There is no obligation to use the card once you have it and you can cut it up if you don't plan to use it.

Also, remember you really can negotiate with your credit card company to lower the interest they charge and to waive the annual fee. Just be careful of the 'low introductory rate' offered by many banks. They may offer a finance charge of 4.9% for the first 6 months but then the rate could jump up to 15% to 20%. Don't be fooled by the introductory rate. If you shop around you will find rates of 10% or less year round (not just for a limited time.)

Free Haircuts

Did you know that free haircuts are available through many of your local beauty and barber schools? Check your phone book and give them a call. Some may ask a small fee or a tip for the trainee. Some of your larger hair designers may offer free style and cuts certain months or certain times of the year. Call your favorite salon and find out when they are training their students. You benefit by getting the designer him/herself for free. (In their salon they may charge anywhere from $50.00 and up.) Companies like Clairol often offer free hair coloring styling when they are testing new products. Don't hesitate to give any of them a call. Remember, if you don't ask you'll never know.

Want to try free perfume or have a makeover? Try any one of your larger department stores. You are never obligated to buy and some of the companies will even give you free product samples. You could have a ball going from store to store. Next time you need a new look, try your local department store.

Free For Consumers

Supermarket bulletin boards offer free items that neighbors may want to get rid of or trade.

Credit card companies offer free month trials on discount shopping clubs, travel, insurance and offer all kinds of specials. The one thing you have to remember is if you don't want it, after the month is up, cancel it.

You can even get free magazine subscriptions, tapes and CD's just for asking. Always remember to look in your local paper for deals at the supermarkets for *"buy one item, get one free."* On nonperishable items that you will use (like paper towels, soft drinks, canned soups, etc.), stock up when they are on sale.

'Grand' Magnet For 'Grand'parents

"My Grandchild Did This" refrigerator magnet is a perfect addition to include when sending along a child's art work to a grandparent. This will really show off those delightful creations of your grandchildren. Send $1.00 with a long SASE with 2 stamps to:

PRACTICAL PARENTING
DEPT MG BEST
15245 MINNETONKA BLVD.
MINNETONKA, MN 55343

Free Top Soil and Fire Wood

When they excavate a building site, contractors frequently have a problem of what to do with the dirt they remove. Often they will offer free land fill and free top soil to anyone who wants it. The only catch might be that you have to remove it (or pay a nominal delivery charge.) If you have a piece of property that needs top soil or landfill, check out construction sites. Also, you can often get free fire wood when they are clearing the land.

Free Birthday Dinner

Don't forget that there are quite a few restaurants that offer you a free dinner on your birthday. All you have to show is a license or some proof of your birthdate. Check with your favorite restaurants to see if they offer this courtesy.

Also check the ads for local restaurants that offer those great coupons for buy-one dinner get-one free.

Enjoy A Free Concert

Don't overlook all the free concerts and theatre productions in all community parks outdoors especially during the summer months. Check with your local parks and recreation department or your local newspaper.

Many local movie theatres have deals on slow nights. For example, a local movie theatre offers a special on Tuesday nights: Buy one ticket, get one free. Check it out.

If you like concerts and drama some theatre and opera companies offer volunteer ushers free tickets in exchange for their work.

These are just a small handful of the tons of free and practically free offers all around you all the time. The important thing is to keep an eye out for them and take advantage of them where they are of interest to you.

Keeping Your Breath Fresh

Did you know that eating parsley keeps your breath fresh? Well instead of going around with a spray of parsley hanging from your mouth, you can have the next best thing,

BreathAsure™. BreathAsure™ is sunflower oil and parsley seed oil in a soft gelatin shell. BreathAsure™ is the all natural "Internal Breath Freshener®," send a self-addressed stamped envelope to:
BREATHASURE
FREE SAMPLE
26115 MUREAU ROAD
CALABASS, CA 91302-3126

'Seniors Today'

If you are a senior and would like a free issue of *Seniors Today* magazine, chuck full of helpful information and articles of special information just for seniors, just call:
1-800-557-7204

Life Advice

Met Life has a series of educational brochures called *Life Advice*. There are more than 70 topics from doing your taxes, to starting a business or planning for retirement. They all offer you valuable advice. For a specific brochure or for a listing of all of the topics available, call them at:
1-800-638-5433
Or visit their web site:
http://www.lifeadvice.com.

Trace Your Family Tree

Many diseases run in families. One of the first things a doctor might ask you is for a family tree to see if you may have a predisposition for a particular disease. If you are interested in tracing your family history, the first place to start might be asking your relatives. Next, your local library often has a family history center where you can track your lineage. The family history library of the Church of Latter-day Saints has the largest collection of genealogical records

in the world. For the free booklet, *Discovering Your Family Tree,* write to:
FAMILY HISTORY LIBRARY
35 NORTHWEST TEMPLE ST.
SALT LAKE CITY, UT 84150
Another resource for genealogical research is the National Genealogical Society. You can call them toll-free at:
1-800-346-6044

Free Miracle Polishing Cloth

If you are looking for a business you can start or a product you can sell, be sure to check out the *Miracle Polishing Cloth.* It cleans and polishes any surface, metal, wood, glass, tile and restores jewelry and silverware... virtually anything. For a free sample ($3.98 value) plus information on how to make money selling this miracle cloth, just write to:
R & S INDUSTRIES CORP.
8255-SB BRENTWOOD IND. DR.
ST. LOUIS, MO 63144-2814

Consumer Complaints

We've all had this happen to us. You buy a product that turns out to be of inferior quality. When you return it to the store, they refuse to give you a refund or exchange. You leave in frustration and wonder what to do about this problem. Next time you have a serious complaint about a product or service you purchased and aren't sure where to write or who to complain to, get this free brochure and learn more about complaining effectively. For a free copy of *How to Resolve Your Consumer Complaint*, send a long SASE to:
COMPLAINT RESOLUTION
CONSUMER FEDERATION OF AMERICA
1424 16TH ST. N.W.
WASHINGTON, DC 20036

Help For Consumers

For more help in resolving your complaint be sure to get a copy of *The Consumer's Resource Handbook*. It includes a directory of government, nonprofit and corporate consumer complaint assistance sources you can contact. This is something no one should be without. For a free copy, write to:

CONSUMER RESOURCE HANDBOOK
CONSUMER INFORMATION CENTER
PUEBLO, CO 91009

Don't forget that you can also check the *Directory of Consumer Protection Agencies* at the back of this book. In it you will find the phone numbers of your local consumer protection agency. Call the office closest to you and explain your complaint to them.

Consumer Action

If you ever wanted to complain to a company about one of their products but didn't know how to go about it, this is for you. *How To Talk To A Company And Get Action* should help you get your problem solved—fast. You'll also receive the *Story of Coca Cola*. Write to:

CONSUMER INFORMATION CENTER
COCA-COLA CO.
DEPT. FR, P.O. DRAWER 1734
ATLANTA, GA 30301

Consumer Complaint Tip...
Go Right To The Top

Whenever you have a complaint with a larger company, get their phone number and call them directly. If the person you speak to tries to give you the brush off, ask to speak to their supervisor and if you still don't get satisfaction, ask to speak to the supervisor's supervisor all the way up to the top. If none of that works, ask for the name and mailing address of the president of the company, and write him/her a polite letter explaining your complaint in detail. You'll be amazed. Nine times out of ten the president will hand the matter over to someone who will contact you with an offer to resolve the complaint to your satisfaction. Try it...it works!

Book Bargains

Catalog of Book Bargains is for all book lovers that want to save 90% or more off original prices. Some recent best sellers are sold in this 50 page catalog at very sharp discounts. The catalog is free from:
P. DAEDALUS BOOKS INC.
BOX 9132
HYATTSVILLE, MD. 20781
OR CALL: 1-800-395-2665

Get Rich At Home

Have you ever dreamed of starting your own business from your home? If so you will want to get the *Mail Order Success Secrets report*. Learn how to start your own successful business in your spare time with little money and grow rich in the most exciting business in the world. Send a SASE to:
ROBLIN-BSR
405 TARRYTOWN RD. SUITE 414
WHITE PLAINS, NY 10607

"The Good Life Catalog"

If you're a cigar smoker or know someone who is, this catalog is a must. Not only will you find every cigar you can think of, but all the accessories that go with them. There is a *Cigar Hall of Fame* and even some unusual and interesting gifts for people who don't smoke. Drop a postcard to:
THE THOMPSON COMPANY
5401 HANGAR COURT
P.O. BOX 30303
TAMPA, FL 33630-3303

Surprise Gift Club

We've all faced the problem of what to give someone as a gift. Finally there's help. The Surprise Gift of the Month Club has developed an innovative solution. They offer you a broad selection of items from kites, iron-ons, coasters, stickers, and records to crewel and needlepoint kits plus many more items to select from. Anyone young or old will be delighted to receive a surprise gift each month. It's a beautiful way to say "I'm thinking of you" to someone special. For a sample of the assorted crewel and needlepoint kits, send $1.00 for postage and handling to:

SURPRISE GIFT OF THE MONTH CLUB
55 RAILROAD AVE.
GARNERVILLE, NY 10923

Go On A Learning Vacation With Elderhostel

Elderhostel offers moderately priced learning vacations across the United States and Canada as well as 70 nations abroad for senior citizens who enjoy adventure and travel but who have a limited amount of money to spend. The subjects taught on these vacations range from astronomy, to zoology. For a catalog of courses and travel itineraries, or to be added to their mailing list, contact:

ELDERHOSTEL
75 FEDERAL ST., THIRD FLOOR
BOSTON, MA. 02110-1941
OR CALL TOLL-FREE: 1-877-426-8056

House Of Onyx

If you like gems and gemstones...whether in the rough or finished into fine jewelry or artifacts, this catalog is for you. You will find some fabulous closeout buys on some fantastic gemstones, geodes even Mexican onyx and malachite carvings. If you are just a collector or need some great gifts, send

for this catalog. Write to:
HOUSE OF ONYX
THE AARON BUILDING
120 MAIN ST.
GREENVILLE, KY 42345

What To Look For In A Gem

Buying a valuable gem can be a tricky affair unless you are prepared. Have you ever wondered what makes one diamond more valuable than another that may look the same to the naked eye? Before buying any gemstone it is essential to learn exactly what to look for. For example do you know the 4 'C's' that determine a diamond's value? They are... Cut...

Color... Clarity... Carat (weight). To learn more about what to look for when buying a diamond, send for a free consumer kit from the American Gem Society. Send a postcard to: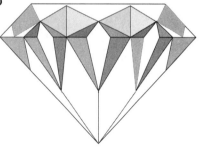
THE AMERICAN GEM SOCIETY
8881 W. SAHARA AVE.
LAS VEGAS, NV 89117

Sleep Tight

A healthful good night's sleep makes for a very productive, pleasant person. Learn all the facts on how to get a healthful sleep, by selecting the right bedding pillows and positions. The makers of Simmons will send you this free book, *Consumer Guide To Better Sleep,* plus several others including *It's Never Too Early To Start Caring For Your Back* and tips for shopping for the right bed. To get your copy, send a business-sized SASE to:
SIMMONS BEAUTYREST
ONE CONCOURSE CENTER, SUITE 600
BOX C-93
ATLANTA, GA 30328

Tips On Buying A Home

Are you considering buying a house? This 160 page book from Lawyers Title Insurance Corp. is a must for you. It will help answer all those questions you have about owning your own home. Ask for *The Process of Home Buying.* Send 75¢ postage & handling to:

LAWYERS TITLE INSURANCE CORP.
DEPT. CW
6630 WEST BROAD ST.
BOX 27567
RICHMOND, VA 23230

Planning To Buy A Home?

If you are thinking of buying a home any time in the near future, there are certain things you should do to protect yourself. For example, before buying a home, it is a good idea to hire a trained inspector to check for defects you might not see such as termites or a roof in need of repair. But first be sure to get a free copy of *Top Ten Home Inspection and Buying Tips* from the American Homeowners Foundation. Call them toll-free at: **800-489-7776.**

Money Saving Tips

The publishers of *Quick, Easy, Cheap and Simple* newsletter would like to send a sample issue. It's loaded with information in the form of a newsletter with handy, easy-to-understand tips, on the all important topics of saving both time and money. You'll also find an assortment of quick and easy recipe ideas. For your free newsletter, mail a SASE to:

QUICK, EASY, CHEAP AND SIMPLE
4057 N. DRAKE-RP5
CHICAGO, IL 60618-2219

Love Letter Newsletter

Love guru, Greg Godek, author of the bestselling book, *1001 Ways To Be More Romantic*, would like to give you a free one year subscription to *LoveLetter Newsletter*, chuck full of great romantic ideas. Put the spark back in your love life. Call Casablanca Press at:

1-800-727-8866

Also, if you would like a romantic idea *"Tip Sheet"* with more love hints from Celebrate Romance, call: **1-800-368-7978**

Before You Buy A Wig

For the best prices on the finest wigs, send for your *free catalog*. You will be amazed at the beautiful selection of wigs from Revlon, Adolfo and many more. So if you are in the market for a wig, write to:

BEAUTY TREND
PO Box 9323, DEPT. 44002
HIALEAH, **FL 33014.**

Easy Reading

This freebie is for adults whose reading levels is grade 4 to 6, and is a great way to help improve their reading skills. Each issue contains articles covering important international news as well as features on education, health, leisure, law, and more in a format that is easy to read and understand. To get a free sample, ask for a sample copy of *News For You*. Write to:

NEW READERS PRESS
DEPT. 100, PO Box 888
SYRACUSE, **NY 13210**

Keeping Your Home Healthy

To help make housework easier and less time consuming, Bounty has developed their new Rinse & Reuse paper towel

that keeps its strength when wet allowing you to reuse the towel. You'll receive a sample plus the booklet, *The New Rules of Cleaning* with cleaning tips. Just call:
1-888-4-NEW-RULES

Shop Easy

Do you like to relax and shop at home? If so, be sure to get a copy of Lillian Vernon's *free catalog.* You'll find that it's full of affordable treasures from around the world. Drop a post-card to:
LILLIAN VERNON
VIRGINIA BEACH, VA 23479

Classic Gifts

Harriet Carter has provided distinctive gifts since 1958. This fun-filled catalog is chuck-full of unique gifts you will find fascinating. Write to:
HARRIET CARTER
DEPT. 14
NORTH WALES, PA 19455

Get That Bug

The makers of Raid bug sprays would like you to have a highly informative chart, *Raid Insecticides - What to Use For Effective Control.* Learn how to deal with crawling, fly-ing and biting pests both inside and outside your home (in-cluding plant pests). You'll also receive a money-saving cou-pon. Send a postcard to:
"INSECT CONTROL"
JOHNSON WAX
RACINE, WI 53403

Free Art Films

To help bring art appreciation to a wider audience, The National Gallery of Art would like to send you a video without charge. They have dozens of videos and slide programs to lend to individuals, community groups and schools. Your only obligation is to pay the postage when sending the video back. For a complete *catalog and reservation card* send a card to:

NATIONAL GALLERY OF ART
EXTENSION PROGRAM
WASHINGTON, DC 20565

Free Tickets To TV Shows

The TV networks will provide you with free tickets to any of their shows that have audiences. If you plan to be in Los Angeles or New York and would like to see a TV show write to the network (care of their 'Ticket De-  partment') before your visit. Generally you will get a letter you can exchange for tickets for any show open at the time of your visit. Write to:

ABC
7 WEST 66TH ST.
NEW YORK, NY 10023
or in California the address is:
4151 PROSPECT AVE.
HOLLYWOOD, CA 90027

NBC
30 ROCKEFELLER PLAZA
NEW YORK, NY 10020

In California the address is:
3000 W. Almeda Ave.
Burbank, CA 91523

CBS
524 W. 57th St.
New York, NY 10019
In California the address is:
7800 Beverly Boulevard
Los Angeles, CA 90036-2188

Oprah
PO Box 909715
Chicago, IL 60690
Or call: (312)591-9222

The New Maury Show
15 Penn Plaza
Grand Ballroom
New York, NY 10001
212-244-7545

Ships And The Sea

This 100 page *catalog is* full of decorative nautical ideas for the home. If you're looking for a ship model, marine painting or ship's wheel you'll find it here. Drop a postcard to:
Preston's
174-A Main St. Wharf
Greenport, NY 11944

Free For Chapped Lip Sufferers

If you suffer from dry chapped lips or mouth sores, this is especially for you. You will receive sample packets of *Blistex Lip Ointment* plus two informative brochures and a *money-off* coupon too. Send a long SASE to:
Blistex Sample Offer
1800 Swift Dr.
Oak Brook, IL 60521

For The Larger-Sized Or Taller Woman

Lane Bryant offers a stunning collection of dresses, coats, jeans, sportswear, lingerie and shoes for the woman who wears half size or large size apparel. You'll find name brands and designer fashions in their free *catalog*. If you are 5'7" or taller also ask for their *Tall Collection catalog*. Write:

LANE BRYANT
DEPT. A
INDIANAPOLIS, IN 46201

Are You Milk Sensitive?

If you are allergic to milk you will want to get a copy of 'Ross's Educational Materials Catalog' designed specifically for those with a lactose intolerance. Write to:

EDUCATIONAL SERVICES
ROSS LABORATORIES
COLUMBUS, OH 43216

Your Own Flag Flying Over The U.S. Capitol

Your Congressman will provide a unique service for you free of charge. If you'd like to have your own flag flown over the U.S. Capitol Building write to your congressman. The flag itself is not free (prices range from $8.00 to $17.00 depending upon size and material) but the service of having the flag purchased, flown and sent to you is free. This also makes a unique gift for someone special. Write to your own Congressman,

CONGRESS OF THE UNITED STATES
WASHINGTON, DC 20515

Grow Your Own Moneytree

Wouldn't it be great to have your very own moneytree grow-

ing in a corner of your kitchen? American companies give away billions of dollars of gifts, cash, sweepstakes and freebies every year. The editors of *MoneyTree Digest* show you how to get your share of the Great American Giveaway. To get a free issue of this terrific magazine, send $1.00 postage & handling to:
MoneyTree Digest
648 Central Ave. Suite 441-BSR
Scarsdale, NY 10583

How To Buy Life Insurance

Buying the right amount and the right type of life insurance is one of the important decisions you must make. Before you make any decision, be sure to get your copy of *How To Choose A Life Insurance Company*. To get your copy of this informative booklet, simply send a postcard to:
Occidental Life
Box 2101 Terminal Annex
Los Angeles, CA 90051

You'll Save A Lot Of Dollars With These Great Scents

If you love all those expensive perfumes and colognes advertised on TV, radio and magazines but hate those high prices, this is a must for you. This company makes an affordable line of perfumes and colognes that are almost identical to brands costing as much as ten times as much money. For your free list and scented cards, send a postcard to:
Essential Products Co. Inc.
90 Water St.
New York, NY 10005

Soft And Warm

You know how terrific it feels to have something super soft gently touching your body. If this sounds appealing to you, check this one out. The Company Store offers a superior blend of hand selected white goose and duck down feather comforters, pillows or outerwear. Send a postcard and ask for their *free catalog* to:

THE COMPANY STORE
500 COMPANY STORE ROAD
LA GROSSE, WI 54601

Words of Wisdom

If you need words of encouragement to keep going in the face of adversity and failure (and who doesn't), *Portrait of An Achiever* will make an inspirational addition to your home. It tells of how one famous man (we'll keep his name a secret) turned a lifetime of failures into one overwhelming success. This beautiful parchment reproduction is suitable for framing and makes an excellent gift. Send $1.00 s&h to:

ROBLIN PRESS
405 TARRYTOWN RD SUITE 414 - POA
WHITE PLAINS, NY 10607

Preserve Our History

If you'd like to participate in the preservation of sites, buildings and objects that are important to American history and culture, there is something you can do. Drop a card asking for the *Historic Preservation package* to:

NATIONAL TRUST FOR HISTORIC PRESERVATION
1785 MASSACHUSETTS AVE. N.W.
WASHINGTON, DC 20036

Cure For Bad Breath Is Here

If you are plagued with bad breath these great *Fresh Breath Capsules* will help you cure your bad breath right where it actually starts...in your stomach. Dont worry...the next time you eat garlic or spicy food, pop one of these Breath Fresh capsules. They also have other great products like Retinol

A, Ultramins plus Vitamins and Thigh Cream. To try the Breath Freshener, send $1.00 to cover postage and handling to:

21st Century Group
10 Chestnut Street
Spring Valley, NY 10877

Mail Order Buying

When you buy by mail do you know your rights? Here's a practical and informative guide detailing the protection you have under the F.T.C.'s Mail Order Merchandise Rule. A free copy of *Shopping By Phone & Mail* is yours by writing to:

Shopping by Phone and Mail
Department P
Federal Trade Commission
Washington, DC 20580

Flags Of All Kinds

If you are looking for any kind of flags, poles and accessories, custom designs states, nations, historic and nautical, this *free catalog* has them all. Write to:

Chris Reid
P.O. Box 1827SM
Midlothian, VA 23113

Free Gift From The President

Can you imagine the excitement of getting a letter from the President of the United States! The President will send a signed card embossed with the Presidential seal to any couple celebrating their 50th anniversary (or beyond) or to any citizen celebrating their 80th (or subsequent) birthday. At the other end of the spectrum, the President will also send a congratulatory card to any newborn child. If you'd like, you can also have the card sent to you so you can frame it and give it as a great one-of-a-kind gift! Send your requests at

least 4 weeks in advance to:
THE GREETINGS OFFICE
THE WHITE HOUSE
WASHINGTON, DC 20500

Free Photo Of The President

How would you like a full color autographed photo of the President and First Lady? To get your photo simply request it by mail or fax from:
GREETINGS OFFICE
OLD EXECUTIVE OFFICE BUILDING
ROOM 39
WASHINGTON, DC 20502
FAX: 202-395-1232

Free From The White House

The President would like you to have a beautiful full color book, *The White House, The House of The People.* It features a room-by-room photo tour and history of the White House. For your free copy write to:
THE WHITE HOUSE
WASHINGTON, DC 20500

The President Requests Your Opinion

Yes, your opinion really does count. That's one of the great things about our country. And whether you agree or disagree with his policies, the President would like to hear what you have to say. In fact there's a phone number you can call that will connects right into the White House where you you will be asked to express your opinion on the subject that concerns you most. So if you always wanted to give them a piece of your mind, now you can just be calling...
202-456-1111

Are You Planning A Move?

If you are planning to move soon, be sure all of your important mail gets to your new home. To do that you will need to send out a notification to everyone you want to have your new address. To help you do that be sure to get your free *Address Express Kit* from State Farm Insurance. Call them toll-free at:
1-800-MOVE-299

Once You've Decided To Move

How To Stretch Your Moving Budget - The Interstate Moving Guide is a useful pamphlet that will help you make your interstate move run smoothly. It tells you how to prepare for moving day, how moving costs are calculated, a glossary of moving terms and lots more. It's yours free from:
ATLAS VAN LINES
1212 ST. GEORGE RD.
EVANSVILLE, IN 47703.

A Moving Experience

To help you with your next move United Van Lines has set up a toll free number you can call. Their Community Profile

Center is set up to answer any specific questions you may have. For example, they can answer your questions about employment, educational facilities, housing, and more, in 7,000 cities and towns throughout the 50 states (and foreign countries too). They can also provide you with guides which make preplanning a lot easier and they'll give you the local phone number of the United Van Lines nearest you. Call:

1-800-325-3870:
COMMUNITY PROFILE CENTER
UNITED VAN LINES
ONE UNITED DR.
FENTON, MO 63026

Free Moving Kit

Mayflower has a nice packet of moving materials free for the asking. It includes labels to mark your boxes with plus tips to make your move run smoother and faster. Ask for your *Moving Kit* from your local Mayflower mover or send a postcard to:

MAYFLOWER MOVERS
BOX 107B
INDIANAPOLIS, IN 46206

Free Trout To Stock Your Lake

If you would like to restock your lake or pond, contact the Federal Hatcheries first. They offer free assistance in your restocking plans. If their production is sufficient, they may be able to supply the trout you need. They also have an interesting booklet you might want, *Endangered & Threatened Wildlife and Plants*. Write to:

U.S. DEPARTMENT OF THE INTERIOR
FISH & WILDLIFE SERVICE
WASHINGTON, DC 20240

Getting Rid Of Facial Hair

If you're a woman bothered by unsightly facial hair, you'll want to call the Nudit Hotline. Nudit allows women to discuss with experts the sensitive issue of hair removal treatments. Their hotline number is:
1-800-62-NUDIT

Free Home Economics Classes And Lots More

You may not even be aware of it but your local cooperative extension office offers an amazing range of free information and services to all who request them. Free cooking classes, home and garden seminars, soil analysis, 4-H information, home economics classes and money-management workshops are just a few of the services available. To find your local Cooperative Extension Service or Agricultural Extension Office, just check the Blue pages of your local phone book. Call the one in your state and they will tell you exactly what services they offer and will give you the address and phone number of their office closest to you.

Free Help Writing A Will

Another little known service offered by many Extension offices is free help in writing your will. Often they will have will forms and pamphlets as well as an instructor to help you write that will. Check the Extension offices in the blue pages of your phone book.

Free Medical Care & Health Information

Free Prescription Drugs

Yes it's true there are actually free prescription drugs available to those who can not afford them. Most people are not aware of the fact that drug manufacturers have programs that provide drugs to those who need them but do not have the money or insurance coverage to pay for them.

You may be suffering from cancer, a heart ailment or some other disease that requires a medication that's an essential part of your treatment, but one you cannot afford to pay for. Through these special indigent programs, drug companies will supply the medication free of charge directly to your pharmacy or to your doctor (if he must administer it).

Your first step is to tell your doctor that you will not be able to afford the medicines needed. Next ask him if he has any information on the *'indigent patient drug program'* for the medication you need. Suprisingly a lot of doctors don't even know these programs exist.

Since the majority of doctors will not have information on the program you need, in the back of this book you will find a *Directory of Free Prescription Programs* with full information on the drugs covered, who is eligible for the program and how to contact the pharmaceutical company.

Also, many states have programs that will provide prescripton drugs to you for as little as $1.00 or even free.

Check the *State Pharmaceutical Programs Directory* in the back of this book.

Another place to check is the Pharmaceutical Manufacturers Association. They have up-to-date information on the various drug manufacturer's patient programs. Contact PMA at:

1-800-PMA-INFO (THAT'S 1-800-762-4636)
OR YOU CAN ACCESS THIS INFORMATION ON THE INTERNET AT
www.phrma.org/patient

Striking Back At Strokes

There's great news in the battle against strokes! Modern medical treatments have reduced the death rate from strokes by 50% in the last 25 years.

Many doctors now feel that by taking a small dose of aspirin daily, controlling high blood pressure and practicing more healthy nutrition and exercise programs, we can reduce the health threat from stokes even more. To find out what you can do to avoid a stroke, *Preventing Strokes* is a one publication you will want to get. To get your free copy contact:

NATIONAL INSTITUTE OF NEUROLOGICAL DISORDERS & STROKES
PO Box 5801
BETHESDA, **MD 20824**
OR CALL TOLL-FREE: **1-800-352-9424**
Or visit them on the Internet at:
www.ninds.nih.gov

Free Hospital Care

If you don't have insurance coverage, even a very brief hospital stay can easily cost you tens of thousands of dollars and put you on the edge of bankruptcy. Fortunately now there is something you can do. If you need hospital care but can not afford it and have no insurance or if you already been in the hospital and can't afford to pay the bill, try calling the *Hill-Burton Hotline*. With this program over 1,000 participating hospitals and other health facilities provide free or low-cost medical care to patients who can't afford to pay.

You can qualify for this program even if your income is double the poverty income guidelines and even if the bill has already been turned over to a collection agency. For more information, call the Hill-Burton Hotline at:
1-800-492-0359

Controlling Chronic Headaches

If you suffer from migraine or chronic headaches, you'll definitely want to get this *Headache Information Package*. You will learn about the latest research, new drug treatments, biofeedback and lots more. In the package you will find articles, reports and resources for headache suffers. To get your free package, contact:

NATIONAL INSTITUTE OF NEUROLOGICAL DISORDERS & STROKES
PO BOX 5801
BETHESDA, MD 20824
OR CALL TOLL-FREE: 1-800-352-9424
Or visit them on the Internet at:
www.ninds.nih.gov

Free Medical Care

How would you like to have the finest medical care money can buy...and not spend a cent for it? That's exactly what thousands of people are doing every year thanks to the National Institutes of Health Clinical Center. The NIH is funded by the federal government and is one of the nation's leading medical research centers.

At any one time they have as many as 900 programs under way in dozens of hospitals throughout the country studying the newest procedures in the treatment of every imaginable disease including all types of cancer, heart disease, and Alzheimer's to mention just a few.

And if your condition is one that is being studied you may qualify for free medical care at their 540 bed hospital in Bethesda, Maryland. To find out about their ongoing research projects and clinical trials and whether you qualify for treatment, call their toll-free hotline:

1-800-411-1222
NATIONAL INSTITUTES OF HEALTH CLINICAL CENTER
BETHESDA, MD 20292

Free Eye Care

One of the key ingredients to enjoying a good quality of life is having good eye sight. This means taking care of eye problems like cataracts and glaucoma before they ruin your eye sight.

Your first step is to find out just what you can do to keep your eyes healthy. The National Eye Institute has a number of informative publications you will want to have. They will tell you about various eye diseases and what you can do about them. For a complete list of booklets available, contact:

NATIONAL EYE INSTITUTE
INFORMATION OFFICE
9000 ROCKVILLE AVE.
BUILDING 31 ROOM **6A32**
BETHESDA, MD **20892**
301-496-5248

Next, check the community service pages of your local newspaper for announcements that organizations such as the Kiwanis or Lions Clubs are offering free eye glasses and eye exams to elderly people who can not easily afford to pay for them.

Finally, check with your local Office of the Aging (see the directory in the back of this book). There are a wide variety of eye care programs that are offered that include free eye exams and free eye glasses.

Choosing the Right Nursing Home

What should you do if a loved one needs the continuing care they can only get in a nursing home? What can you do to insure they get the proper care? How do you know how good a particular nursing home is? Your first step would be to get *A Guide To Choosing A Nursing Home*. In this great guide you'll find a step-by-step approach to evaluating and choosing the right nursing home. It's available free from the Medicare Hotline:
1-800-638-6833

Free Health Care For Both You And Your Pet

Remember, if you live near a university that has a medical, dental and even veterinary school, they very often offer all kinds of medical, dental or veterinary services for free or for just a nominal charge. Just give them a call and ask.

Extend Your Life

The Life Extension Foundation is committed to helping people who are well, live longer and healthier lives. They publish an excellent magazine, *Life Extension*, that will keep you informed and up-to-date on all the new advances in how certain vitamins and nutrients keep our minds alert and our bodies healthy and strong.

Life Extension is a magazine that carries 'insider' reports on revolutionary research projects that might one day extend the healthy human life-span to 150 and beyond! They will send you a copy of *Life Extension* magazine along with information on how to become a member. So if you think it might be fun to live for a century and a half, write to:
LIFE EXTENSION FOUNDATION
PO Box 229120
HOLLYWOOD , FL 33022-9120

Healthy Golden Years

Being a senior can sometimes bring with it special problems that can be easily solved if you have the right kind of
information. And to bring this important information to you,
The National Institute on Aging can help you in several ways.
First, they act as a referral agency which means that if you
have a problem they don't handle, they will refer you to the
agency that can provide you with the help you need (usually with a toll-free phone number.) Next, their Internet 'Age
Pages' offers valuable information on diseases, disorders and
conditions. They also have a series of booklets you will find
extremely useful. Some of the most popular ones are: *Aging
and Alcohol Abuse, Dealing with Diabetes, Forgetfulness: It's
Not What You Think, Osteoporosis: the Silent Bone Thinner,
Stroke: Prevention and Treatment, Urinary Incontinence.*
Their brochures will help you with questions you may have
regarding medical care, medications, safety, even health
promotion and disease prevention...all the topics that are
important to every senior. They also have a long list of free
booklets available in print or online. To get a copy of any
booklet that interest you, contact them at:

NATIONAL INSTITUTE ON AGING
PUBLIC INFORMATION OFFICE
PO BOX 8057
GAITHERSBURG, MD 20898

Or call their toll-free order line:

1-800-222-2225
Or you can visit their Web site at:
www.nih.gov/nia
and click 'Health Information.'

Here's a partial list of the booklets
and reports you can get:
* *Alcohol Abuse*
* *Aging and Your Eyes*
* *Arthritis Advice*

- *Crime and the Elderly*
- *Constipation*
- *Don't Take It-Exercise!*
- *Foot Care*
- *Health Quackery*
- *Hearing and Older People*
- *High Blood Pressure: A Common But Controllable Disorder*
- *Hypothermia: A Hot Weather Hazard for Older People*
- *Life Extension: Science or Science Fiction?*
- *Medicines: Use Them Safely*
- *Pills, Patches, and Shots: Can Hormones Prevent Aging?*
- *Pneumonia Prevention: It's Worth A Shot*
- *Sexuality in Later Life*
- *Shots for Safety*
- *Skin Care and Aging*
- *Taking Care of Your Teeth and Mouth*
- *What To Do About Flu*

Alzheimer's Disease Helpline

If someone you love has been diagnosed with Alzheimer's disease, there is a toll-free hotline you can call for information. It's called the Alzheimer's Disease Education and Referral Center and they will be happy to send you a several helpful publications such as the *Forgetfulness* booklet and the *Alzheimer's Disease Fact Sheet*. Call them at:
1-800-438-4380
Or visit them on the Internet at:
http://alzheimers.org/adear

Healthy Smiles

Colgate Total wants you to have shiny healthy teeth and gums. They'd like to send you information on how their formula works even after you stop brushing... fighting plaque,

gingivitis, and cavities. You can call them toll free at:
1-800-763-0246
You can also visit Colgate's World of Healthy Smiles Website:
www.colgate.com.

Seniors Health Care

Seniors Today: Go For It! is an enjoyable and very useful resource guide from Cigna Senior Health Care. In this informative guide you'll learn creative ways to spend your free time.
It explains why along with maintaining a healthier life style
through proper diet and exercise, we must also be open to
trying new things and opening new horizons to keep our minds
healthy too! Cigna says *'Go For It!'* and see the effects volunteering, working and playing has on seniors and their com-
munities. *Ask for The Senior Health Care Kit.* Write to:
CIGNA HEALTH CARE KIT
195 BROADWAY, 7TH FLOOR
NEW YORK, NY 10007
OR CALL: **1-800-781-2058**

How To Check Yourself For Thyroid Disease

The American Association of Clinical Endocrinologists would
like you to stick your neck out a little. They've developed a
new self-test for thyroid diseases, including cancer. It's as
easy as drinking a glass of water, if you know what to look
for. If you should notice a bulge or lumpiness below your
Adam's apple as you swallow, it's a warning sign to see your
doctor. Just be sure you're not confusing your Adam's apple
with a bulge. For a free copy of *The Thyroid Neck Check*,
send a SASE to:
THE AMERICAN ASSOCIATION OF ENDOCRINOLOGISTS
RADIO CITY STATION
PO BOX 1512
NEW YORK, NY 10101-1512

Medicare Supplemental Insurance

Health insurance today is an absolute must for everyone, no matter what age they are. It becomes more confusing when you have to deal with all the questions involved with HMO's and their coverage. If that wasn't enough, you reach retirement age and realize that Medicare doesn't cover all your needs. You discover that you must supplement your Medicare insurance and the options become overwhelming. Every company has a different idea about how you should supplement your health plan. To help you decide what is best for you, the Health Insurance of America puts out a very informative 29 page book that answers questions regarding Medicare Supplemental insurance. It even includes an extensive list of where to find more information in your area. Ask for your free *Medicare Supplemental Insurance Guide.* Write to:

HEALTH INSURANCE ASSOCIATION OF AMERICA
555 13 ST. NW, SUITE 600E
WASHINGTON, DC 20004

Do You Have Trouble Sleeping?

Did you know that 88% of all Americans suffer from some form of sleep disruption. To learn more about sleep, sleep disorders, and drowsy driving, visit the National Sleep Foundation Web site at:
www.sleepfoundation.org.
Or send long self addressed envelope with 2 stamps to:
THE NATIONAL SLEEP FOUNDATION
729 15TH ST. NW, 4TH FL., DEPT. UW
WASHINGTON, DC 20005

Dry Mouth Relief

If you suffer from dry mouth due to radiation therapy or age related problems, you'll want to try Salivart. Salivart is an easy spray application of synthetic saliva that will quickly add moisture to your mouth. For a free spray can of Salivart, send your name and address plus $2.00 for shipping and handling to:

GEBAUER COMPANY
9410 ST. CATHERINE AVE., DEPT. RX
CLEVELAND, OH 44104-5526.

Nasal Moist Gel

Do you suffer from dry crusted inflamed nasal membranes, and have trouble breathing freely every day and every night? Now there may be a solution to your discomfort...Nasal Moist Gel from Blairex. For samples of this gel, send $1.00 postage and handling to:

BLAIREX
PO BOX 2127, DEPT. RX
COLUMBUS, IN 47202-2127

First Aid In A Jar

If you suffer from the pain of arthritis, carpal tunnel syndrome, back and shoulder pain even heel spurs, you will want to try *Therapeutic Pain Rub (TPR)*. This cream has been called 'first aid in a jar.' TPR is a homeopathic topically applied cream that relieves pain. TPR combines 11 approved natural homeopathic medicines that have been proven safe and effective for over 200 years for those who suffer from painful ailments. TPR is also effective as a first aid treatment for poison ivy, minor burns, sunburn, mosquito bites and bruising. Try it for yourself and see. They are also happy to answer any of your questions. Call for your free sample today:

1-800-959-1007

Or visit their Web site:

www.webyellowpages.com/tpr.htm

Daily's Food Supplement Sample

Many health professionals feel that taking antioxidants food supplements may help you avoid certain diseases. Now you can receive an informative chart of the antioxidants considered to be most important, their benefits and their natural dietary sources. You'll also receive a sample of Daily's One-A-Day tablets. Write to:

DAILY'S FOOD SUPPLEMENT
4360 VIEW RIDGE
SAN DIEGO, CA 92123

Lower Your Cholesterol

Cholesterol is a natural fat-like substance that the body needs to function properly. Unfortunately some people's bodies produce too much of the wrong type of cholesterol. This can lead to clogging of the arteries and can put you at risk of a heart attack. To find out what you can do to bring your 'bad' cholesterol to more moderate levels, write for the booklet, *High Blood Cholesterol.* It's yours free from:

NATIONAL CHOLESTEROL EDUCATION PROGRAM
NHLBI INFORMATION CENTER
PO Box 30105
BETHESDA, MD 20824

Cholesterol & High Blood Pressure Help

The National Heart, Lung and Blood Institute has a toll-free number you can call for helpful tips on lowering your cholesterol level and reducing your high blood pressure. In addition to recorded tips, you can also leave your name and address for printed booklets on these important life extending subjects. Call:

1-800-575-WELL

Taking Care of Your Feet

How many times have you ignored an ingrown toenail until you couldn't stand the pain anymore? Did you ever stub or injure your toe and find that it swells up like a balloon? Do you wear the wrong kind of shoes just because they look good? The American Orthopedic Foot and Ankle Society has some great information for you that will turn your sore feet into dancing feet. To get your free copy of *The Adult Foot,* just send a long SASE to:

AMERICAN ORTHOPEDIC FOOT AND ANKLE SOCIETY
701 16TH AVE.
SEATTLE WA 98122

Put Your Best Foot Forward

When your feet ache and you are looking for some kind of relief, what can you do? For answers to that question and for help with your aching feet, The Podiatric Association of America has a toll-free number you can call to get assistance. Call them at:

1-800-FOOT-CARE

Free Health Guide

If you are concerned about nonprescription drugs and what effect they may be having upon you, be sure to get a copy of *Nonprescription Medicines: What's Right For You?* It's yours free from:

CONSUMER INFORMATION
DEPT 556D
PUEBLO, CO 81009

"Breathe Right"

Did you ever wonder why all those professional football players were wearing band aids across their noses? Well it's not a band aid, it's a "Breathe Right" nasal strip. These strips

are great for anyone who snores or has nasal congestion and stuffiness, or needs relief from breathing difficulties associated with a deviated septum. Each strip is lined with a special backbone consisting of two parallel strips. When these strips are properly placed across the bridge of the nose, they lift and open the nasal passages, providing immediate and continual relief without drugs. They even come in clear so they can be worn during the day. Call for your free sample and you'll also receive a $1.50 rebate to use when you purchase Breath Right. Call:
1-800-858-NOSE (6673)

"Glide Floss"

How many times have you started to floss your teeth when the floss sticks between your teeth and half of it shreds and the rest is stuck there. The makers of *Glide Floss* have made flossing easier with their new patented fiber technology. It's easy to use, slides easily between teeth without shredding and is clinically proven to remove plaque. Call for your free sample:
1-800-645-4337
Or check them out on the web:
www.glidefloss.com.

Keeping Your Lungs Healthy

Do you know what the warning signs of lung disease are or what to do if you have emphysema? Are you aware of the common hazards around us in our everyday environment that affect our lungs? Would you like helpful hints on quitting smoking? For answers to these questions and lots more, The American Lung Association has a number of booklets you will find useful. To find out more about lung related problems and solutions, call The American Lung Association at:
1-800-LUNG-USA

Help For Stutterers

If you stutter or know anyone who has a stuttering problem, you are not alone. The Internet has some excellent sites you might want to check out.

National Stuttering Project at:
http://members.aol.com/nsphome/

The site includes essays about stuttering, contacts for local support groups, information on upcoming workshops and links to related sites.

The Stuttering Foundation of America at;
http://www.stuttersfa.org.

Helpful information on stuttering, lists of upcoming workshops and referrals to speech pathologists and clinics. The nonprofit group can also be reached at:
1-800-992-9392

Free Remedy Magazine

With the rapid breakthroughs in medicine today, it's hard to stay on top of it all. One way of doing that is to get a free two year subscription to *Remedy Magazine, Prescriptions For A Healthy Life.* In each issue you will find useful information like medically proven ways to lower your blood pressure, what the lowdown on salt really is, are there really vaccines that can keep you from getting cancer, arthritis, diabetes and multiple sclerosis? To get your free subscription all you need to do is fill out and return a simple health survey. Write to

REMEDY MAGAZINE
SUBSCRIPTION DEPT.
120 POST ROAD WEST
WESTPORT, CT 06880

Also visit their web site at:
www.remedyonline.com

Keep Yourself Cancer Free

The American Institute For Cancer Research has tons of valuable information available for those suffering from cancer and for those who want to keep themselves cancer-free. If you already have cancer, you'll want to learn more about how to maintain a healthy diet while fighting your illness. You'll also want to receive information on how you can help prevent certain cancers by living a healthy lifestyle, through exercise and by following a well balanced diet. These booklets are free, but if you want to help further the research and education on the link between diet and cancer, a small donation would be greatly appreciated. Write to:

AMERICAN INSTITUTE FOR CANCER RESEARCH
1759 R STREET N.W.
PO Box 97167
WASHINGTON, DC 20090-7167

Breast Cancer Support

Y-ME Breast Cancer Support Program was created in 1978 by Ann Marcou and Mimi Kaplan, who turned their own difficult experience into a positive network of volunteers that provides counseling and information to thousands of women suffering from breast cancer. For a free copy of *Y-ME Hotline* newsletter write to:

Y-ME
212 W. VAN BUREN
CHICAGO IL 60607

You may also call their 24 hour support hotline:
1-800-221-2141
Or visit their Internet site at:
www.y-me.org

Get Rid Of Heartburn Before It Starts

Do you suffer from the agony of heartburn or other acid distress because of the acid in the foods you eat? Now you can enjoy all those spicy foods without having to worry about chewing antacids. *Prelief* is not a drug but a dietary supplement. It works on the food, not on you. It's tasteless and doesn't change the taste of your food in any way. They will gladly send you a free sample. It comes in tablet or granule form and you'll even receive a money saving coupon. Call: **1-800-994-4711**

Free Dental Care For Seniors

You know just how expensive dental care can be especially if you need dentures, tooth implants or gum surgery. Fortunately if you need expensive dental work but can not afford it, help is close at hand. Top quality dental care is available at little or no cost at local dental clinics and at dental colleges nationwide. Also, the dental societies in each state have a list of dentists who volunteer their services to help those who can not afford proper dental care. (See the *Directory of Free & Low Cost Dental Programs* at the back of this book).

Kick That Fungus

If you suffer from discomfort or embarrassment stemming from a fungal growth under your finger or toe nails there is something you can do to get rid of this problem. Your first step is to get the free *Kick-It Kit,* free from Sporanox. Call them toll-free: **1-800-595-NAILS**

Cold Facts

The folks who make Halls cough tablets want you to know the 10 myths about the common cold. They'll even send you a coupon that will save you money on your next purchase of Halls Cough Tablets. Try them they really do work! Write: COLD HARD FACTS 500 N. MICHIGAN AVE., SUITE 100 CHICAGO, IL 60611

HERE ARE SOME IMPORTANT TOLL FREE NUMBERS FOR INFORMATION ON MEN'S AND WOMEN'S HEALTH. FOR MORE INFORMATION ABOUT MEN HEALTH ISSUES:

Call *Men's Health Consulting* for information on men's health reform and what you can do to help.
1-800-WELL-MEN

Men's Maintenance Manual. A free booklet by the founders of Men's Health Week and the Association of American Family Physicians that deals with stress management, sexual health and weight control and lists health hotlines for 23 helpful organizations that will provide information on topics ranging from aging allergies to sports medicine and stress. Contact them at:
MEN'S MAINTENANCE MANUAL
14 EAST MINOR ST
EMMAUS, PA 18098
1-800-955-2002
Or you can reach them at their web site:
www.menshealth.com

FOR MORE INFORMATION ABOUT WOMEN'S HEALTH ISSUES:
Call the National Women's Health Network Information Clearinghouse. They can provide you with free information packets on women's health issues including fibroids, contraception and estrogen replacement therapy. Call them at:
202-628-7814

Also, for more information on women's health issues, The Office of Research on Women's Health, National Institutes of Health has a list of useful publications you'll want to get.
301-402-1770

What Are Your Pension Rights?

If you have questions about your pension and your rights, the Pension and Welfare Benefits Administration has a toll-free number you can call to order free publications about pensions and health coverage. They have over 30 free booklets you can request including:

- *What You Should Know About Your Pension Rights.*
- *Protect Your Pension- A Quick Reference Guide.*
- *Women and Pensions-What Women Need to Know and Do.*
- *How to File A Claim for Your Benefits; Health Benefits under COBRA*
- *Pension and Welfare Brief.*
- *Can the Retiree Health Benefits Provided By Your Employer Be Cut?*

There are also free guides for small business owners that outline *Simplified Employee Pensions* (called: 'SEPS') and *Savings Incentive Match Plans for Employees of Small Employers* (called: 'SIMPLE'). For your free information, call them 9am-8pm Monday-Friday toll-free at:
1-800-998-7542

Controlling Your Cholesterol & Blood Pressure

We all know how critically important it is to keep our cholesterol and blood pressure at safe levels. To find out what you can do, call the National Heart, Lung and Blood Institute for recorded information on cholesterol and high blood pressure. When you call, you can also leave your name and address for written information. Call:
1-800-575-WELL

Taking Care Of Your Heart

When you call The American Heart Association's toll-free hotline, your call will be routed to your local AHA office for the latest information on heart disease, strokes, high blood pressure and diet. Many offices can tell you about local support groups or low-cost or even free screenings for blood pres-

sure and cholesterol in your area. Call:
1-800-AHA-USA-1

Staying Young At Heart

The National Institute on Aging would like you to have a copy of *For Hearts and Arteries: What Scientists are Learning About Age and the Cardiovascular System.* Learn how the latest research can help keep your heart running younger no matter what your age.
NIA INFORMATION CENTER
PO Box 8057
GAITHERSBURG, **MD. 20898-8057**
OR CALL **1-800-222-2225**

Free Holistic Herbal Healthcare Guide

This herbal guide will give you basic information about herbs, herbal combinations and homeopathic medicines. You'll learn the five main benefits of herbs, why people use herbs, what herbs are sources of vitamins, minerals and trace minerals and important points that should be considered when purchasing herbs for personal consumption. If you would like a copy of *The Holistic Herbal Healthcare Guide,* send your name, address and 4 first class stamps to cover postage to:
DEBORAH COBLE
1420-E3 STEEPLE CHASE DRIVE
DOVER, **PA 17315-3784**

Discover the World of Natural Medicine

If you are interested in learning about natural remedies and natural products and their effect on your body, send for this *catalog of homeopathic remedies.* Enzymatic Therapy and

Learning offers you some of their natural methods of feeling better. They will even send you a $3.00 coupon to try *Herpilyn*, a cold sore remedy. To get answers to your questions, you can call their consumer information line.
1-800-783-2286

COLD SORE TIP:

Incidentaly, if you are prone to cold sores, ask your doctor about *Denavir* which is a new prescription medication. Research shows that applying the cream immediately after a cold sore first appears and then reapplying it every two hours helps cold sores disappear a full day earlier.

Using Biofeedback To Stay Healthy

Did you ever wonder how the process of reward gratification works? (When you accomplish something you're given a reward). Today's alternative methods of treating people include 'biofeedback' where your body learns to detect and control various functions. Learn more about these techniques and how they can make us healthy and happier. For information about certified biofeedback professionals, send a long SASE to:
BIOFEEDBACK CERTIFICATION INSTITUTE OF AMERICA
10200 W. 44TH AVE., SUITE 304
WHEAT RIDGE, CO 80033

Help For Back Troubles

The BackSaver catalog has a wonderful assortment of all types of products for your back, including chairs, seat and back support cushions, sleeping supports, reading tables and more. It's free from:
BACKSAVER PRODUCTS CO.
53 JEFFREY AVE.
HOLLISTON, MA 01746

Dealing With Bladder Problems

Did you know that nearly half a million people suffer from interstitial cystitis an often misdiagnosed chronic bladder disorder. The National Institutes of Health has published a free booklet that gives basic information in easy-to-understand layman's terms on the disease. Ask for *Interstitial Cystitis* when you contact:

IC BOOKLET
NATIONAL KIDNEY AND UROLOGIC DISEASES INFORMATION
CLEARINGHOUSE
3 INFORMATION WAY
BETHESDA, MD. 20892
301-654-4415

How to Curb Teen Smoking

If you have a teenager, you know that one of the most harmful things peer pressure may cause them to do is to start smoking. Without the proper guidance, they may begin a lifelong battle with this dangerous habit. The Centers for Disease Control's Offices on Smoking and Health will help you tackle questions on what you can do to curb teen smoking. For specific advice, call them at:
1-800-CDC-1311

Keeping Your Heart Healthy

The American Heart Association has a valuable toll-free helpline you can call. By calling that helpline, you can get free copies of a host of booklets dealing with your heart. Topics include blood pressure, CPR, cholesterol, diet, exercise, heart disease and strokes to mention just a few. Learn the best ways to eat smart and healthy by reducing fat in your diet. You can also learn you how to read the new food labels to help you shop for healthier foods. Ask for *How to Read the New Food Label,* and *Save Food Dollars and Help*

Your Heart and any other heart-related topics you are interested in. Write to:

THE AMERICAN HEART ASSOCIATION NATIONAL CENTER
7272 GREENVILLE AVE.
DALLAS, TX 75231.
OR CALL TOLL-FREE: 1-800-242-8721

Before Having A Joint Replacement

If you or anyone you know ever needs joint replacement, you will want to read this valuable information. You will learn why and when it is necessary... how it is performed, benefits versus risks and lots more. Ask for *Total Joint Replacement*. Send a SASE to:

AMERICAN ACADEMY OF ORTHOPEDIC SURGEONS
BOX 2058
DES PLAINES, IL 60016

Sleep Hotline

The American Society of Travel Agents and Searle are happy to provide you with tips on how to feel your best while traveling. Request a free booklet called *Sleep Well... Stay Fit - Tips for Travelers*. Call toll-free:
1-800-SHUTEYE

Now Hear This

If you are experiencing hearing loss and your doctor has recommended a hearing aid, you may need help in determining what kind of device you need. The American Speech -Language-Hearing Association, offers general information about hearing aids and their costs, insurance coverage, proper fit and care. For your free copy of *How to Buy a Hearing Aid,* call toll-free:
1-800-638-8255

The Latest Information On Cancer

To help you keep informed about the most up-to-date information about cancer, the National Cancer Institute has a toll-free number you can call. When you call you can ask for free publications, ask for help locating FDA-approved mammography facilities or talk with cancer specialists.
1-800-422-6237

What You Can Do About Prostate Cancer

Did you know that next to lung cancer prostate cancer is the #2 cancer killer of men? Almost all men will have some kind of prostate problem if he lives long enough. Fortunately, with the modern advances in medicine and drug therapies, help is close at hand. Your first step is to inform yourself about this problem and the newest treatments for it. To get a copy of the free *Prostate Information Package* or for answers to specific questions you may have contact:
NATIONAL KIDNEY AND UROLOGIC DISEASE INFORMATION
CLEARINGHOUSE
3 INFORMATION WAY
BETHESDA, **MD 20892**
301-654-4415
Or check out their web site at:
www.niddk.nig.gov

The Facts About Prostate Cancer

Early Detection of Prostate Cancer answers the most often-asked questions about prostate cancer. Although the disease is of prime concern to men over 55, it explains that the disease can often exist without symptoms and that men over 40 should be tested annually. The National Cancer Institute also includes a list of problems that might indicate pros-

tate cancer. It also covers the specifics of diagnosis, treatment, and prognosis. Incidentally the prognosis is excellent if the condition is caught early enough. For your free copy or to speak with a specialist, call:
1-800-422-6237

Essential Cancer Hotline

If you had been diagnosed with an advanced cancer, imagine how great it would be to find out there was a clinical trial program with new and promising treatments for the type of cancer you had. The good news is that there *is* a toll-free number you can call for help. The National Cancer Institute's Information Service provides the latest information about cancer, including causes and medical referral to low-cost clinics, medical consultation, referral to patient support groups and publications on request. They can provide you with literature and answer questions concerning various types of cancer and the standard treatment. Contact them at:
NCI, Cancer Communications Office
31 Center Drive MSC 2580
Building 31, Room 10A07
Bethesda, MD 20892
or call 1-800-4-CANCER (that's 1-800-422-6237)
You can also visit their web site at:
www.nci.nih.gov
At their web site for information on clinical trials, click on the *"Clinical Trial"* option

For Allergy and Asthma Sufferers

If you have questions about allergies or asthma, here's how you can find answers. The Asthma and Allergy Foundation will answer any questions you have regarding the symptoms of allergies to different substances, foods and how all these can be related to asthma.
Call: 1-800-7-ASTHMA

Parent Resource Guide

It's important for children to develop good eating habits when they are young so that they can grow up to be healthier, more active adults. The American Academy of Pediatrics has some important nutrition information just for the asking. Send a business sized SASE to:

NUTRITION BROCHURES DEPT. C
AMERICAN ACADEMY OF PEDIATRICS
PO BOX 927
ELK GROVE, IL 60009

"A Healthier You"

Research shows that eating fresh fruits and vegetables puts more fiber in your diet and helps you stay healthy. Finding out more about the vitamins, minerals and fiber in fruits and vegetables is essential to a healthier you. The booklet, *A Healthier You*, from the American Institute for Cancer Research also includes healthy recipes. Send a SASE to:

THE AMERICAN INSTITUTE FOR CANCER RESEARCH
DEPT. AP
WASHINGTON, DC 20069

ABC'S Of Eyecare

The Better Vision Institute has some important information about your eyes and how to take the best care of them.

Topics include everything from the proper selection of eyeglass frames, to eye care for children & adults, tips on correct lighting, correct type of sunglasses and more. Send a business-sized SASE to:

BETTER VISION INSTITUTE
PO BOX 77097
WASHINGTON, DC 20013
OR CALL 1-800-424-8422

There Is Something You Can Do About Depression

Today even when we are very aware of everything around us we sometimes blot out or deny the signs of depression in ourselves and those around us. There is some highly informative information on depression published by the National Institute of Mental Health. Learn all the facts and become aware. Send a business-sized SASE and reques the *Depression Awareness information package*:

D/ART, NIMH
5600 FISHERS LANE, ROOM 10-85
ROCKVILLE, MD 20857
OR CALL: **1-800-421-4211**

Tips On Handling Tension & Depression

Chronic tension and depression are two emotionally debilitating illnesses that you can do something about. The National Mental Health Association has a ton of information on how to handle the problems of both tension and depression. If you have any questions about these conditions, they have a toll-free number you can call for help. They will also send you helpful information you can use. Call them at:

THE NATIONAL MENTAL HEALTH ASSOCIATION,
ALEXANDRIA, VA
1-800-969-6642

Healthy Teeth

Teeth - we only get one set of permanent healthy adult teeth so it's essential to learn how to keep them strong and cavity free. Dental care is also a very important career opportunity that also allows you to help others take care of their teeth. If you know someone who may be interested in finding out more about career options, ask for a copy of *Dental Hygiene - A Profession of Opportunities* and also *Facts About*

Dental Hygiene. Send a long SASE to:
AMERICAN DENTAL HYGIENISTS' ASSOCIATION
444 N. MICHIGAN AVE.
CHICAGO, IL 60611
ATTN: NUTRITION DEPARTMENT

Free Wellness Guide For Older Adults

As the body ages, it changes in a variety of ways. To help
you adapt to these changes, now you can get a free *Wellness
Guide* which offers you advice on health issues and preven-
tive care. The *Wellness Guide* is designed to provide practical information on matters such as sensory changes, diet,
exercise, legal and financial considerations of interest to the
older adult as well as common health problems - all designed
to help you remain vibrant, active and independent throughout your entire life. Write to:
MARKETING SERVICES
PENNSYLVANIA HOSPITAL
800 SPRUCE STREET
PHILADELPHIA, PA 19107

Using Your Mind To Heal Your Body

When used properly the mind is a powerful instument you
can use to stay well. To learn just how powerful your mind
can be in controlling your body and how your mind can help
you heal yourself, be sure to get the free *Resource Directory*
which comes to you from The Institute Of Noetic Sciences.
CALL TOLL-FREE: **1-800-628-4545**

Do You Really Need A Hysterectomy?

The American College of Obstetricians and Gynecologists
has published a free brochure, *Understanding Hysterectomy*
which outlines what constitutes a medically necessary hys-

terectomy and describes what the surgery involves. Before having this operaton, request a free copy from:
ACOG
409 12TH ST. SW
WASHINGTON, DC 20024

Energizing Your Brain

The brain affects all your vital body functions. If we don't nourish it and exercise it like any other organ it becomes dull. If you want more information on feeding and energizing the brain with the Brain III Formula, call:
1- 800-NU-BRAIN

Hiking Safety

Whether you are walking to lose weight, exploring a tourist attraction, or hiking to enjoy scenic trails, there are a number of guideline you should follow. Send a SASE and ask for *Hiking Safety* from:
AMERICAN HIKING SOCIETY
DEPT T, PO BOX 20160
WASHINGTON, DC 20041

"Megabrain"

Now you can actually improve your creativity, enhance mental functioning, induce deep relaxation and reduce stress. Sounds to good to be true but the people from Comptronic Devices say it can be done through the use of a product called 'DAVID' Light and Sound devices. There's even a special application to improve sports performance. To get your free information on this amazing device write:
COMPTRONIC DEVICES LIMITED
9860A 33RD AVENUE
EDMONTON, ALBERTA, CANADA, T6N 1C6

Nature's Way To "Rev Up"

"Rev Up" is an herbal energy capsule that will help you handle the pressures, deadlines and overloads in your life. The ancient civilizations believed that natural herbs worked wonders for you, and today there seems to be a lot of merit to those old ideas. Learn all about this personal fatigue fighter and also get a 15% discount.

CALL **800-63-REV-UP**

Massage Therapy

Stress got you down? Maybe you need a good massage. The *Massage Therapy* booklet will give you detailed information about different methods of massage and the benefits of each type. It will also answer many of your questions about stress and the reasons massage therapy works. Write to:

AMERICAN MASSAGE THERAPY ASSOCIATION
820 DAVIS ST., SUITE 100
EVANSTON, IL 60201

Asthma Relief

Asthma patients who use inhalers may be masking the physical cause for their symptoms. Doctors have come up with a checklist for asthma patients who rely on those inhalers to open their airways. If you use your inhaler more than three times a week, if you go through more than one canister a month, and if your asthma awakens you at night...you may be suffering from an inflammation of the airways that is the real cause of your symptoms and may need drug treatment to clear it up. To receive a copy of the list, write to:

ASTHMA INFORMATION CENTER
BOX 790
SPRINGHOUSE, PA 19477

Speak To A Dietician On The Toll-Free Nutrition Hotline

Find out how your diet is affecting your health. Call the American Institute for Cancer Research, Nutrition Hotline and ask a registered dietician your personal questions on diet, nutrition and cancer. When you call you can leave your question with an operator and a dietician will call you back within 48 hours with answers to your questions.

CALL BETWEEN 9AM-5PM, EST MONDAY-FRIDAY:
1-800-843-8114

Free Health Publications

The AICR also has a variety of free publications designed to help you live a healthier lifestyle. A small contribution gets you a very informative newsletter and you can ask for the following booklets by name: *Get Fit, Trim Down* - how to lose weight sensibly. *Alcohol and Cancer Risk: Make The Choice For Health.* - find out how alcohol affects your cancer risk. *Diet & Cancer* - are you eating enough fiber, something that's been linked to lower cancer risk? *Reducing Your Risk of Colon Cancer* - learn steps you can take that may reduce your risk of one of the most common cancers in the United States. Also ask for *Everything Doesn't Cause Cancer* which will calm many of the concerns you may have about what causes cancer. You can ask for one of these or all. Write to:

AMERICAN INSTITUTE FOR CANCER RESEARCH
WASHINGTON, DC 20069

Free Child's Health Record Book

This easy to use health record log is great for parents and kids alike. Keep your child's vital health records in this handy easy-to-read log. With it you will keep track of illnesses, allergies, health exams, immunizations and tests, family history and health insurance. It features the ever popular Peanuts gang (Charlie Brown, Snoopy and friends) and is sure to be popular with the little ones. Ask for *Your Child's Health Record.* Send a long SASE to:

MET LIFE INSURANCE (16UV)
BOX HR
ONE MADISON AVE.
NEW YORK, NY 10010

Does Your Child Have An Iron Deficiency?

To understand the effect that iron and iron deficiency has on health development of your child, be sure to get this free brochure on iron from Carnation, makers of Good Start Infant Formula, and Follow-Up Formula. Ask for the *Iron Brochure.* You'll also learn that although iron is essential for your baby, it is just as essential to a mature adult. Send a long SASE to:

CARNATION NUTRITIONAL PRODUCTS
IRON BROCHURE OFFER
PO BOX 65785
SALT LAKE CITY, UT 84165

Health At Home

This Home Health catalog is the official supplier of Edgar Cayce products for health, beauty and wellness. You'll find over 50 products to help you feel and look your best. There is everything from juices, vitamins, even minerals and salts from the Dead Sea. Write to:

HOME HEALTH
949 SEAHAWK CIRCLE
VIRGINIA BEACH, VA 23452

Your Family Health Record

Every member of the family should keep a written medical

record. The family's medical record will be useful to you in filling out insurance forms, as well as school and travel records. It can also be vital in helping a physician diagnose a medical problem a family member might have. If you would like, they will also send you information on prenatal and natal care, guide to healthy pregnancy and information on how your baby grows. They also have informative brochures for teens about drugs and sexually transmitted disease. Write to:

MARCH OF DIMES
1275 MAMARONECK AVE.
WHITE PLAINS, NY 10605

Help For The Visually Handicapped

A great series of publications are free to those with impaired vision. Printed in very large type are instructions for knitting, crocheting, and gardening plus children's books and more. Also available are guides for the partially sighted including a dial operator personal directory. There are also 2 free newsletters...*IN FOCUS for youths* and *SEEING CLEARLY* for adults. For a complete listing write:

NATIONAL ASSOCIATION FOR VISUALLY HANDICAPPED
305 E. 24TH ST.
NEW YORK, NY 10010
(IN CALIF. ONLY—3201 BALBOA ST., SAN FRANCISCO, CA 94121).

Johnson & Johnson Hotline

Who can you turn to for answers to your questions concerning hygiene, personal care and baby care? To help you with answers to these questions, Johnson & Johnson has set up a toll-free consumer information hotline you can call. Call them with your questions Monday thru Friday between the hours of from 8:00am to 6:00pm EST.

THEIR TOLL-FREE HOTLINE IS:
1-800-526-3967

What To Do About Hearing Loss

Straight Talk About Hearing Loss, is a fact-filled book about hearing loss and hearing aids. If you're concerned about your loss of hearing and wondering just what you can do about it, get the facts about Miracle-Ear. For your free book CALL: **1-800-582-2911**

Do You Need A Hearing Aid?

If you are experiencing hearing loss and your doctor has recommended a hearing aid, you may need help determining what kind of listening device suits you. The American Speech-Language-Hearing Association, offers general information about hearing aids and their costs, insurance coverage, proper fitting and care. They can also make referrals to certified audiologists and speech-language pathologists. To get your free copy, ask for *"How to Buy a Hearing Aid,"* CALL **800-638-8255**

Help For The Deaf

Every year over 200,000 children are born deaf or suffer hearing loss in their first years of life. *Speech and Hearing Checklist* tells parents how to detect possible deafness in their children. Another nice booklet, *Listen! Hear!* is for parents of children who may be deaf or hard of hearing. Both are free from:
ALEXANDER GRAHAM BELL ASSOCIATION FOR THE DEAF
3417 VOLTA PL. N.W.
WASHINGTON, DC 20007

How To Keep Your Bones Strong

Supplements can help replace the calcium in your bones that age takes away. Just two of these soft chewy, vanilla-flavored squares give you 1200 mg. of calcium daily. For more information on keeping your bones healthy and staying fit,

call toll free weekdays between 9:00 am and 5:00 pm EST:
1-800-STAY-FIT

Free Medical Supply Catalog

If you have a disability or illness that requires you to use medical equipment or supplies, now you can order your medical supplies from your home by phone and save up to 60%. Send for this free catalog from America's leading mail order medical supply catalog. Drop a postcard to:
BRUCE MEDICAL SUPPLY
DEPARTMENT 712
411 WAVERLY OAKS RD.
WALTHAM. MA 02154

Questions About Medicare? Call This Toll-Free Hotline

If you have questions or problems regarding Medicare, now there's a toll-free number you can call for help. When you call you can get additional information regarding a Medicare claim you may have, general information about Medicare and the services it provides. They can also help you with information regarding insurance supplements to Medicare, mammograms and lots more. Call:
1-800-638-6833

Physical Fitness For Seniors

It's always a great idea to get in shape and stay in shape. Just remember that if you take better care of your body, it will take better care of you. The President's Council on Physical Fitness & Sports has useful information that can help add years to your life. You'll get an introduction to exercise, weight control, physical fitness, sports, running and lots more. Here are a few titles you will want to ask for
• *Pep up Your Life*—fitness for seniors

- *Older American Fact Sheet* - what to do to stay in great shape
- *Exercise & Weight Control*-they go hand in hand.
- *Fitness Fundamentals* - how to develop a personal fitness program

Drop a card to:
THE PRESIDENT'S COUNCIL ON PHYSICAL FITNESS & SPORTS
200 INDEPENDENCE AVE. SW ROOM 738H
WASHINGTON, D.C. 20201
202-690-9000

What To Ask Your Doctor Before You Have Surgery

If you are considering having any type of non-emergency surgery, be sure to get your free copy of *Questions to Ask Your Doctor Before Surgery*. It will help you be informed about the options and risks involved. Call toll-free:
1-800-358-9295

Sexually Transmitted Diseases Hotline

If you suspect you may have contracted a sexually transmitted disease, there's a toll free hotline you can call for help and for information. Their specialists will answer your questions concerning STDs and tell you the symptoms that are the warning signs of disease and how to get help. You'll be referred to free or low-cost public health clinics or doctors in your area. They will also send you free brochures concerning STDs. Call Monday thru Friday between 8 am and 8 pm at:
1-800-227-8922

Eat Your Way To A Healthy Heart

If you would like a copy of the American Heart Association's

recommendations for a healthy heart including lists of good and bad foods, plus practical suggestions for cutting out the bad stuff. Ask for *Exercise Your Heart, An Eating Plan For Healthy Americans; Cholesterol & Your Heart* and *Recipes For Low-Fat, Low Cholesterol Meals.* Just send a SASE to:
AMERICAN HEART ASSOCIATION, NATIONAL CENTER
PO Box UCB
7320 GREENVILLE AVE.
DALLAS, TX 78531

Avoiding Skin Cancer

Prevention is always far better than a cure. And one of the most preventable diseases is skin caner. To find out what you can do to prevent this disease, be sure to get a copy of the free booklet *Skin Cancer: If You Can Spot It You Can Stop It.* Send a long SASE to:
THE SKIN CANCER FOUNDATION
Box 561
NEW YORK, NY 10156

Free Guide To Strokes

For up-to-date information on strokes and the most effective treatment and therapy for those who fall victim to a stroke, ask for your free copy of *Guide To Strokes.* Write to:
STROKE
NINCDS-W
9000 ROCKVILLE PIKE, BLDG 31, RM 8A16
BETHESDA, MD 20892

Overcoming Your Lactose Intolerance

Millions of people suffer from a condition know as 'lactose intolerance'. That simply means that they can become very ill if they eat any product that contains dairy or a dairy by-

product. Until now the only solution was to avoid all foods that contain lactose. But now there may be an easier way to deal with this problem. That solution is called 'Lactose Ultra' and taking one tablet before eating a dairy product allows you to easily and naturally digest the lactose. To try a free sample of Lactose Ultra, simply call their toll-free phone number:
1-888-ULTRA-NOW

Free Guides To Healthy Living

America's pharmaceutical companies would like you to have their *Guides To Healthy Living*. The subjects covered include breast cancer, heart attacks, strokes, menopause, and prostate cancer. For information on any or all of these topics call this information hotline toll-free:
1-800-862-5110

Headache Hotline

If you are plagued with headaches and don't know where to turn, The American Council for Headache Education may be able to offer you a solution on how to lessen your pain and discomfort. Call them toll-free:
1-800-255-ACHE

For Asthma Relief

If you suffer from asthma, you'll want to get a free copy of *Making The Most of Your Next Doctor Visit*. In it you'll discover what you can do to assist your doctor in helping you relieve your asthma suffering. Call toll-free:
1-800-456-2784

Free Contact Lenses

If you wear contact lenses or are thinking of getting them, Johnson & Johnson would like you to try their Acuvue contacts. They have made arrangements with local optometrist throughout the country to supply you with a your first pair. Just ask an optometrist in your area who carries *Acuvue* contacts for a free pair.

Free Focus Contacts

If you always wanted to try soft contact lenses but weren't sure you'd like them, here's your chance to try a free pair. For a certificate you can take to your local eye care store for a free trial pair of *Focus Contact Lenses* plus a $25.00 rebate form to use on your next pair, call toll-free:
1-800-215-7749

Save 50% On Contact Lenses

To save up to 50% on your contact lenses, consider buying them by mail order from a company called 1-800-CONTACTS. They carry a full line of first quality contact lenses in all prescriptions from all manufacturers. Their toll-free order line is easy to remember since it's the same as their company name...
1-800-CONTACTS (THAT'S **1-800-266-8228**).

Important Health Hotlines

To help answer various health questions you may have there are a number of toll-free hotlines you can call:

CALCIUM INFORMATION CENTER:
1-800-321-2681

MILK CONSUMER HOTLINE:
1-800-WHY-MILK

NATIONAL CENTER FOR NUTRITION & DIURETICS
1-800-366-1655

NATIONAL OSTEOPEROSIS FOUNDATION
1-800-223-9994

FOOD ALLERGY NETWORK
1-800-929-4040

CONSUMER NUTRITION HOTLINE
1-800-366-1655

If You Have Cancer, Call This Hotline First

If you've been diagnosed with any type of cancer, be sure to call the *Cancer Toll-free Hotline.* They will put you in touch with someone who has had the same type of cancer and will help you deal with the initial fear. Speaking with another person who's had to deal with the same life-threatening disease that you have can be highly informative and enormously comforting. Call:
1-800-433-0464

Health Web Sites

There is so much material on the World Wide Web that people new to the Internet often find searching for information a bit overwhelming at first. To help make your search simple and successful there are a number of useful search resources you can use to locate a wide range of information.

For example, if you would like to explore the area of health Lycos, Excite and Yahoo are three of the best 'search engines'. Just by typing in their web address and following the directions below, you will instantly be able to find the latest health related news, information and answers to health questions you may have.

EXCITE
www.excite.com
They have what they refer to as their *Health Channel*. Click on that and you'll find listings for Mayo Health Oasis, Healthy Ideas and New England Journal of Medicine Online.

LYCOS
www.lycos.com
Click on *Health* and you'll get a general web page on Health plus another page with options like Health News, Eating & Exercise and Health Care.

YAHOO
www.yahoo.com
This may be your best bet. Yahoo Health, offers a breakdown of about 50 categories ranging from alternative medicine to hospitals to transplant resources.

**HERE ARE SPECIFIC HEALTH SITES YOU MAY
WANT TO VISIT ON THE INTERNET:**

HEALTH A TO Z
www.healthatoz.com
This is designed to be a health navigational tool. Health A to Z is useful both for medical professionals and consumers. To locate information, you can either enter your own search words or click on one of 30 categories for a listing of related sites.

HEALTHFINDER
www.healthfinder.gov
This is a consumer health and human services information Web site from the U.S. government. It leads you to online publications, clearinghouses, databases, Web sites and support groups, including government agencies.

MEDSITE
www.medsite.com
Enter a medical or health key word and click on the search button and you're on your way.

MEDSURF
www.medsurf.com
You can do a word search for specific health questions or sift through the categories under General Information, Practitioners' Information or Researchers' Information.

IF YOU SUBSCRIBE TO AMERICA ONLINE:
AOL has a Health and Fitness "channel" (key word: *'Health'*). You'll find a health library, the Better Health and Medical network, plus health resources, support groups and the Medline database you will find useful.

IF YOU SUBSCRIBE TO COMPUSERVE:
CompuServe has a useful health database (go: *'Health'*) and Health-Net. They also use information provided by John's Hopkins and include resources on alternative medicine, women's health and specific ailments.

NATIONAL INSTITUTES OF HEALTH INFORMATION
www.nih.gov/health.com
This includes Medline, Medscape, patient information and journals. Very well organized.

MAYO HEALTH OASIS:
www.mayo.ivi.com
You get the Oasis Library, The Cancer Center, Heart Center, Women's Health and medicine Center. The Library has great resources and links to other sites.

ASK DR. WEIL:
www.drweil.com
Dr. Andrew Weil's site is for those who are interested in finding an alternative to traditional medicine.

FAMILY CAREGIVER ALLIANCE
www.caregiver.prg
This site combines a clearinghouse for publications, newsletters, diagnoses and research with a resource center for care services, public policy and links.

ATLANTA REPRODUCTIVE HEALTH CENTRE
www.ivf.com/home.shtm
One of the oldest Web sites, it has a host of information on women's health.

WEEKEND MAGAZINE
www.usaweekend.com
For helpful information on men's and women's health, visit *Weekend* magazine's website

THE BLACK HEALTH NET
www.blackhealthnet.com
This site provides information and resources on topics such as AIDS and African Americans, sickle cell and other diseases.

ARTHRITIS FOUNDATION
www.arthritis.org
For comprehensive information on arthritis call the Arthritis Foundation toll-free at **1-800-283-7800** or for a brochure on rheumatoid arthritis, call toll free **1-877-467-3472** or visit their web site.

For more information on on the latest research on arthritis, you will also want to visit the following web sites:
www.rheumatology.org
www.nih.gov/niams

NEW CANCER DRUG
www.entremed.com
Entremed, the new cancer drug that cures cancer in mice will begin clinical trials on humans by the middle of 1999. A toll free number will be posted on the company Internet site at that time to recruit participants. It's too soon to say, but this could be a major breakthrough for those suffering from cancer and certainly adds hope to all those afflicted with that disease. Log onto their web site for the latest on their clinical trials.

Health Tips

What You Can Do To Help Your Doctor Help You

Next time you are suffering from pain and discomfort and can't easily pinpoint exactly what hurts, follow this checklist. It will not only help you identify the problem but will help the doctor diagnose the ailment .

- When did the pain or symptoms start?
- Did it follow an accident?
- Does it happen before meals or after meals?
- Did symptoms develop gradually or suddenly?
- Are the symptoms intermittent or constant?
- Are symptoms worse in certain positions, such as sitting or lying down, or at certain times such as morning or evening, or during certain activities?
- How have the symptoms affected your normal activities?
- Make a list of prescription and nonprescription drugs you are taking.
- Describe your pain. Words like cramping, sharp, throbbing, aching, all give different information to your doctor.

This is the best way to assist your doctor by providing accurate information about your medical concerns.

Can Apples Reduce Your Cancer Risk?

In a Finnish study of 10,000 adults, eating three apples a week appears to have shown a reduction in lung-cancer risk by 58%. It seems apples are high in quercetin, an antioxidant that appears to be protective against lung cancer.

Everyday Exercise

Looking for a great exercise routine, well no need to look any further. Here are a few tips to get you going!
• Do some spring cleaning around the house and scrub the floor a little harder
• Do some gardening and yardwork
Clean out that attic and garage
• Walk, don't drive !
• Looking for a fun aerobic workout...dance. Try learning one of those new funky dance steps.

Caesar's Garlic Wars?

Many claims have been made in recent years about the important medicinal value of garlic. But did you know that the Greeks favored garlic to ward off evil, while the Romans ate whole cloves for strength and courage, preparing themselves for battle with doses of it. Could it be that their breath sent their enemies into retreat?

Why Doctors Use Vitamin E

In a recent survey of medical doctors as to what vitamins they took on a regular basis, it was found that 40% of the doctors took vitamin E. A study of men aged 50 to 69 found that those who took 50mg of vitamin E daily for five to eight years lowered their risk of prostate cancer by 32%. Even among those who did get cancer, vitamin E reduced their chances of dying from it by 41%.

No one is quite certain just how vitamin E protects us against this cancer but it is said that its antioxidant powers prevent cell damage that sets the stage for cancer. Other studies suggest that vitamin E may reduce the risk of heart attacks too. If taken as a supplement, you may want to consider taking one with 400 IUs of E for maximum protection.

Make sure to buy the natural vitamin E with is better absorbed than the synthetic form.

Chew Away Your Heartburn

If you're prone to getting heartburn after eating a hearty meal, try chewing gum for a half hour after meals. It seems chewing gum boosts saliva production which neutralizes stomach acid and washes it away from the esophagus where it can irritate tender tissues.

Another Reason To Stop Smoking

Along with all of the serious health risks that have been linked to smoking, there is now a new risk. A study shows that smokers are twice as likely to suffer age-related hearing loss as nonsmokers. Researchers speculate that smoking reduces blood flow to the ear.

To Cut Your Risk Of Heart Attack

In a new study of 80,000 women, Harvard researchers found that there was a greater risk of having a heart attack among women who eat lots of *partially hydrogenated vegetable oils* also known as *'trans fats'* (found in margarine and thousands of other processed foods) than in those who eat lots of saturated fats (found in butter, steak and other animal foods). Check the food packages and cut back on those that list hydogenated vegetable oils as an ingredient. If you use margarine, remember that the harder the spread the more trans fats it contains. Use soft or liquid margarines instead.

Volunteer Just For The Health Of It

We all know that *"it's better to give than to receive"* but did you know that studies have shown that people who volunteer actually live longer, happier, healthier lives? Volunteering has been shown to reduce anxiety plus it provides you with a renewed sense of purpose and a feeling of fulfillment.

Besides seniors (folks 50+ years young) have a lot to give. They have a wealth of knowledge, talent and experience (not to mention a wealth of wisdom) that they can now share with others. Remember, giving of your time to help someone else, helps you as well. Plus one day you may be on the receiving end of this aid.

If you have a little time and would like to make a difference in your life and in the life of someone else or if you currently need help, here are a few places to start.

The National Senior Service Corps for National Service

This is a network of more than a half million seniors who are making a difference through the following programs:

FOSTER GRANDPARENTS
In this program seniors are caring for kids. They help children who have been abused or neglected; they mentor troubled teenagers and young mothers and care for premature infants or children with physical disabilities.

Senior Companion Program (SCP)

Isn't it wonderful to help a friend in need? With this program there's help for seniors who have difficulty with day-to-day tasks or who have lost family and friends and need help getting things done. Senior Companions not only provide assistance and friendship but help with chores like paying bills, grocery shopping, providing a ride to a medical appointment and more. Senior Companions also receive training in Alzheimers, strokes, diabetes and mental health, so they are able to alert doctors and family members to potential problems.

Retired Senior Volunteer Program (RSVP)

This program has helped those 55 and older put their skills and life experience to work for others. As an RSVP volunteer, you might teach English to immigrants, organize a neighborhood watch, or help people recover from natural disasters. The number of hours you serve is flexible. You will receive appropriate on-the-job training from the agency or organization where you are placed.

For all of the above, call the National Senior Service Corps at: 1-800-424-8867

Or contact them at their Internet site:
www.senior.com/npo/nssc.html

Service Corps Of Retired Executives (SCORE)

This program, sponsored by the U.S. Small Business Administration, matches volunteers with small businesses that need advice. So if you're thinking of joining the ranks of entrepreneurs - this is the place to get free advice from a seasoned pro. On the other hand, if you are a retired executive and would like to help other budding businessmen get started on the right foot, call them for information on how you can be of service at:
1-800-634-0245

Global Volunteers Make A World Of Difference.

If you've always thought about joining the Peace Corps but hesitated because you couldn't commit for two years, Global Volunteers may be for you.

For the last 14 years Global Volunteers has sent people to 18 countries around the world for a 2-3 week stay. You will be a part of a team of 10-20 volunteers plus host country participants, working on projects that include teaching English, improving health care, working on forest trails and teaching business practices. Since Global Volunteers is a private nonprofit organization, participants pay their own transportation as well as a land package and administration fee that averages $1,000-$2,000. But their entire outlay is tax deductible, including transportation to and from the country. What a great way to see the world and to help your fellow man at the same time. For more information about Global Volunteers, call:
1-800-487-1074.

American Association Of Retired Persons (A.A.R.P.)

A.A.R.P. provides a variety of volunteer programs, services and activities that help older Americans. One example is the *'Widow Person'* referral program (for widows and widowers). With this program, a widowed person can meet with another widowed volunteer in their area for mutual friendship and support. Another service offered is a program that will refer you to organizations in your area either to volunteer your services or to be helped by a volunteer. For a full information package on all of the services offered, call the A.A.R.P. Volunteer Talent Bank.
CALL: 1-800-424-3410

Peace Corps

The Peace Corps can give you the chance to immerse yourself in a totally different culture while helping to make an important difference in other people's lives. If you like helping people and want to get involved, get the *Peace Corps information package.* Call toll-free:

1-800-424-8580

ALSO, CONSIDER VOLUNTEER OPPORTUNITIES IN YOUR TOWN AND CHECK IN YOUR PHONE BOOK FOR YOUR LOCAL CHAPTER OF:

- American Cancer Society
- Chamber of Commerce
- Forest and Wildlife Service
- Forest Service Volunteers
- Hospice, Lions Club
- National Parks Service
- Red Cross
- Vista
- Respite
- Rotary Club
- The United Way

Also check out these web sites with volunteer opportunities: SERVEnet:

www.servenet.org/)

or IdealLIST9

www.contact.org/)

Free Health & Beauty Aids

For many large companies the best way to promote their products is directly to the consumer. And what better way of doing it, than by giving you a free sample. You'll like it, pass it on to your friends and family and the company will have more loyal customers. Everyone comes out ahead!

Some of the free samples listed below may have limited availability, so call now!

10 Steps To Healthy White Teeth

The makers of Rembrandt toothpaste want you to be aware of how you can keep your teeth healthy and white and to show you how to do that they want you to have, *Top Ten Oral Care Problems Have One Solution- Rembrandt.* They also have valuable information they will send you on aging teeth. Along with your free sample of Rembrandt whitening toothpaste they will also send you $1.00 off coupons for all of their products. To get your free sample and money-off coupons call toll-free:
1-800-548-3663

Plus, if you have canker sores in your mouth, call this toll-free hotline for information on a toothpaste specifically designed to relieve your problem.
1-800-433-6628

Taking Care Of Your Skin

Alpha Hydroxy will be happy to send you information about all their skin products and how they will work for you. They

also have a consumer hotline updated monthly that tells about their products and where they are available. If you are interested in finding out about their facial, body care and foot care products, call:
1-800-55-ALPHA

If You Suffer From Migraine Pain

For anyone who suffers from the excruciating pain of a migraine headache, *Chart Your Route To Relief,* is a personal migraine management program that actually helps you find relief. It includes a comprehensive chart that will help you and your doctor pinpoint the cause. To get your free chart simply request it when you write to:
CHART YOUR ROUTE
BOX 816
MEDFORD, NY 11763

Migraine Relief

If you suffer from migrane headaches, you will want to get the *Excedrin Migraine Tablets and Relief Guide.* When you request it, you'll also receive a free sample of their new migraine tablets plus helpful information on dealing with migraine headaches. Call them toll-free:
1-800-580-4455
Or visit their web site at: www.excedrin.com

Milk Sensitive?—Now You Can Enjoy A Milk Shake

Do you have trouble digesting milk and milk products? Now for the first time you can enjoy a big glass of milk or even a delicious ice cream sundae with the help of Lactaid Ultra tablets. To have your questions answered and to receive a free sample plus a coupon to save money on your next purchase, call: **1-800-LACTAID (that's 1-800-522-8243)**

Skin Secrets

Celebrity Skin Secrets is a free booklet from Vaseline. You will be amazed to discover the makeup secrets famous celebrities use to look good. Plus you'll find some quick and easy tips you can use to look great. Call:
1-888-449-8477

Free Earrings

Do your ears sting, turn black or just kill you when you put on your favorite gold earrings? Here's the answer to those sensitive ear woes. Once again you'll be able to wear those fashionable earrings you always dreaded to put on because you were allergic. Simply Whispers will not only send you a catalog of their quality earrings made of top-quality surgical steel with the look of silver or 24-karat electroplated for gold lovers, but a free pair to try as well. Best of all they are guaranteed for life. You have a choice of pierced or clip. Write to them at:

SIMPLY WHISPERS
430 COURT ST.
PLYMOUTH, MA 02360
OR CALL THEM TOLL-FREE AT: **1-800-445-9088**

Pantyhose Problems?

The National Association of Hosiery Manufacturers would like to help you overcome your fear of stocking runs, snags and droops. They will provide you with valuable information and helpful tips on how to determine your correct size, stocking care and how to make your hosiery last. When you call them you can also ask them any specific questions you may have about stockings. Call:
1-800-346-7379

Leg Talk

Has this ever happened to you...you're down to your last pair of stockings and late for an important meeting when, for no apparent reason, the stockings 'run'? Would you like to find out why this happens and what you can do about it? Write for your free copy of *Sheer Facts About Hosiery*.
NATIONAL HOSIERY ASSN.
200 N. SHARON AMITY BLVD.
CHARLOTTE, NC 28211

Ask The Hair Coloring Experts

Are you thinking of changing your hair color? Having trouble finding the right shade? Can't cover that problem gray? The experts at Clairol have a toll-free hotline you can call for answers to all your hair coloring questions. Their color consultants will also provide you with helpful tips that will help you look your very best. Call them Monday-Friday 8:30am-8:30pm or Saturday 9am-6pm EST at:
1-800-233-5800.
You can also visit the Clairol Women's Link site on the Internet at:
www.womenslink.com

Hair Care Guidance & More

If you would like advice on how to manage your hair, how to color it or just how to keep it looking good, L'Oreal has the answers for you. Next time you can't decide which shampoo or conditioner is best for your hair type, call the toll-free L'Oreal Guideline Monday-Friday, 10am-7pm EST at:
1-800-631-7358 or you can write to them at:
L'OREAL CONSUMER AFFAIRS
PO BOX 98
WESTFIELD, NJ 07091

Healthy Diet-Healthy Looks

We've all heard the expression, 'you are what you eat.' Well it's true, the basics of looking good and feeling good, start with healthy eating habits. The American Dietetic Association is making a concerted effort to get us back on a healthy eating track. They have a toll-free phone line you can call weekdays for more information on healthy eating and for a referral to a local dietician. Call the Consumer Nutrition Hotline at:

1-800-366-1655

Keep It Clean

The makers of Moisturel Products would like to show you just how well their skin cleansers and lotions work. If you drop them a card they will send you a $1.00 discount coupon good on your next purchase of Moisturel products. Send a postcard to:

Westwood Pharmaceuticals
468 DeWitt St.
Buffalo, NY 14213

Cooking Up A Storm

If you love to try new things, you're going to love the recipe collections we've found for you. The companies giving away these free cookbooks and recipe collections do so at great expense as their way of saying "thank you" to their loyal customers and also as a way of attracting new customers. They want to inspire you to even greater use of their products by showing you new and innovative ways of using them to create meals you and your family will LOVE.

Wonderful Cajun Style Cooking!

Get a free copy of Chef Paul Proudhomme's Magic Spice book and learn some of his cooking secrets. Imagine using the very same spices in your kitchen that he uses at his famous K-Paul's Louisiana Kitchen in New Orleans. You can receive his *Mail Order Sourcebook*, with 8 different recipes from Chef Paul himself. If you send $1.00 he'll also send you a $5.00 certificate for future purchases along with 2 sample packs of his Magic Seasoning Blends. Send $1.00 to:

"CHEF PAUL PRUDHOMME'S MAGIC SEASONING BLENDS"
PO Box 23342
HARAHAN, LA 70183-0342
OR CALL TOLL-FREE:1-800-457-2857

Delicious M&M Deserts

Everyone knows just how great M&M's are all by themselves. But did you know they also make a great ingredient in mak-

ing deserts? The M&M's Recipe booklet tells you how to make delightful and fun deserts using M&M's. (That is if you don't eat them all first). For your free copy call them toll-free at:
1-800-627-7852

Yummy Cranberries

Ocean Spray would like to show you some of the great things you can do with cranberries. When you call, they will send you four different recipe collections of tasty things to do with cranberries. Just ask for *Cooking With Cranberries*. Call them toll-free at:
1-800-662-3263

Sample A Wonderful Gourmet Coffee

Peerless coffee has been providing the San Francisco area with the freshest and best quality coffee for years. The Peerless Colombian roast has been chosen number one by a panel of experts, and they will be happy to send you a free sample to try. You'll also receive a free catalog of all their delicious coffees and an equally distinctive selection of teas. Their catalog offers not only selected coffees and fine teas but a collection of coffee related gifts from around the world. Write to:
PEERLESS COFFEE CO.
260 OAK ST.
OAKLAND, CA 94607
OR YOU CAN CALL TOLL FREE:**1-800-310-5662**

Hints For A Healthier Diet

Today everyone is focusing on maintaining a healthy diet. Saco Foods will send you their excellent, *Hints For a Healthier Diet*, which discusses oils, fats, fiber, snacks, meats and dairy products, fish...even canned foods are best for you. You'll also receive a free sample of their low-fat cultured buttermilk powder (makes great pancakes) and also free recipes for their sinfully delicious cookies made with Saco's delicious chocolate chunks. They are really the best! Write to:

SACO FOODS
PO BOX 620707
MIDDLETON, WI 53562
OR CALL TOLL-FREE: 1-800-373-SACO (7226)

Fiesta Time

If you love salsa and like to cook up those spicy Southwestern dishes, you'll love this catalog of salsas and seasonings. You'll even get a free sample of their fiesta mix to try. It makes a great addition to those dips, chile, even pasta sauces. You'll really enjoy the unique taste and the fun of trying some new ideas. To get a free catalog and a sample of their tasty 'fiesta mix', contact them at:

SALSA EXPRESS
100 N. TOWER RD.
ALAMO, TX 78516
OR CALL THEM TOLL-FREE: 1-800-43-SALSA
(1-800-437-2572)

Wonderful Low-Fat Meals

If you would like to improve your diet with more low fat meals, be sure to get *Make Over Recipes* from *Swanson Food's Low-Fat collection*. You'll find a wide variety of healthy low-fat meals that are quick and easy to make. To get your collection, call them toll-free at:
1-800-479-2676

It's Herbal Tea Time

If you really enjoy sampling all those wonderful herbal teas, this catalog is a must for you. Here's your chance to try Ginseng Power-Plus or one of their other popular teas. Along with their catalog, they'll also send you some free samples to try. Send an long SASE to:

SATORI FINE HERBALS
825 W. MARKET ST.
SALINAS, CA 93901

Low Salt Recipes

If you would like to cut down your salt intake without cutting down on taste, here's your chance. Try some of the tasty recipes using Nu-Salt, the salt substitute from the makers of Sweet 'N Low. In *Cooking With Nu-Salt* you will find a wide variety of sodium-reduced recipes ...everything from light and healthy Spinach & Pasta Soup to Trout Almondine and Coq au Vin. For your free copy, write to:

NU-SALT
PO BOX 1526
NORTH BRANCH, NJ 08876
OR CALL THEM TOLL-FREE:
1-800-206-9454

Eat More Grain

Near East Company, the makers of great tasty rice, wheat and grain products would like to send you their free recipe booklet with yummy new ways of using healthy grains in your next meal. Call them toll-free at:
1-800-399-4488

Vegetarian Delight

Have you been thinking of becoming a vegetarian? Well now is your chance to join the group of people who have decided they would rather be kind to animals and go vegetarian. It's easy to stay on a vegetarian diet while you are home, but when you go on vacation will you have to bring your own food? The Vegetarian Resource Group has a list of places throughout the U.S. and Canada where you can enjoy vegetarian dining in addition to your regular menus. To get your copy, send a long SASE to:

THE VEGETARIAN RESOURCE GROUP
BOX 1463
BALTIMORE, MD 21203

200 Treats Under 200 Calories.

Imagine trying some delicious low calorie treats for under 200 calories. This is a great low calorie guide to low calorie eating. This low calorie guide to low calorie eating gives you some great tips on calorie counting as well as tasty daily menus. They'll even give you a diet nutrition plan to follow and some yummy recipe collections including different baking ideas. Write:

ROMAN MEAL CO.
PO BOX 11126
TACOMA WA 98411

"The Little Book Of Secrets"

Did you know that soy sauce was first used as a vegetarian seasoning hundreds of years ago? Today millions of people now use it to intensify the natural flavor of meat. Kikkoman Soy Sauce, the big secret in the little bottle, is a great seasoning for all kinds of meats and vegetables. For more ideas, ask for *The Little Book of Big Secrets.* Call toll-free:

1-888-KIKKOMAN

"Clam Lover's Delight"

Gorton's Seafood is delighted to send you their great recipe

collection, *Clam Lover's Delight*. You'll be amazed at all the tasty ways you can use Gorton's chopped or minced clams. You will learn new ways to make tasty appetizers as well as stuffed seafood, or just delicious pasta recipes. Call them toll-free:
1-800-222-6846

The Art of Light Tortillas

Mission Light Tortillas has a wonderful recipe collection using their light tortillas. You can start with the delicious strawberry breakfast crepes or try meatless tortilla lasagna. You'll be amazed at all the tasty dishes you can make from appetizers to main meals. They will also send you some coupons to try their products free. Ask for, *The Art of Light Tortillas*. Write to:
MISSION FOODS CORPORATION
5750 GRACE PLACE, SUITE A
LOS ANGELES, CA 90022

"What's For Dinner"

The makers of Rice a Roni and Pasta Roni have some quick and delicious recipes to help make life easier for you. You'll want to try their Jazzy Jambalaya, lemon garlic chicken or quick taco salad. This collection of easy recipes all can be cooked in 30 minutes or less. These ten delicious recipes come to you on colorful cards which are easy to file with all your other recipes. Write to:
THE GOLDEN GRAIN COMPANY
PO BOX 651230
SALT LAKE CITY, UT 84165

A-1 Steak Sauce Recipe Book

We all know that A-1 Sauce makes a terrific addition to your meat once it's on your plate but did you know that it also

make a great seasoning for all kinds of foods while they are being cooked? Learn all of the great tasting meals you can make by using A-1 Steak sauce in new and innovative ways. Ask for *A-1 Steak Sauce Recipe Book* from:
NABISCO FOODS, INC.
PO BOX 1928
EAST HANOVER, NJ 07936-1928

Meat & Poultry Hotline

The USDA has a meat and poultry hotline to help you with questions dealing with food safety. There are a full series of recorded answers to the most commonly asked questions or if you have specific questions, you can speak with a food safety expert. Call weekdays from 10:00am

- 4:00pm EST to speak to a specialist.
For recorded messages, you can call 24 hours a day.
1-800 535-4555

Simple And Tasty Recipes

The folks at College Inn Broth have a great recipe book to show you how to enhance all your dishes by using their chicken, beef & vegetable broths in new ways. To get your copy, call them toll-free:
1-800-55-BROTH

Flavorful Ways To Cut Back On Fat

Today we know just how important it is to cut back on our consumption of fat. But how do you do that without cutting back on flavor? For starters try using these great recipes

using reduced fat sour cream. Just ask for the *Changing Courses Recipe Collection.* Call:
1-800-782-9602

For Great Meals In Half The Time – Call the Noodle Helpline

Are you always in such a hurry that you never have the time to prepare a new nutritious main dish. Well now's the time to call the *Rice-A-Roni / Noodle-Roni Main Dish Helpline.* Calling this computerized phone service will help you put together a great meal in less than 30 minutes. You will also receive quick to prepare rice and pasta recipes. Call them toll-free at:

1-800-421-2444 OR WRITE TO:
GOLDEN GRAIN CO.
PO BOX 651230
SALT LAKE CITY, UT 84165

Hot Potato

Are you constantly wondering what you can do to make dinner more interesting? Learn why potatoes are America's favorite vegetable and new ways to prepare and serve this healthy vegetable. Ask for *Dinnertime Dilemma: Answers to That Age-Old Question.* Send a long SASE to:
"DINNERTIME DILEMMA" DEPT PA
55 UNION STREET
SAN FRANCISCO, CA 94111

Great For Cookie Lovers

The ultimate cookie is here. Saco Foods will send you these *ten delicious recipes* plus a money-off coupon. Create a chocolate sensation today with these delicious chocolate chunks. Remember, it's the chocolate that makes the difference. Now it's easy to get more sweet satisfaction in each bite! They

even have a *'Bake Your Best' hotline*:
1-800-373-SACO. OR SEND A **SASE** TO:
SACO FOODS
FREE COOKIE OFFER
PO BOX 616
MIDDLETOWN, **WI 53562**

Prize-Winning Beef Recipes

If you would like to sample some of the best beef recipes in the nation, be sure to get a copy of the *National Beef Cook-Off Prize Winning Recipes*. You will find a host of delicious easy-to-prepare meals ranging from Chile Pizza to Gecian Skillet Ribeyes. Send a SASE to:

NATIONAL BEEF COOP-OFF RECIPES
DEPT **NBCO-1997**
444 N. MICHIGAN AVE **18**TH FLOOR
CHICAGO, **IL 60611**
OR CALL TOLL-FREE: **800-848-9088**

Deli-Delicious

Easy Entertaining-Award -Winning Deli Meat Recipes contains 12 recipes for perfect party platters. Preparation times and even calorie counts accompany the recipes. This wonderful freebie comes to you from the National Live Stock and Meat Board. Ask for the *Easy Entertaining Brochure*. Just mail a SASE to:

NATIONAL LIVE STOCK AND MEAT BOARD
444 N. MICHIGAN AVE., DEPT. **EE**
CHICAGO, **IL 60611**

When In Rome

History shows that the Romans used clay cookware many centuries ago. Clay retains moisture which is released slowly during cooking resulting in savory self-basted food. For a terrific collection of recipes using clay Brique Ware, ask for

Brique Ware Recipes and *Microwaving with Nordic Ware.*
Both come to you free from:
NORDIC WARE CUSTOMER SERVICE
HIGHWAY 7 AT 100
MINNEAPOLIS, MN 55416

Sizzlin' Hot Stuff

Red Devil Hot Sauce is a zesty hot sauce that has dozens of
uses—in soups, stews, sandwiches and just about anywhere
you want to add a lively taste to your food. For a compact
collection of dozens of recipes, send a postcard asking for
Seasoning With Trappey's Red Devil Hot Sauce to:
B. F. TRAPPEY'S SONS
DRAWER 400
NEW IBERIA, LA 70560

Snap, Crackle &...Nutrition

When is a Rice Krispie more than a Rice Krispie? When it's
part of a well-balanced nutrition program. The folks at
Kellogg's would like to show you how to serve your family
more nutritious meals using their outstanding line of food
products. Send for *Kellogg's Favorite Recipes,* which is free
from:
DEPARTMENT OF HOME ECONOMICS
KELLOGG CO.
BATTLE CREEK, MI 49016

Fish Really Is Good For You

Research has proven that eating fish really is good for you.
According to a study by the National Fisheries Institute,
the average person eats a total of about 15 pounds of fish a
year, or 4 1/2 ounces per week. Among the top 10 choices are
salmon and catfish. The Catfish Institute has three recipe
brochures waiting for you. In them you'll find a variety of

ideas besides traditional high-fat frying. They can be ordered free just by calling:
1-888-451-FISH

Cooking Light

We all know that what we eat affects our health. But exactly what foods are the best for our health? How do you prepare foods that are good for you? Now there's a toll-free number you can call for answers to these and other questions you may have. This hotline sponsored by the *Healthy Cooking* magazine will put you in touch with registered dietitians who will answer your questions about cooking light. Call between 9 a.m. and 5:30 p.m. weekdays
1-800-231-3438

Bakers Hotline

The Fleishmann's Yeast Bakers Help Line, specializes in answering all your questions about yeast and bread-baking, including advice on using bread machines. Call weekdays between 10 am and 8pm.
1-800-777-4959

Tasty Sweet Nectar

Many people say that Golden Blossom Honey is the tastiest honey there is. To show you how to use their sweet and healthy necter in new ways, they will send you a nice collection of recipes. Just call and ask for the *free Golden Blosssom recipes collection*. Call toll-free:
1-800-220-2110

The Perfect Grill-Out

If you love to barbacue, you're gonna love *A Barbecuer's Dozen Of Rib Ticklin' Recipes.* You can get yours just by calling the Weber Grill Hotline at **1-800-GRILL-OUT.** This toll-free phone number is in operation from April 1st to Labor Day each year. You can also call this same hotline to get answers to all your barbecue questions including cooking methods, fat trimming tips and proper methods of clean up and lots more.

Fascinating Food Facts

The Department of Agriculture has a large package of fascinating and educational materials including a handy food pyramid guide waiting for you. Learn exactly what the USDA does in the areas of consumer services, food safety, nutrition and lots more. Excellent teaching and learning tool. Write to:

U.S. DEPARTMENT OF AGRICULTURE
PUBLICATIONS DIV.
WASHINGTON, DC 20250.
OR YOU CAN ACCESS THEIR HOME PAGE ON THE WORLDWIDE WEB AT
INTERNET ADDRESS:
http://www.usda.gov

Eating Healthy

AARP has a nutrition guide with information on dietary guidelines, the food pyramid, the new food labels and special diets for a better quality of life. To get a free copy of *Healthy Eating For a Healthy Life* (stock #D15565), send a postcard to:

AARP FULFILLMEMNT EE0924
601 E STREET N.W.
WASHINGTON, D.C. 20049

Fine Cheese Recipes

Six cheese recipes on file cards are available free from Marin

French Cheese Company. Also included will be a mail order price list for their fine line of cheeses. Free from:
MARIN FRENCH CHEESE CO.
7500 RED HILL RD.
PETALUMA, CA 94953

Poppin' Fresh Dough

In their new collection, Pillsbury brings you prize winning recipes including cakes from scratch, easy yeast baking and all kinds of new dough ideas. All this to help make your next dessert a sweet and tasty delight. It's yours free from:
PILLSBURY CO.
CONSUMER RESPONSE
P.O. BOX 550
MINNEAPOLIS, MN 55440

De-light Tortillas

To help you add a 'south of the border' touch to your next meal, the folks at Mission Foods would like to send you *The Art of Light Tortillas*. Learn how to make a delightful Spanish Pizza, Strawberry Breakfast Crepes, Fiesta Crab Crisps and lots more.
CALL TOLL FREE: 1-800-600-TACO

Just For Popcorn Lovers

If popcorn is a favorite of yours, the *Favorite Popcorn Recipes* collection is a must. It features mouth-watering popcorn balls, zesty treats and sweet 'n munchy snacks. Drop a postcard to:
AMERICAN POPCORN CO.
BOX 178
SIOUX CITY, IA 51102

Do You Have A Sweet Tooth?

Looking for new dessert ideas your whole family will enjoy?

You'll find lots of yummy dessert recipes and also learn how to cut the fat from sweets with *Plum Good Recipes*. For your free copy and discount coupon, write to:
Sokol & Co.
5315 Dansher Rd.
Countryside, IL 60525

Pasta – A Food For All Times

Here are three excellent booklets for the health conscious. There are terrific recipes plus lots of things you can add to pasta to come up with a new meal. There are even quick microwave dishes you can make. Ask for *Hershey Pasta Recipes* from:
Hershey Pasta Group
Consumer Relations
PO Box 815
Hershey, PA 17033

What's A Porcupine Meatball?

Roman Meal Company makes an excellent line of whole grain breads. *The Roman recipe collection* will show you how to make meals your family will love—like Porcupine Meatballs or Sloppy Joe's. You'll also receive budget stretcher ideas and low-fat diet menus. Free from:
Roman Meal Co.
PO Box 11126
Tacoma, WA 98411

Great Apple Sauce Recipes

This great cookbook has some of the most delightful recipes using Lucky Leaf Apple Sauce. You'll find recipes for everything from entrees to desserts to give your family new taste treats. It's yours free from:
Knouse Foods
Peach Glen, PA 17306

Do You Love Sausage?

Discover a host of tasty new ways of enjoying sausages with the *Hillshire Farm Sausage recipe collection*. For your free copy, send a postcard to:
HILLSHIRE FARMS
ROUTE 4, BOX 227
NEW LONDON, WL 54961

Dinner Pancakes

From the makers of Mrs. Butterworth's buttered syrup, comes a nice collection of great budget recipes that will appeal to any palate. Send a postcard asking for *Mrs. Butterworth's Inflation Fighting Recipes,* to:
LEVER BROTHERS CO.
390 PARK AVE.
NEW YORK, NY 10022

Not For Dieters

Here's a yummy collection of *Hershey's Favorite Recipes* with selections like Chocolate Peppermint Whirlaway Pie. It makes your mouth water just thinking about it. Your diet can wait 'til next month. Also ask for *A Profile Of Hershey Foods.* Drop a card to:
CONSUMER INFORMATION
HERSHEY FOODS
HERSHEY, PA 17033
OR CALL: 1-800-468-1714

Potatoes–A Heart's Good Friend

It's been known for many years that potatoes are one of the healthiest foods you can eat. Now with the *Heart Healthy recipe collection* you will learn how to enjoy this nutritious vegetable in new ways. In addition to tasty recipes you will discover some handy tips on buying and storing Idaho pota-

toes. Send a postcard to:
IDAHO POTATO COMMISSION
P.O. BOX 1068
BOISE, ID 83701

Enjoy A Georgia Peach

Like peaches? You're gonna love Georgia Peach Cobler, Peach Salsa, and other low fat recipes using peaches. Send a long SASE and ask for *Enjoy Georgia Peaches: A Southern Tradition,* to:
GEORGIA PEACH COMMISSION
BOX 38146
ATLANTA, GA 30334

Super Suppers

If you are afraid to enjoy pasta meals just because you're on a diet— this one's for you. With *Super Solutions For Super Suppers,* you will enjoy delicious Italian meals that are nutritionally balanced and still allow you to lose weight. You'll also receive a discount coupon. Send to:
RAGU FOODS, INC.
33 BENEDICT PL.
GREENWICH. CT 06830

Spice Up Your Life

Grey Poupon Dijon Mustard has a sixteen page recipe book that features over 35 different ways to spice up your menu with Grey Poupon Dijon Mustard. Here are tasty recipe ideas for red meat, chicken, pasta, fish and more. Ask for *Excellence Made Easy.* Write to:
NABISCO FOODS GROUP
GREY POUPON
PO BOX 720
HUDSON, WI 54016

Sweet As An...Onion?

An onion is probably the last thing you think of when you think of sweet foods. Vidalia Onion would like to change your mind. These special onions are mild and tasty. They're grown only in a small section of Georgia where weather and soil conditions blend to make the World's Sweetest Onion. Send today for the *Vidalia Onion recipe collection* which will also show you how to freeze and store these unique onions. Send a SASE to:

VIDALIA ONION COMMITTEE
P.O. BOX 1609
VIDALIA, GA 30474

Salmon Delight

This compact collection of seafood recipe ideas comes to you from Lassco Smoked Salmon. You'll find tasty delights that'll make your next barbecue more fun and gourmet delicacies to liven up any meal. Ask for *Seafood Recipes From Lassco.* It's yours free from:

LASSCO
778 KOHLER ST.
LOS ANGELES, CA 90021

Why Fish For Kids

Learn why fish is an important food for kids as well as adults. Send for a free copy of *Why Fish For Kids.* Plus, for the youngsters there's a fun comic book called *Ricky & Debbie in SardineLand* that will entertain while it informs young people about the great benefits of eating fish. All are free from:

MAINE SARDINE COUNCIL
470 N. MAIN ST.
BREWER, ME 04412

Basket Of Fresh Ideas

Just about everyone loves fresh strawberries. Now this collection of yummy strawberry recipes will show you how to use this tasty fruit to make mouth watering desserts and drinks. Send a postcard to:

CALIFORNIA STRAWBERRY ADVISORY BOARD
P.O. BOX 269
WATSONVILLE, CA 95077

Sugarless Sweet Recipes

NutraSweet Company has a nice package of easy to prepare recipes. Some of the things you will receive include *Home Sweet Home With Equal - NutraSweet Spoonful Recipes*, plus some simple tips for making food label information easy to understand and discount coupons. To get your free kit, write to:

E-Z SURVIVAL KIT
THE NUTRASWEET COMPANY
PO BOX 830
DEERFIELD, IL 60015
OR CALL THEIR TOLL-FREE NUMBER: **800-632-8935**

Cooking With Honey

Here's a double-barreled special. First, you'll find some fascinating facts about bees and honey plus a collection of taste tempting recipes using golden honey. Just ask for *Cook It Right With Honey*. Send a card to:

DADANT & SONS
HAMILTON, IL 62341

Top Hits From Frito Lays

This new recipe collection *Baked Low Fat - Taste The Fun Not The Fat* will provide you with a host of innovative new

ways to enjoy Tostitos Tortilla Chips. Enjoy Chicken Curry Nachos or Italian Nachos. You'll also learn *The Story of Frito-Lay*. Free from:
FRITO-LAY,
PO Box 35034
DALLAS, TX 75235

Eat A Yam For Dessert

How would you like to enjoy a marshmallow yam dessert or yam orange cookies? These are just two of the tasty treats you'll find featured in the *Sweet Potato recipe collection* with dozens of prize winning yam recipes. Free from:
LOUISIANA SWEET POTATO COMMISSION
P.O. Box 2550
BATON ROUGE, LA 70821-2550

Birthday Party Planner

Before you plan your child's next birthday party, be sure to send for this freebie. Skippy has put together some great party ideas from invitations to decorations and activities. Ask for *Skippy Peanut Butter Party Planner* from:
SKIPPY PEANUT BUTTER
DEPT. SPP, Box 307
COVENTRY, CT 06238

Spice It Up

Add a little zest to your next meal with these recipes using Tabasco sauce. Send a card asking for *From The Land of Tabasco Sauce*. This cookbook features dozens of tangy and tasty meal ideas and recipes for everything from Holiday Turkey to Cream Onion Dip. Put a little spice in your life and your meals. Write to:
McILHENNY CO.
AVERY ISLAND, LA 70513

New Adventures In Good Eating

Looking for new meal ideas your whole family will enjoy? Meals such as Stuffed Pork Chops and Tangy Chicken are among those you'll find in the *Heinz Recipe Collection*. Also ask for *Heinz Cooking With Beans*. All are free from:
H. J. HEINZ
PO BOX 57
PITTSBURGH, PA 15230

Red Hot Stuff

If you like your food red hot, you'll definitely want to send for this. *Tempting Recipes With Red Devil Hot Sauce* will show you some great ways to spice up your meals. You will also receive a Red Devil discount coupon and a Tabasco catalog. Send a card to:
B. F. TRAPPEY'S SONS. INC.
BOX 400
NEW IBERIA, LA 70560

Fabulous Figs

The fig has been with us ever since Adam and Eve decided that fig leaves made nifty apparel. Now *Buyers Guide To Dietary Fiber* along with *Fabulous Figs - The Fitness Fruit* and *This Fig Can Teach You A Lot About Nutrition* will give you delicious new ways to use this delightful and nutritious fruit. Free from:
DRIED FRUIT ADVISORY BOARD
BOX 709
FRESNO, CA 93712

Being Creative With Olive Oil

When dinner's done you may receive a standing ovation from your family for the meal you just made with the help of this

recipe collection. *How To Change Your Oil & Recipes* will give you a couple of dozen creative meal ideas using olive oil. You will also receive a store discount coupon. Send a postcard to:
POMPEIAN OLIVE OIL
4201 PULASKI HIGHWAY
BALTIMORE, MD 21224

Millionaire Manhattan's & More

The makers of the original cream sherry - Harvey's Bristol Cream have a great recipe collection just for the asking. You'll find 'Peachy Cranberry Sauce' for pork, 'Millionaire's Manhattan' plus lots more. Send a long SASE and ask for *HBC's Recipes* to:
HBC RECIPE COLLECTION
PO BOX 767
HOLMDEL, NJ 07733

Salad Dressing Recipes

This compact collection gives you 5 recipes using Uncle Dan's Salad Dressing and shows how you can use it as seasoning, for party dips and even as a sandwich spread. Write to:
UNCLE DAN'S
PO BOX 980
YAKIMA, WA 98907

Cookouts Are Fun

How would you like a grill chef's hat or a new set of barbacue tools? Be sure to get a free copy of the *Grill Lovers Catalog*. In it you'll find something every barbecue chef will enjoy having. It's yours free from:
W. C. BRADLEY
BOX 1240
COLUMBUS, GA 31902

Ummm ... Good

Campbell has a special collection of recipes along with a discount coupon waiting for you. They feature their tasty line of soups. When you write, ask for the *Golden Corn Soup Chronology.* Write to:

CAMPBELL SOUP CO.
HOME ECONOMICS DEPT.
CAMPBELL PLACE
CAMDEN, NJ 08101

Wonderful Almonds

For a change of pace try using almonds to flavor your next meal. The *Fast & Fabulous collection* will show you how to use almonds in everything from chocolate-almond apricot bread, turkey tetrazzini almondine and almond-blueberry fruit cake. Free from:

ALMOND BOARD OF CALIFORNIA
12TH STREET, BOX 31307
MODESTO, CA 95354

Saucy Recipes

The Light & Elegant Cookbook includes recipes of all kinds with everything from soups to nuts. All these exciting meals feature Lea & Perrins Sauce. There's even a nice index to help you easily find the recipe you want. Free from:

LEE & PERRINS SAUCE
POLLITT DR.
FAIRLAWN, NJ 07410

Butter Recipe Of The Month

One call to the *Best of Butter Hotline* will reveal a world of ideas, recipes and tips on how to use Kellers Hotel Bar Butter in delightful new ways. When you call you will be taken step-by-step through the special recipe for that month. To find out more about their new recipes, cooking tips and product information, contact:

KELLER'S/HOTEL BAR FOODS
CALL THEM TOLL-FREE AT: **1-888-KELLERS**
Web site address: **http://www.butter1.com**

"Cooking With Sweet Potatoes"

Here's a collection of 28 tasty meals using sweet potatoes. You'll enjoy the main dishes and colorful casseroles featuring sweet potatoes in combination with other vegetables and meats. For your free copy, write to:

SWEET POTATO COUNCIL
PO BOX 14
1475 MARSH HILL RD.
MCHENRY, MD 21541

Free Sweet 'N Low Samples

For an envelope full of Sweet & Low samples plus a handy carry case, just send a SASE and request *"Sweet & Low Samples."* Send to:

SWEET & LOW, CUMBERLAND PACKING CORP
2 CUMBERLAND ST.
BROOKLYN, NY 11205

Fresh Ideas From Florida

What a wonderful package this is—an outstanding collection of recipes and information on seafood and aquaculture. Discover how to make a Seafare Saute & lots more. Send a long SASE to:

BOB CRAWFORD
COMMISSIONER OF AGRICULTURE & CONSUMER SERVICES
BUREAU OF SEAFOOD & AQUACULTURE
2051 EAST DIRAC DR.
TALLAHASSEE, FL 32310-3760

Thomas' Promises..

If you like Thomas' English Muffins plain—you'll love 'em fancy. To get their *English Muffins Recipes* plus a discount coupon, send a postcard to:

S.B. THOMAS. INC.
930 N. RIVERVIEW DR.
TOTOWA, NJ 07512

"Texasweet Citrus Recipes"

This collection of mouth-watering citrus recipes comes to you from TexaSweet. Their Ruby Red grapefruit has a sweet, juicy flavor. The recipes cover breakfast, dinner, dessert and drinks using this delectable citrus. Send a postcard to:

TEXASWEET
P.O. BOX 2497
MCALLEN, TX 78501

A Sweet Way To Cheat

If you love sweets (and who doesn't) but must watch your weight *26 Ways To Get Back To Nature* is for you. For your free copy of this booklet plus four others including *Cakes For All Occasions*, send a postcard to:

SUGAR FOODS CORP.
9500 EL DORADO AVE., P.O. BOX 1220
SUN VALLEY, CA 91352

Spread The Nutrition

Oscar Mayer sandwich spreads are easy and versatile to use. Try the spreads on crackers, breads and in other recipes. For a nice collection of recipe ideas called *Nutrition Facts,* send a postcard to:

OSCAR MAYER
DEPT. ST, P.O. BOX 7188
MADISON, WI 53707

Nuts About Nuts

If you're crazy about nuts, *All The Goodness of Hawaii* is the catalog for you. You can order anything from Macadamia Nuts to Kona Coffee. For your free copy, send a postcard to:

MAUNA LOA
MAINLAND GIFT CENTER
PO BOX 1772
PEORIA, IL 61656

Staying Young At Heart

Are you one of the 60 million Americans with high blood pressure? If so you should learn how to eat right. Send for the free booklet, *So You Have High Blood Cholesterol* from:

INFORMATION CENTER
NATIONAL HEART, LUNG, & BLOOD INSTITUTE
7200 WISCONSIN AVE., PO BOX 30105
BETHESDA, MD 20824

'Ole' Fashioned Creole Cooking

If you enjoy the unique taste and flavors of Cajon and creole food, this one's for you. Tony Chachere's Creole Foods, featured in Oprah Winfrey's cookbook, *In The Kitchen With Rosie,* would like to send you a free cookbook showing you how to use their creole seasoning to create old-fashioned Louisiana taste delights. Write to

TONY CHACHERE'S CREOLE FOODS
533 NORTH LOMBARD ST.,
PO BOX 1687
OPELOUSAS, LA 70571

Sizzling Lamb Recipes

The American Lamb Council has several recipe collections that will show you exciting ways to make your dinners more delightful. The collection includes *Make It Simple, Make It*

Sizzle, and *Festive Lamb Recipes,* plus several others. You'll find wine-basted, marinated, grilled, roasted and broiled recipes using fresh American lamb. Send a long SASE to:
THE AMERICAN LAMB COUNCIL
6911 S. YOSEMITE ST.
ENGLEWOOD, CO 80112

Bringing Home The Bacon

If you like bacon, be sure to get your copy of *Savor The Flavor, Round The Clock With Oscar Mayer Bacon.* In it you'll discover tasty recipes and cooking ideas featuring bacon. They will also include party & cookout recipes using Oscar Mayers Little Wieners & Little Smokies plus Nutrition Facts. Send a postcard to:
BACON BOOKLETS
OSCAR MAYER CONSUMER CENTER
PO BOX 7188
MADISON, WI 53707

Delicious Skinny Beef

Looking for something easy but delicious for your family's meals? How about meals that are perfect for anyone watching their weight? Try something different... like 'beef, pasta & artichoke toss' or 'quick steak & vegetable soup'. Send a SASE and ask for *Delicious Easy Beef Recipes From Skinny Beef.* Send to:
MEAT BOARD TEST KITCHENS
DEPT. DEBR, 444 N. MICHIGAN AVE
CHICAGO, IL 60611

How To Comfort

Now you can make some great desserts, drinks and even coffee using that versatile liquor from Kentucky — Southern Comfort. If you would like some delicious recipe ideas, write to:

SOUTHERN COMFORT COMPANY
DEPT. GT, BOX 1080
LOUISVILLE, KY 40201

Wine And Dine With Gallo

The Gallo recipe collection will show you dozens of palate pleasing ways of using Gallo to enhance your next meal. Included is a delightful recipe for a Goumet Pizza and lots more. These recipes will help you turn everyday cooking into an adventure. Write to:

E & J GALLO WINERY
MODESTO, CA 95353

New Recipes For Using White Wine

Wine lovers delight in trying new wines and new ways to enjoy familiar wines. With this compact collection of recipes called, *White Wine Recipes,* you'll create tasty new meals using the fine wines of Widmer. Free from:

WIDMER WINE CELLARS
NAPLES, NY 14512

Free Wine Tasting Tour

Beaulieu Vineyards describes and pictures the Beaulieu line of fine wines. Also includes a card for a free wine tasting tour of their vineyard. Write to:
BEAULIEU VINEYARDS
PO BOX 329
RUTHERFORD, CA 94573

Virgin Island Rum

Cruzan Rum is an exceptionally clean tasting rum that works well with mixers or on its own. For your copy of the free *Imported Rum Recipes*, write:
CRUZAN RUM DISTILLERY
PO BOX 218, FREDERIKSTED
ST. CROIS, VL 00840

The Finest Cordial Recipes

Hiram Walker has put together a selection of over 30 famous food and drink recipes from around the world. These recipes all feature their fine line of cordials. Just ask for their free, *The Best Of Kahlua*. Pink Chinchilla Pie anyone? Write to
HIRAM WALKER
P.O. BOX 33006
DETROIT, MI 48232

The Marvelous Liqueur

Chambord is a liqueur made with small black raspberries plus other fruits & herbs combined with honey. For new ways to enjoy this magnificent liqueur, send for the free *Chambord Recipe Book* from:
CHAMBORD RECIPES
LA MAISON DELAN ET CIE
2180 OAKDALE DR.
PHILADELPHIA, PA 19125

For Home & Garden

"Trash The Germs"

The makers of Bounty paper towels want to send you their informative booklet *Trash the Germs,* to help reduce the spread of household germs. Most of us are not aware of how we can prevent the spread of household germs before they cause serious problems. Using paper towels to dry your hands and discarding it after handling meat or poultry products reduces the risk of leaving any bacteria to linger and multiply on a cloth dish towel. Learn to have good home hygiene ask for *Trash the Germs.* Call toll-free:
1-888-554-3767

Easy Cleaning From Pledge

Dust Control brochure and *Home and Gardens Simple Solutions Booklet* are yours from the makers of Pledge. These handy guides will give you all kinds of tips to make your cleaning chores a breeze. After reading and using some of their handy tips you'll have more free time to relax and enjoy the day. When you call, the recorded voice mail will ask you a number of automated questions including your name and address. Call them toll-free at:
1-888-647-5334

Dirty Secrets

Wisk will be happy to send you their free *Dirty Secrets* brochure with tips on how to handle all those dirty laundry problems. To get your copy, just call them toll-free at:
1-800-ASK-WISK

Powerful Hand Cleaner

Ink Solv is great hand cleaner that will remove those ugly hard to clean ink and paint stains from your hands. If you are tired of scrubbing ink and paint stains, give them a call. They're offering a free sample if you need a heavy duty soap in your work. Call them toll-free:
1-800-383-0251

Free Potpourri Bonnets

These delightful miniature straw hat bonnet magnets are filled with potpourri and ready for your refrigerator door or bathroom. They are yours for two first class loose stamps. Send to:
VALERIE'S HATTERY
4494 POLK
DEARBORN, MI 48125

Putting Solar Energy To Work

One day your home may be heated and powered with free energy from the sun. Here are the answers to many of the most frequently asked questions about putting solar and other kinds of renewable energy to work for you. Write to:
RENEWABLE ENERGY INFORMATION
BOX 8900
SILVER SPRINGS, MD 20907

There is also a toll-free phone number you can call to get in touch directly with an expert who can answer specific questions you may have about renewable energy. There are also a large number of free booklets dealing with every aspect of renewable energy. They are all available by calling the same toll-free number.
CALL: **800-523-2929.**

Finally, if you have a computer and modem you can access the Department of Energy and Renewable Resources, on the

Worldwide Web. They even have free software you can download. Their web site is located at:
www.eren.doe.gov
Their bbs can be reached at:
http://erecbbs.nciinc.com

Important Tips To Save Energy

Saving energy not only makes America less energy dependent on other nations - it will save you a tidy sum of money too. The Department of Energy has put together a package chuck full of useful energy-saving information they would like you to have. Ask for the *Energy Saver booklets.* They're yours free from:
D.O.E. Technical Information Center
Box 62
Oak Ridge, TN 37830

How Does Fiberglas Work?

All About Insulation and *Owens-Corning Fiberglas* are two of the useful guides found in the *Fiberglas information series.* You'll find out how Fiberglas is made and how it's used for insulation, dust-stops and air filters. It's yours free from:
Owen Corning Fiberglas
Fiberglas Tower
Toledo, OH 43659

Let The Sun Shine In

If you're planning on building or remodeling a house, have you thought about which new windows and doors are right for you? *Window Scaping* pictures and describes all of the various types of windows and doors available to help you decide for yourself. It's free from:
Rolscreen Co.
Pella, IA 50219

Home Remodeling Ideas

Are you getting ready to build or remodel a home? If so the *Insider's Look At Building Your Home* and *Insider's Look At Remodeling Your Home* are an absolute must. Your creative juices will begin to flow as you thumb through these beautifully illustrated idea books. The answer books will provide help in solving your remodeling problems whether you're adding a room or simply changing a window. Write to:

ANDERSEN CORP.
BAYPORT, MN 55003
1-800-426-4261 EXT 2837
Or visit them on the web at: www.andersenwindow.com

Emergency Stain Removal

This helpful *Emergency Spot Removal Guide* will help you get rid of some of the trickiest stains you may get on your carpets or draperies. It is free for the asking and will come with discount coupons. Drop a postcard to:

COIT DRAPERY & CARPET CLEANERS
DEPT. ABJ, 897 HINKLEY RD.
BURLINGAME, CA 94010

Beautify & Protect Your Home

Red Devil would like to show you the right way to beautify your home with wall coverings and protect it from cracks and drafts with caulk. Ask them for the *free wallcovering and caulk booklets*. Write to:

RED DEVIL INC.
CONSUMER RELATIONS
PO BOX 3133, UNION, NJ 07083

"The Story Of Hardwood Plywood"

If you are a handyman, you'll enjoy this informative booklet which tells the whole story of plywood. Best of all you'll receive a set of 4 different plans showing you how to build a bookcase, room divider, saddle seat desk and TV trays (planter/desk/stereo, etc.) All free from:

HARDWOOD PLYWOOD MANUFACTURERS
PO BOX 2789
RESTON, VA 22090

Building A House You Can Afford

You may still be able to afford the home you've always wanted. For the past quarter century DeGeorge Homes has helped over 15,000 people enjoy home ownership with their step-by-step instructions and pre-cut material. For a free copy of their 80 page *color catalog* with 50 exciting models to choose from, contact:

DEGEORGE HOMES
55 REALTY DRIVE
CHESHIRE, CT 06410
1-800-342-7576

"Save Water"

Wasting water even from a slow leak over time can cost you a bundle. To help you prevent this, here's a fully illustrated guide on how to pinpoint water waste in your toilet and what to do about it. You'll also receive a packet of dye you can use to detect leaks. Drop a postcard to:

FLUIDMASTER
PO BOX 4264
1600 VIA BURTON
ANAHEIM, CA 92803

The Right Way To Clean A Carpet

Hoover will send you a free guide to carpet care. *The Con-*

sumer Guide to Carpet Cleaning is loaded with carpet care tips and facts, cleaning alternatives, a stain removal chart and more. This 16 page booklet provides important information you should know. Ask for *Consumer Guide to Carpet Cleaning.* Send a long SASE to:

THE HOOVER COMPANY
CONSUMER EDUCATION, DEPT. FC
101 E. MAPLE ST.
NORTH CANTON, OH 44720

For A Worry-Free Septic System

If you have a septic system, time may be running out before your system fails. Before that happens, the makers of RID-X would like to send you this informative booklet, which can help you avoid septic system failure. Send a postcard to:

RID-X
DEPT. MBD
MONTVALE, NJ 07645

Save On Wallpaper By Mail

This great *catalog* offers you an excellent selection of high quality wall covering products at low, low prices. To make your selection easier, they will send you free swatches of the paper and even matching fabrics. Send a postcard to:
ROBINSON'S WALLCOVERINGS
225 WEST SPRING ST.
TITUSVILLE, PA 16354

"Guide To Paint & Varnish Removal"

In this handy guide you will learn some great and easy ways to improve the appearance of your house. There are quick and easy methods for removing both mildew stains and paint or varnish from all interior and exterior surfaces. These helpful hints are a must for any tough cleaning or renovat-

ing job. Send for your free guide to:
Savogran Company
P.O. Box 130
Norwood, MA 02062

Alarm Your Home For Security

To protect your family and home, a home security alarm system is essential. To help you decide on what type of protection is best for you and your family, ask for the free *Amgard Security Planning Guide.* Write to:
Amgard Security Offer
Amway Corporation-33A-2J
Ada, MI 49355

The All-Purpose Wonder

Want to save money and look good too? Send for *This Little Box With A House Full of Uses.* In it you will learn how to use baking soda in ways you never thought of...in the kitchen, bathroom, basement, even on your pet. Write to:
Arm & Hammer
Consumer Relations
Church & Dwight Co.
Princeton, NJ 08547

Stain Removal Guide

Most stains can be removed if you know how. The people at Maytag have an excellent stain removal guide they will send you just for the asking. Remember, once you master the steps it's easy to remove just about any stain by referring to this handy guide. You'll also receive *Facts of Laundry.- Choosing The Right Laundry Additives.* Send a postcard to:
Maytag Company
Customer Education Dept.
One Dependability Square
Newton, IA 50208

Carpet Care

If you are thinking of adding or changing carpets in your home but are confused by the many choices you have to make, call The Carpet and Rug Institute's information line for answers to your questions related to carpeting your home **1-800-882-8846**

How To Stay Warm This Winter

Stay warm this winter with insulated clothing, outdoor equipment and toasty down comforters that you make yourself — with the help of a Frostline kit. For a copy of their free catalog, send a postcard to:

FROSTLINE KITS
2525 RIVER ROAD.
GRAND JUNCTION, CO 81505

Slip-Free Bathtub

If you've always wanted to have a slip-free bathtub, here's your chance. You'll never have to use messy bathtub stickems or a rubber mat. The makers of Trusty Step have great news for you...a simple 3 minute treatment can make your tub slip-free forever. Send a SASE to:

TRUSTY STEP
405 TARRYTOWN RD. SUITE 414
WHITE PLAINS, NY 10607

Keeping Your Silver Glistening

If you would like to keep your silverware shining like new, try storing it in Hagerty's Tarnish Intercept Bags. Once the silverware is placed inside and the bag zipper is closed, it locks out tarnish. The inside of the bag will blacken when it has absorbed all the corrosion-causing gases. You then remove the silver and place it in a new bag. For information

on their line of precious metal care products, call:
1-800-348-5162 x137
W. J. HAGERTY SONS, LTD.
P.O. BOX 1496
SOUTH BEND, IN 46624.
OR VISIT THEIR WEB SITE AT:
www.hagerty-polish.com

Shingle Your Home Inside & Out

Lots of remodeling ideas are contained in this great *Red Shingle & Shake package.* It shows how to use shingles and shakes outside and inside your house. These guides also show how to do-it-yourself and save. Drop a card to:
RED CEDAR SHINGLE & HANDSPLIT SHAKE BUREAU
SUITE 275, 515 116TH AVE. N.E.
BELLEVUE, WA 98004

Stain Out Hotline

Do you have questions about problem stains on your favorite garments? What do you do if it's an unknown mystery stain and you don't know where to begin? The Dow Stain Experts, the makers of Spray 'N Wash, have the answers for you. Give them a call at on their toll-free hotline:
1-800 260-1066

Free Spot Removal Guide

Here are lots of helpful tips from the clean clothes professionals at Clorox on keeping your clothes clean, bright and stain free. Ask for *Emergency Spot Removal Guide.* Drop a postcard to:
THE CLOROX CO.
PO BOX 24305
OAKLAND, CA 94623

How To Choose The Right Carpet

If you are thinking of buying new carpets, Dupont Company would like you to have this free booklet *Consumer's Guide To Choosing Carpets* to help answer all your questions about carpet selection and care. Send a postcard to:
DUPONT CO.
ROOM G 40284
WILMINGTON, DE 19898.

Brighten Up Your Garden

Would you like to add a colorful look to your garden next spring? Consider planting Holland or domestic tulip bulbs. For a full color catalog, write to:
VAN BOURGONDIEN
PO BOX A, 245 FARMINGDALE RD.
ROUTE 109
BABYLON, NY 11702

Start An Herb Garden On Your Window Sill

This catalog is packed with everything you can imagine to start your vegetable, flower or fruit garden. They have seed starter kits and plants. You'll even find garden helpers, bird houses and fun seed kits for kids. Grow your own herb garden right on your kitchen window sill. When you call or write mention *OFFER #82* and in addition to their new *Flowering Bulb and Perennial Catalog*, you'll also receive a special $5.00-off coupon. Free from:

W. ATLEE BURPEE & CO.
WARMINSTER, PA 18974
OR CALL **1-800-888-1447**

Start A Community Garden

In the last few years backyard community gardens have been popping up all over the nation. Bring your community together add beauty to your community and save money too - start a community garden. You'll also receive teaching tools to help young minds grow. Ask for *Growing Ideas*. It's yours free from:

NATIONAL GARDEN ASSOCIATION
180 FLYNN AVE.
BURLINGTON, VT 05401

Why Plants Fail

The question of why some plants fail to grow even when they are carefully tended to, has always been somewhat of a mystery. Now Gurney Seed and Nursery would like to throw some light on the subject so you can have a more beautiful garden. They will also send you the new *Gurney Catalog*. It features over 4000 items—many shown in full color. You'll find how-to-grow-it tips plus planting charts and moisture guides along with many special offers. If you'd like a packet of giant sunflower seeds, include a quarter. Write:

GURNEY SEED & NURSERY CO.
DEPT. 84, 1130 PAGE ST.
YANKTON, SD 57079

Growing An Organic Garden

How To Grow An Organic Garden will get you started raising your own delicious and naturally pure vegetables. It even includes a plan for a sample garden. Get your free copy and let Mother Nature do her thing. Write to:

ORGANIC GARDENING & FARMING
33 E. MINOR ST.
EMMAUS, PA 18049

1,300 Exotic Imported Plants

Do you enjoy unusual and out-of-the ordinary type plants? If so, this one's for you. The new *Stokes seed catalog* features 1300 varieties including many imported from England, Europe, and Canada. Get your free catalog from:
STOKES SEEDS INC.
BOX 548
BUFFALO, NY 14240

Terrific Nursery Guide

In this nursery catalog and planting guide, you'll find a new seedless grape, virus-free berries and several pages of tested recipes and a whole lot more. Miller Nurseries has put together a broad selection of their most popular nursery items. Ask for their new *Catalog & Planting Guide*:
J. E. MILLER NURSERIES
DEPT. 706
WEST LAKE RD.
CANAN-DAIGUA, NY 14424

To Grow The Perfect Lawn

Here's a super 5-star special for anyone with a lawn or garden. To help improve lawn, flowers, vegetable garden, trees and shrubs - call the experts at Scott Lawn Products on their toll-free phone. They have the answers to any and all questions about lawn growing, diseases, fertilizing, problem areas and more. They'll also give you a free subscription to *Lawn Care* with loads of useful information (plus money saving coupons). They're happy to send you any of the dozens of booklets, magazines and brochures that will help you grow the perfect lawn or garden. Excellent. Call toll free:
1-800-543-TURF OR WRITE:
SCOTT LAWN PRODUCTS
14111 SCOTTS LAWN RD.
MARYVILLE, OH 43041

Would You Like A Great Lawn?

Loft's Grass seeds will be happy to send you a free *Lawn Care Guide* chuck full of useful information to help you create a great lawn. Call them toll-free at:
1-888-775-6387

Imagine – Full-Sized Fruit From Dwarf-Size Trees!

If your yard is too small to grow as many fruit trees as you'd like, take a look at this free catalog. These dwarf trees grow only 8 to 10 feet tall but grow full size apples, peaches, pears, cherries, and nectarines. This catalog features almost 400 varieties of fruit, shade and nut trees plus shrubs, vines, ornamentals, and award-winning roses. Send a postcard for

the catalog and special offers to:
STARK BROTHER NURSERIES & ORCHARD CO.
BOX A12119
LOUISIANA, MO 63353

Free Fertilizer

Free manure is available to gardeners through Extension Services located throughout the country. To find the one nearest you, call your local U.S. Department of Agriculture Extension Service. You'll find their phone number in the blue pages of your local phone book.

Great Gardens

The Burreil Seed Growers have a nice seed catalog every home gardener will want to have. It features all kinds of wonderful ideas on creating a beautiful garden. Before you get ready to plant your next garden, be sure to get a copy of this catalog. Send a postcard to:
D.V. BURREIL SEED GROWERS
PO BOX 150H
ROCKY FORD, CO 81067

Gardener's Handbook

If you want to learn how to have a beautiful fruitful garden, be sure to get a free copy of *The Park Gardener's Handbook*. In it you will find all kinds of useful information that will help you to get more productive results from your gardening efforts. You can also choose from over 3000 new and rare varieties of flowers and vegetables as well as the more familiar types—all available in the full color Park catalog you'll receive. Send a postcard to:
GEORGE W. PARK SEED CO. INC.
254 COKEBURY ROAD
GREENWOOD, SC 29647

For Pet Lovers

Being Kind To Animals

If you care deeply for animals, The American Society For The Prevention of Cruelty to Animals...the ASPCA has an information packet including booklets about caring for or traveling with your pets. To get a full list of their helpful information, write to:

AMERICAN SOCIETY OF PREVENTION OF CRUELTY TO ANIMALS
PUBLIC INFORMATION DEPT.
424 E. 92ND ST.
NEW YORK, NY 10128

Or visit them on the Internet at:
www.aspca.org

How About A Free Pet?

If you have ever stopped by a pet shop in the mall to play with the delightful puppy they had sitting in the window, you learned that to take that puppy home would make a deep dent in your wallet. There's no reason to spend hundreds of dollars when your local newspaper and supermarket bulletin boards may have ads giving away free kittens and pups when their pets have litters. Also, don't forget that animal shelters also have delightful free pets dying for a home. Usually they'll only ask you to pay for the shots. Call your local animal shelter for more information.

Free Animal Calendar And Datebook

For pet lovers everywhere, The Animal Protection Institute has a handy informative *Animals Calendar and Datebook*. In addition to being a datebook and calendar it is full of hundreds of fascinating facts about animals plus a listing of important animal events. If you love animals, this is definitely for you. Write to:

ANIMAL PROTECTION INSTITUTE
2831 FRUITAGE ROAD
SACRAMENTO, CA 95820
1-800-348-PETS
Internet: www.onlineapi@aol.com

Caring For A Dog With Arthritis

Does your dog have difficulty getting up after a nap or a hard time climbing? Most people just assume that it's old age and that nothing can be done about it. The problem may very well be osteoarthritis which afflicts 1 dog in 5. Pfizer Dog Care has a toll-free number you can call for information on what you can do for your dog if it suffers from this problem. Call:
1-800-720-DOGS

Taking Special Care Of Your Cat

Special Care for Special Cats is a cat chow that helps maintain the urinary tract health for your cat. It's made with real chicken for a great taste. For information call:
1-800-CAT CARE

Your Dog Will Love You More

Purina One Reduced Calorie Dog Formula is made with real turkey, that makes it nutritious and tasty. Your dog will love

it! For your free sample plus useful information, call:
1-800-787-0078 Ext. 43

Breath Friend For Your Pet

Did you know that regular dental care may actually pro-long a pet's life? Breath Friend is a pet oral cleanser that cleans teeth and eliminates bad breath without brushing. You will receive absolutely free a *Breath Friend* sample and information about the importance of oral health in pets. You'll even get a $1.00 rebate on your first purchase. Send a long SASE to:

American Media Group
7300 W. 110th St., Suite 960
Overland Park, KS 66210
Or visit their website: www.breathfriend.com

If You're Allergic To Pets

If you would love to have a pet but are allergic to animal hair and dander, there may be a new way to help eliminate those allergies around the house with a new vacuum by Nilfisk, Inc. of America. Call:
1-800-241-9420 Ext 2

Free Vet Care For Your Pet

Remember if you live near a university that has a Veteri-nary school, you may be able to get free vet care for your pet especially if you are a senior citizen. Call them and ask about the services they offer.

Also, if you need assistance with an ailing pet, contact:
Center for Veterinary Medicine
U.S. Food and Drug Administration
7500 Standish Place
Rockville, MD 20855
301-295-8755

You And Your New Puppy or New Kitten

Are you thinking of getting a new puppy or kitten? If so, this freebie from Iams Company is for you. *You & Your New Puppy* and *You & Your New Kitten* will give you useful advice on feeding, house-training, health care, grooming, training of a new pet and lots more. Write to:

**The Iams Company
Puppy/Kitten Information Center
Box 1475
Dayton, Ohio 45401**

Caring For Your Pet

If you have a dog or are planning to get one, make sure you write for *free pet information* from the folks at Ralston Purina dog food products. They have an excellent freebie that will not only give you a brief history of dogs, but also give you tips on feeding your dog, grooming, obedience training, keeping your dog healthy and traveling with your dog. They may also include discount coupons and a Purina dog food guide to balancing nutrients to meet your dog's needs. Also ask for *Guide To Caring For Your Dog* and *Help...My Pet Refuses To Eat*. These freebies are a must if you've ever thought of getting a dog for a pet. Write to:

**Ralston Purina
Dog Food Division
Checkerboard Square
St. Louis, MO 63164.**

This Cake Is For The Birds

Lafeber's Avi-Cakes Gourmet Bird Food will provide a perfectly nutritious snack to satisfy bird munchies. Avi-Cakes is a nutritionally complete bird treat with proper vitamins and delicious flavors. Get your free trial size sample now. Ask for the *Avi-Cakes Sample* Write to:

LAFEBER COMPANY
24981 N. 1400 EAST RD
CORNELL, IL 61319

Fish Are Fun

Fish are educational, fun and something the whole family can enjoy. Now you can learn step-by-step how to set up a year round backyard pond and stock it with hardy fish. Send for your free *We Are The Water Garden Experts*. Drop a postcard to:

TETRA POND
3001 COMMERCE ST.
BLACKSBURG, VA 24060-6671

Raising A Healthy Pet

If you have a cat or dog, Gaines Foods has a number of useful and informative publications that will show you how to care for and raise a healthy pet. They are yours just for the asking. Just ask for the free publications list from:

QUAKER PROFESSIONAL SERVICES
585 HAWTHORNE COURT #14
GALESBURG, IL 61401

More Than A Friend

To millions of people their pet is a real member of the family. And love of animals has inspired many to follow a career path to becoming a veterinarian. For these people, the American Veterinary Association has an interesting booklet called *Today's Veterinarian* about the opportunities available today in this interesting field. For your free copy, send a postcard to:

AMERICAN VETERINARY ASSOCIATION
1931 NORTH MEECHAM RD. SUITE 100
SCHAUMBURG, IL 60196

Caring For Your Pets

The American Humane Association has a whole series of informative booklets available for pet owners. These booklets tell how to care for dogs, cats, horses, birds and fish. For a complete listing, write for their free *catalog of publications*. From:

AMERICAN HUMANE ASSOCIATION
P.O. BOX 1266
DENVER, CO 80201

Better Pet Care And Nutrition

If you'd like any information about proper pet care and pet nutrition, the makers of Kal Kan pet food would like to help you. They will send you *Understanding Your Dog* and *Understanding Your Cat*. Write to:

KAL KAN CONSUMER ADVISORY SERVICE
3386 EAST 44TH ST.
P.O. BOX 58853
VERNON, CA 90058

Craft & Hobbies

Free Bead Supply Catalog

Are you looking for an interesting and challenging hobby? The Frantz Bead Company has put together an informative newsletter and supply catalog to help teach you the art of bead making. You'll get the free newsletter plus a catalog with a full assortment of terrific bead supplies. Simply send a postcard to:

FRANTZ BEAD COMPANY
1222 SUNSET HILL ROAD
SHELTON, WA 98584

Beautiful Christmas Ornament

If you love to collect truly unique Christmas ornaments, you will definitely want to get this one. It's a beautiful hand-made angel that will quickly become the centerpiece of your holiday decorations. Simply send $2.00 (or 7 loose first class stamps) for shipping and handling and request the *'Christmas Angel'* from:

ANGELIC CREATIONS
PO BOX 4620
TRAVERSE CITY, MI 49685

Fun With Ribbons

Learn to create colorful and fun projects with ribbons. You'll be amazed at what you can create using ribbons of all sizes, colors and textures. This is a great rainy day project and

you can even use the finished projects to raise money for a special cause. Write to:
CON OFFRAY & SON
ROUTE 24, BOX 601
CHESTER, NJ 07930

If You Like Duplicate Bridge

Do you enjoy playing duplicate bridge? If so you'll want this *catalog and product source guide* with just about anything you might want or need for this game. Write to:
AMERICAN CONTRACT BRIDGE LEAGUE
2990 AIRWAYS BLVD.
P.O. BOX 161192
MEMPHIS, TN 38116

Playing Better Chess

Learn the official rules of this challenging game of chess and also receive another publication to join the U.S. Chess Federation. Chess helps you develop your ability to think analytically. Ask for *Ten Tips To Winning Chess*. Send a long SASE to:
U.S. CHESS FEDERATION
DEPT. 17, 186 ROUTE 9W
NEW WINDSOR, NY 12553
OR CALL: 1-800-388-KING

Crocheting A Doll

If you love to crochet you'll want this free pattern for a pair of Raggedy Ann and Andy dolls. Crocheting these dolls are just half the fun ...giving them as a gift and seeing the joy they bring is the rest. Send a long SASE and $1.00 postage and handling to:
NP PATTERNS
341 4TH TERRACE
EGG HARBOR, NJ 08215

For Collectors of Mechanical Toys

If you are a collector of fine mechanical toys, this beautifully illustrated catalog is for you. In the 32 pages of this catalog you will find a unique collection of classic cars. Ask for Lilliput Catalog from:

LILLIPUT
PO BOX 447
YERINGTON, NV 89447
OR CALL: **1-800-TIN-TOYS**

Trap Your Bad Dreams With A Dream Catcher

The Dakota and Chippewa Indian legend says that the 'dream catcher' will trap your bad dreams but will let the good dreams pass through so that they can come true. Tandy Leather will send you a *Dream Catcher Kit* so you can make your own. Send $2.00 postage and handling to:

TANDY LEATHER
PO BOX 791, DEPT FED
FORT WORTH, TX 76101

Star Search

Do you have a favorite recording artist or special movie star? Well here's your chance to get an autograph of that famous star. You'll receive a listing of over 100 superstar names and addresses along with a brief bio as well as helpful hints on making your star search productive. Send a long SASE to:

JIM WEAVER'S AUTOGRAPHS IN THE MAIL
322 MALL BLVD., #345
MONROEVILLE, PA 15146-2229

Free Celebrity Autograph

Have you always wanted to collect a celebrity's autograph

but didn't know how to get it? Now there's someone who will teach you how. When you write, you'll receive a free address of a celebrity and instructions on how to request an 8x10 autographed celebrity photo. The first time you write, the celebrity's address you receive will be Mr. Greenhill's choice. He's been doing this for 10 years so he knows what he's doing. To get on the celeb bandwagon, send a long SASE to:

DAVID GREENHILL
2306 CEDAR WAY
DALLAS TX 75241

Help From Kodak on How To Take Great Photos

This 48 page guide in full color shows you how to take the best snapshots under any circumstances. It's easy to understand and deals with topics such as lighting, flash photography, action and more. So start taking better pictures now. Ask for *Hot Shots With Any Camera*. Call:
1-800-242-2424

Crochet Time

These free crochet instructions will show you how to make some beautiful hand made ornaments, that you could sell, give as gifts or enjoy yourself. You can make seven simple thread snowflakes and 10 easy yarn ornaments. So get started now and send for your free instructions. Ask for: Crochet Tree-Trim Pattern, SASE to:

LORRAINE VETTER-SR
7924 SOPER HILL ROAD
EVERETT, WA 98205

Home Sewing Basics

If you're thinking of decorating anything from a single room

to an entire house, be sure to get, *Sewing - It's Sew Soothing*. Discover how much fun it is to make your own curtains, slip covers and pillow shams. To get your copy, send a long SASE to:
AMERICAN HOME SEWING AND CRAFT ASSOCIATION
1375 BROADVIEW
NEW YORK, NY 10018

Blackjack Strategy Card

A free Black Jack Strategy Card is yours for the asking. This pocket-sized card gives you invaluable strategies, based on what you are dealt and what the tester is showing. Various combinations of hands and dealer show cards are printed right on an easy to read chart. Gambling, blackjack in particular, can be fun if you're able to combine luck with a little strategy. Ask for *Black Jack Strategy Card*. Write to:
THOMAS GAMING SERVICES
PO BOX 1383
GOLETA, CA 93116

Beat The Odds In BlackJack

Thousands of people love the challenge and excitement of blackjack. If this describes you, you may have wondered if there was any way you could improve your chances of winning. To help you better your odds, send for a wallet-size free mini-magnetic strategy card. Send a SASE and ask for *Winning Blackjack Strategies* to:
S. J. LEE ENTERPRISES
PO BOX 333-H, DEPT. BSR
SCARSDALE, NY 10583

Having Problems With Your Polaroid?

Have your Polaroid photos been coming out the way you'd

like? If not there's a toll-free hotline to call where an expert will answer any questions you may have. Call toll free 8AM -8PM Monday through Saturday at: **800-343-5000.** Polaroid has a wonderful policy of complete customer satisfaction. Your problem may lie with defective film which they'll replace at no charge. Send defective film or photos to:

POLAROID CUSTOMER CARE SERVICE
784 MEMORIAL DR.
CAMBRIDGE, MA 02139

Just For Knife Collectors

This catalog is packed with hundreds of knives, swords, specialty and novelty knives, sharpening systems, accessories and more. Now you can find that special carving knife for meat, cheese or fruitcake. If you are a collector of swords and sheaths there are several to choose from. Write:

SMOKY MOUNTAIN KNIFE WORKS
BOX 4430
SEVIERVILLE, TN 37864

Taking Better Photos

Kodak has a terrific freebie for anyone who wants to take perfect (or at least better) photographs. Call their toll-free phone number and ask for the beautifully illustrated book, *365 Days to Better Pictures.* Call:

1-800-599-5929

Can You Picture This?

Kodak has a great web site that will help you take better photos. You will find... Top 10 techniques for good photos; Problem-pictures remedies; Picture taking tips for any situation plus a host of other topics and chat rooms relating to digital, general and professional photography.

Also be sure to visit their web site at:

WWW.KODAK.COM

What's Your Hobby?

If you'd like to develop a new and interesting hobby consider paper crafts (origami, paper sculpture, quilling or paper snipping) or decoupage — decorating with paper cutouts. Send a long SASE and ask for *Have A Hobby*. Write to:

HOBBY INDUSTRY OF AMERICA
319 E. 54TH ST.
ELMWOOD PARK, NJ 07407

Enjoying Play Clay

Did you know you can create your own unique gifts, decorations and jewelry with 'play clay'? You'll learn how to make play clay from Arm & Hammer Baking Soda. To get this freebie. Send a postcard and ask for *Play Clay to*:

ARM & HAMMER CONSUMER RELATIONS
DIVISION OF CHURCH & DWIGHT CO.
PRINCETON, NJ 08543-5297 OR CALL:
1-800-524-1328

Creating Beautiful Letters

If you are interested in learning how to create handcrafted lettering, this is for you. With the *Hunt Lettering Charts* you will receive a super collection of Roman Gothic, Old English and Manuscript lettering charts plus helpful hints. Send a card to:

HUNT BIENFANG PAPER CO.
2020 W. FRONT ST.
STATESVILLE, NC 28677

The Art of Ventriloquism

Do you remember Howdy Doody, and Edgar and Jerry Mahoney? Well now you can learn all the same techniques they used. Here is your chance to learn about what a ventriloquist is and how to become one. You will also learn how to build a puppet and even put together and market a show. You will learn how to start the show, the direction to go in and lots more. To receive this 32 page booklet on *How To Become A Ventriloquist,* write to :

THE NORTH AMERICAN ASSOCIATION OF VENTRILOQUISTS
BOX 420
LITTLETON CO 80160

If You Collect Zippo Lighters

Somewhere in your attic or basement you may stumble across an old Zippo lighter known for their reliability and quality for over 50 years. Instead of throwing it out as junk, find out whether that old Zippo has any real value. Send for a *Collectors Guide To Zippo Lighters*:

ZIPPO MANUFACTURING CO.
33 BARBOUN ST.
BRADFORD, PA

Just For Comic Book Collectors

While rumaging through the attic many people have stumbled across comic books they've had since they were kids bringing back wonderful memories of their childhood. For some that is the beginning of an enjoyable hobby of collecting old comic books. If that describes you, you'll want to send for a *giant list of back issues of Marvel comics*. Send 50¢ postage to:

R. CRESTOHL
4732 CIRCLE RD.
MONTREAL, CANADA

Old-Time Stamp Collection

There's an old-time collection of 26 different stamps waiting for you. Each stamp is 50 to 100 years old. The stamps are worth $2.00 at catalog prices but are yours for only 50¢ postage. You'll also receive other stamps on approval but

there's no obligation to buy anything. Write to:
FALCON STAMP CO.
072 ST
FALCONER, NY 14733

Start A Stamp Club

If you're interested in collecting stamps, you will probably enjoy the hobby more in the company of other stamp collectors. If this sounds like something you might be interested in, ask for your free copy of *You Can Start A Stamp Club*. Write to:
AMERICAN PHILATELIC SOCIETY
P.O. BOX 8000
STATE COLLEGE, PA 16801.

Free Numismatic News

Here's a newspaper every coin collectors will want to have. Simply write and request a free copy of '*Numismatic Weekly*.' You'll enjoy its many interesting articles on all aspects of this fascinating hobby. Send a card to:
NUMISMATIC NEWS WEEKLY
IOLA, WI 54990

Computers & The Best Internet Sites

They'll be a time in the not too distant future that having a computer will be as common as having a telephone...and just as essential. One of the main reasons for having a computer is to gain access to the Internet (sometimes called the World Wide Web or just the 'Web'). What this means is that just by typing in an address of a web site, your computer is instantly transported to a place that could very well be on the other side of the world...all for the price of a local phone call!

If you don't have a computer yet but would like to see just what the Internet is all about, here are a number of

ways of getting started.

First, virtually all libraries across the nation have computers you can use free of charge with access to the Internet. It's very easy to use and the librarian will be happy to show you how to get started.

Next, if your budget will allow it, you might want to get your own computer and 'modem' (a little box that hooks you up via your phone line to the Internet.) The most affordable way to get started is with a used computer which you can buy for as little as $100-$200 at stores like Computer Renaissance which sells only used computers. (Incidentally, to use the Internet it isn't necessary to have the newest or fastest computer. However it is good idea to get a fast modem (cost: $50-$120) which will speed your access to the Internet.

Finally, if your budget will allow, there is now a computer called the Apple iMac (under $1,000) which is already set up as it comes out of the box with everything including a built-in modem to get you online in a matter of ten minutes.

Free Computer Services

One of the big advantages of owning a computer is that it puts the world right at your finger tips. At a touch of a key you have instant access to people and sources of information that may be on the other side of the globe. In an instant you can surf the Internet with thousands of fascinating web sites. To get started with free software and in many cases with free online trials, call these toll-free numbers:

AMERICA ONLINE GENERAL INFO: **1-800-827-6364**
   TO GET UP TO **100** FREE HOURS TO GET STARTED
   ON AMERICA ONLINE, CALL: **1-888-265-8002**
COMPUSERVE: **1-800-848-8199** (NOW OFFERING **100** FREE HOURS)
AT&T WORLDNET: **1-800-640-4488**
MICROSOFT NETWORK: **1-800-386-5550**
PRODIGY: **1-800-776-3449**
EARTHLINK: **1-800-876-3151**

Computer Photo CD

If you use photos in your computer graphics programs for newsletters or ads, you will want to check out Adobe's vast collection of high quality photos on CD's. For a free Adobe Image Library Browser Demo CD, simply call them toll-free at:
1-800-502-8393

Free Computer Supplies

Right now there's intense competition going on between several nationwide computer retailers. Just to get you into their store, each of them offers free computer supplies with a full rebate. For example, in the last several weeks the authors have received several hundred computer diskettes, surge protectors, laser paper, a keyboard, a computer mouse, and other computer related items all of which came with a 100% rebate. Hundreds of dollars in supplies absolutely free! Check your local newspapers for full page ads and inserts for CompUSA, Circuit City and other chain stores.

Best Deals on PC's & Macs

If you are looking for the best deals around in computers, software and accessories, some of the best prices you will find are from mail order companies. Even if you decide to buy from a local store, calling mail order companies will allow you to comparison shop to get the lowest price. Each of the companies listed here have been in business for a number of years and have an excellent reputation for customer satisfaction. When you call, ask for their latest catalog which will be full of important information to help you make an intelligent buying decision. Most companies have a 24-hour customer service line and your orders arrive promptly, often the very next day
PC CONNECTION: 1-800-800-1111

MAC CONNECTION: 1-800-800-0002
PC WAREHOUSE & MACWAREHOUSE:
1-800 255-6227
DATACOM: 1-800-328-2261
DIRECTWARE: 1-800 490-9273
MACZONE: 1-800-248-0800
PC ZONE: 1-800-258-2088
TIGER: 1-800-888-4437
MACMALL: 1-800-222-2808
EDUCORP: 1-800-843-9497
MEI: 1-800-634-3478

Free Apple Assistance

If you own a Macintosh or are thinking of buying one and have questions you need answered, there's a toll-free number you can call for help.
APPLE HELP LINE: 1-800-SOS-APPL
Or visit their web site: www.apple.com

Free Computer Business Information

Computer Business Services will send you free cassettes and color literature on one of today's quickest growing industries. We all know the computer industry has taken off like a rocket, and now it's possible for you to be a part of it. To receive free cassettes and color literature on their business opportunities, call **1-800-343-8014**, or write to:
COMPUTER BUSINESS SERVICES
CBSI PLAYA, STE. 1180
SHERIDAN, IN 46069

Free Computer Supply Catalog

If you or your company owns a computer, you will want to get a copy of the *Global Computer Supplies Catalog*. This full color catalog lists thousands of computer-related prod-

ucts of all types. Drop a postcard to:
GLOBAL COMPUTER SUPPLIES
11 HARBOR PARK DRIVE
PORT WASHINGTON, **NY 11050**
OR CALL: **1-800-8-GLOBAL** (THAT'S **1-800-845-6225**)

Free On The Internet

Thousands of pieces of software are available absolutely free on the Internet. If you have a computer and a modem, accessing the Internet is a simple and easy way to open up a whole new world. Among other things, you will find 'freeware', 'shareware' and free computer application upgrades waiting for you to download into your computer. You will also find full text of hundreds of useful government booklets and reports on a host of fascinating subjects all of which you can download free.

Exploring the Internet... Web Sites Just For Seniors

Here are the Internet addresses of sites on the World Wide Web that are of special interest to mid-life and older Web users. Be sure that when you type in the address that you are careful to type it in correctly. Even a small change like the addition or deletion of a space or period will mean you will not be able to access the site

AMERICAN ASSOCIATION OF RETIRED PERSONS:
www.aarp.org

A.A.R.P. GUIDE TO INTERNET RESOURCES RELATED TO AGING:
www.aarp.org/cyber/guide1.htm

ACHOO:
www.achoo.com

AGE OF REASON:
www.nih.gov/nia/health/pubpub/pubpub.htm

ANDRUS FOUNDATION:
www.andrus.org

BRINGING THE FUTURE TO SENIOR CITIZENS: CAREGIVER ALLIANCE:
www.caregiver.org

CHRONICNET:
www.chronicnet.org

DIRECTORY OF WEB AND GOPHER SITES ON AGING:
www.aoa.dhhs.gov/aoa/webres/craig.him

ELDERHOSTEL:
www.elderhostel.org

ELDERPAGE: INFORMATION FOR OLDER PERSONS AND FAMILIES:
www.aoa.dhhs.gov/elderpage.html#wal

FAMILYPC'S GUIDE TO SENIOR CITIZEN COMPUTING:
www.zdnet.com/familypc/content/970411/cover/cover.html

FOCUS ON THE INTERNET:
www.aarp.org/cyber

THE GEEZER BRIGADE:
www.thegeezerbrigade.com

GENERATIONS UNITED:
www.gu.org

GRIEFNET:
rivendell.org

HEALTH A TO Z:
www.healthatoz.com

HOBBY WORLD:
www.hobbyworld.com

INTERNET RESOURCES FOR AGING:
www.mcs.net/-grossman/macareso.him

INTERNET DEVELOPMENT FOR THE AGING NETWORK: ONLINE
RESOURCES:
www.aoa.dhhs.gov/aoa/pages/guidrev.html

LIFE EXPECTANCY CALCULATOR:
www.retireweb.com/death.html

MAPQUEST:
www.mapquest.com

NATIONAL AGING INFORMATION CENTER:
www.aoa.dhhs.gov/naic

NATIONAL LIBRARY OF MEDICINE's MEDLINE:
www.nim.nih.gov/databases/freemedl.html

NATIONAL COUNCIL ON THE AGING:
www.ncoa.org

NEW LIFESTYLES:
www.newlifestyles.com

OLD-TIME RADIO WEB PAGE:
www.old-time.com

OLDER JOKES FOR OLDER FOLKS:
seniors-site.com/funstuff/jokes97.html

ONLINE RESOURCES FOR FINANCIAL AND RETIREMENT PLANNING:
www.aoa.dhhs.gov/aoa/pages/finplan.html

PLAY BRIDGE HAND GENERATOR:
playbridge.com

SSA DIRECT: PERSONAL EARNINGS AND BENEFIT ESTIMATE STATEMENT BY MAIL:
www.ssa.gov/pebes

THE SENIOR CENTER
www.senior-center.com
This is a web site especially for seniors. The Senior Center has all kinds information for senior citizens. You can send a personal e-mail message to the President, Majority Leader of the House of Representatives, the Majority Leader of the U.S. Senate or your own Congressman or Senator.

The Senior Center will also tell you about free and low cost travel bargains at:
www.mbnet.mb.ca/crm/other/genworld/sources.html

SENIOR CONNECTION
www.senior.com

SENIOR FROLIC:
www.geocities.com/Heartland/4474

SENIORLAW HOME PAGE:
www.seniorlaw.com:80

SENIORNET:
www.seniornet.org

SENIOR STAFF JOB INFORMATION DATABANK:
www.srstaff.com

THE SANDWICH GENERATION:
members.aol.com/sandwchgen/index.htm

SILVER THREADS:
www.winnipeg.freenet.mb.ca/sthreads

SPRY FOUNDATION:
www.spry.org

THIRDAGE:
www.thirdage.com

VIRTUAL INTERNET GUIDE:
www.dreamscape.com/
frankvad/Internet.html

TIME ZONE CONVERTER:
poisson.ecse.rpi.edu/cgi-
bin/tzconvert

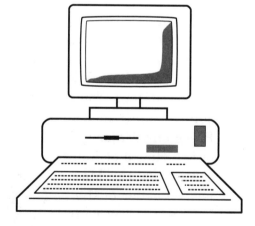

WEATHER CHANNEL:
www.weather.com

TOO OLD FOR COMPUTERS?:
www.portals.pdx.edu/
~isidore/tooold.html

WELCOME TO FOLKS ONLINE:

www.folksonline.com

UNITED CONSORTIUM SENIORS SITE AT
www.seniors-site.com

Use These Web Sites For Online Tips For Navigating The Web

BEGINNERS CENTRAL:
www.northernwebs.com/bc

THE HELPWEB:
www.imagescape.com/helpweb

THE INTERNET LEARNING TREE:
world.std.com/-walthowe/ilmtree.html

INTERNET STARTER KIT:
ss2.mcp.com/resources/genInternet/frame_iskm.html

INTERNET WEB TEXT INDEX:
www.december.com/web/text

Bigtime Savings With Online Auctions

If you love shopping for bargains, you're in for the time of your life with these Internet auction sites. You can bid on everything from cameras to computers and golf clubs... anytime day or night, 24 hours a day, all without ever leaving the comfort of your home. But just remember that as with a traditional auction you must be careful not to get caught in a bidding frenzy and bid too much just to get something you could have bought for less in a store.

A couple of tips: Find out whether the item is new, used or refurbished. New products should come with a manufacturer's warranty. Check the warranty and return policies.

When buying from someone online, be wary of sellers with e-mail accounts which could be used to mask the seller's identity. Wherever possible, pay for your purchase with your credit card since that will offer you the best protection in case there's a problem. In some instances you are b uying from a private individual but in others (like egghead.com) you are buying directly from a large company which adds an additional layer of protection.

Here are several of the most popular Internet auction sites:

www.ebay.com

This is the largest Internet auction site with everything imaginable from antiques to Beanie Babies. To find the items you are interested in you can enter key words and they will do the work of finding a match for the item you are interested in.

www.surplusauction.com

This site is operated by egghead.com. You'll find all kind of computer equipment and other electronics. Also at **www.egghead.com** you'll find a continuous auction on every kind of item imagineable such as Yamaha keyboards and cordless phones. In addition, at egghead.com you'll find an online liquidation center called surplus direct which is a great place to shop for super bargains of all kinds.

www.auctionwarehouse.com

This site focuses strictly on computer-related equipment.

www.onsale.com

Here you'll find an ongoing auction featuring a wide range of items from tech stuff to vacuum cleaners.

www.ubid.com

At this auction site you'll find not only computer products but all kinds of consumer electronics as well.

www.webauction.com

This auction site is operated by one of the largest computer mail order companies, MacWarehouse.

www.auctionx.com

A good site for computers and other tech equipment.

Learning Something New

One of life's true joys is exploring the world and discovering something we never knew before. We enter life with an enormous inborn curiosity about the world around us. Unfortunately once we enter school for many of us learning becomes a chore, a job, something we are forced to do to get good grades or a good job. But once we reach a certain age and the pace of life becomes less frantic, we can once again recapture that excitement of learning something new and feeling like a kid again.

Senior Summer School

That's right Summer School for seniors- two to ten weeks of learning and fun centered around 7 college campuses in the U.S. and Canada. Here's your chance to meet new friends and see the world. The sessions last from 2-10 weeks with no marks, no grades and no mandatory attendance. WOW – school was never like this.

The only requirement is a desire to learn something new. All the programs offer social events too. Write to:

SENIOR SUMMER SCHOOL
PO BOX 4424
DEERFIELD BEACH, FL 33442-4424
YOU CAN ALSO CALL: 1-800-847-2466
OR VISIT THEIR WEBSITE:
www/seniorsummerschool.com

Back To School With Elderhostel

Elderhostel offers senior study programs around the world all year long. You'll live in conference centers on college university campuses and enjoy the cultural and recreational resources that go with them. So if you have an adventuresome spirit and are looking to be challenged by new ideas and experiences, this is for you. You must be 55 years or older to be eligible. Here's your chance to go back to college and experience dorm life as a more seasoned veteran. For information, be sure to get the free catalog of senior study programs from:

ELDERHOSTEL
75 FEDERAL ST.
BOSTON, MA 02110-1941
CALL THEM AT: 1-617-426-8056
OR VISIT THEIR INTERNET SITE AT:
www.elderhostel.org

Free College Extension Courses

If you've always wanted to return to college, there's no time like the present. First, check the *Directory of Colleges With Special Programs For Seniors* in the back of this book. They all offer free or very low cost tuition for seniors.

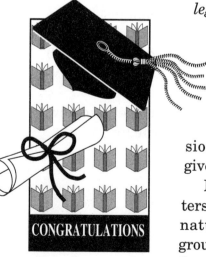

Also, don't forget you can check your local telephone directory for state and community college extension courses. These courses are not given for credit but they are a lot of fun.

Next, contact your local senior centers to see what they have. Museums, nature centers, libraries and church groups also offer courses and seminars that are educational and fun and many instances free or almost free.

Finally, check your local newspaper for seminars and other educational activities in your area.

Are You A Sky Gazer?

If you enjoy studying the heavens, you will want to get a copy of *Essential Magazines of Astronomy* with a catalog of some of the finest astronomy books that will delight all star gazers. Write to:

SKY PUBLISHING CORP.
49 BAY STREET RD.
CAMBRIDGE, MA 02138

A Share Of America

Getting Help When You Invest and *Understanding Stocks and Bonds* and two fascinating guides that tells all about how the stock market works and the important role it plays in our nation's economy. The New York Stock Exchange also has an excellent series of educational aids, huge wall posters, ticker tape, teacher guides and more. Write to:

N.Y. STOCK EXCHANGE
EDUCATIONAL SERVICES
11 WALL ST.
NEW YORK, NY 10005

What Are Quarter Horses?

Whether you are presently an owner of horses or perhaps thinking of buying one - check out American Quarter Horses, the world's most popular breed of horse. Here's an interesting booklet you will want to have, *For An American Quarter Horse*. For a copy of this fascinating booklet (and a colorful bumper sticker too), drop a postcard to:

AMERICAN QUARTER HORSE ASSOCIATION
AMARILLO, TX 79168

Tennessee Walking Horse

Here's one every equestrian will want to have. Send a post-card and ask for the booklet, *Tennessee Walking Horse* plus a colorful postcard showing the three horses chosen by the breeder's association as the world's greatest pleasure and show horses. Write to:

TENNESSEE WALKING HORSE
BOX 286
LEWISBURG, TN 37081

KEEP IN MIND: If you don't have a computer or Internet access at home, most libraries have computers you can use and librarians who are happy to show you how to use them.

Protecting Your Home From Fire

Don't take any chances when it comes to protecting your home from fires. Learn what you can do to protect your family and your house with smoke detectors—a must for all homes. Send a card to:

"HOME FIRE DETECTION,"
NATIONAL FIRE PROTECTION ASSOCIATION
BATTERYMARCH PARK
QUINCY, MA 02269

Look To The Heavens

Man has always been fascinated by the sky at night. With the recent discovery of planets circling around distant stars, one can't help but wonder whether life exists elsewhere in the universe. To find out more about our distant neighbors, send for the *skywatching series of booklets* dealing with our solar system and beyond. Send to:

PUBLIC AFFAIRS OFFICE
HARVARD SMITHSONIAN CENTER FOR ASTROPHYSICS
60 GARDEN ST.
CAMBRIDGE, MA 02138

The Wright Brothers

With men on the moon and rockets to Jupiter it's hard to believe that manned flight began less than a 100 years ago with an historic 120 foot journey that lasted all of 12 seconds. All the fascinating details are found in this historical recap, *The Wright Brothers.* Send a card to:

WRIGHT BROTHERS NATIONAL
MEMORIAL
ROUTE 1, BOX 676
MANTEO, NC 27954

The Truth About Nuclear Energy

Is nuclear energy the answer to our energy needs or are the risks of nuclear disaster just too great? To help you answer this question, here is an excellent package of books that is free for the asking. Topics covered include nuclear power plants, the structure of the atom, magnetic fusion, the story of nuclear energy and a whole lot more. They will also include information about wind energy and conservation. Ask for the *Nuclear Energy information package.* Very informative. All free from:

U.S. DEPARTMENT OF ENERGY
PO BOX 62
OAK RIDGE, TN 37830

What Is Australia Like Today?

What is life like 'down-under'? *Australia Now* will give you a look—in full color-at what's happening in Australia today. You'll also receive vacation planning, travel tips and information on locations, tours and accommodations. Drop a postcard to:

AUSTRALIAN CONSULATE GENERAL
630 FIFTH AVE. SUITE 420
NEW YORK NY 10111

The Facts About Oil

This nicely illustrated guide to petroleum tells all about the history of oil exploration and shows how the search for oil is conducted. Ask for the *energy information series* and you'll receive a great package of excellent booklets dealing with many forms of energy including wind, nuclear, geothermal, coal, oil and more. Send a postcard to:

AMERICAN PETROLEUM INSTITUTE
PUBLICATIONS SECTION
1220 L ST. N.W.
WASHINGTON, DC 20005

How To Shop Smart

Everyone spends money, but not everyone knows how to do it right. Spending money wisely takes skill, time and experience. To help you learn how to shop smart, the FTC and the National Association of Attorneys General have put together a fun activity booklet called *The Real Deal*. To get your free copy, write to:

YOUR STATE ATTORNEY GENERAL
OFFICE OF CONSUMER PROTECTION
YOUR STATE CAPITAL
OR TO: THE FEDERAL TRADE COMMISSION
6TH & PENNSYLVANIA AVE., NW, ROOM 130
WASHINGTON, DC 20580
WORLD WIDE WEB SITE: HTTP://WWW.FTC.GOV

Would You Drive An Aluminum Car?

Today, through greater use of aluminum parts, our cars are getting far better miles per gallon. This is just one of the many uses of aluminum. If you would like a better understanding of the history of aluminum, the ways it is made and how it's used, ask for the free *Story of Aluminum* and *Alcoa* from:

ALCOA
150 ALCOA BUILDING.
PITTSBURGH, PA 15219

Cleaning Up The Environment

Bethlehem Steel would like you to know what they are doing to clean up the air and water. For example, at one plant they have spent over 100 million dollars for air and water quality controls. For a free copy of *Steelmaking & The Environment,* send a postcard to:

BETHLEHEM STEEL CORP.
PUBLIC AFFAIRS DEPT., ROOM 476MT
BETHLEHEM, PA 18016

Learn About Coal

If you're curious about coal and how it is found, extracted, transported and used, be sure to get the informative booklets and poster available free from the American Coal Foundation. When you write, be sure to indicate exactly what your interests are so they can provide appropriate materials for you. A few of the items available include:

Coal Poster - A large colorful poster with important coal information

Coal: Ancient Gift Serving Modern Man

Let's Learn About Coal - includes puzzles and word games explaining how coal is formed.

What Everyone Should Know About Coal Describes the different types of coal, how it is used and how it effects the envirnment.

Coal Science Fair Ideas - to help spark interest in coal plus tips to help you get started with a learning project.
Write to:

AMERICAN COAL FOUNDATION
1130 17TH ST NW, SUITE 220
WASHINGTON, DC 20036-4604

Pitch This One!

Did you know that former President George Bush used to pitch horseshoes? If you think you might find this sport interesting, and would like to find out more about it, now's the time. To discover more about this fun sport and to learn all the rules and tips for throwing the perfect horseshoe pitch, send for your free copy of the *Official Rules For Horseshoe Pitching*. Send a SASE to:

NHPA, RR2
Box 178
LaMonte, MD 65337

Keep Your Mind Sharp At Any Age

The mind is like a muscle...if you want to stay sharp you must stretch your mind by giving it intesting challenges. One great way of doing that is with puzzles and mazes. If you like figuring out puzzles and mazes, you will love this freebie. You will receive a complimentary maze valued at $2.95. Simply send $1.00 for postage and handling and ask for it from:

PDK Enterprises
PO Box 1776
Boyes Hot Springs, CA 95416

Learning To Be More Romantic

Since the beginning of time, women have accused men of not being romantic enough. Finally there's help and it's called *The RoMANtic*. Each 12 page newsletter gives dozens of practical, creative and inspiring ideas and stories on dating, gift-giving, anniversary celebrating and more. To learn how to rekindle the romantic spark and have more fun in your relationships, send 3 first class stamps to:

The RoMANtic Sample Issue Offer
714 Collington Dr
Cary, NC 27511
Or check out sample issues at their Web site:
www.TheRomantic.com

Invite A Bird Over For Lunch

This large colorful poster-like guide will show you how to *Invite Birds To Your Home*. It tells how to attract birds with proper tree plantings that specific species prefer. You also might want to ask for *Your Hometown, Clean Water Town*. For your free copy write:

SOIL CONSERVATION SERVICE
U.S.D.A.
BOX 2890
WASHINGTON, DC 20013

Preserving Our Forests

The book you're reading right now and the lumber in the house in which you live are just two of the many products we take for granted that come from our nation's forests. It is essential that we take care to preserve and renew our forests. The U.S. Forest Service has a booklet you will want to have: *Making Paper From Trees* shows how a tree goes from the forest and ends up as paper. Send a postcard to:

FOREST SERVICE
U.S. DEPT. OF AGRICULTURE
BOX 2417
WASHINGTON, DC 20013

Money For College

If you're a parent with children in college or about to go off to college, you have discovered just how expensive it is. The good news is that there are all kinds of financial assistance programs available for virtually everyone. All that is necessary is to go through a series of steps in your search for the money you will need.

Here we've listed a number of important and easy to use resources to help you effectively direct your search for college money. One of the most efficient ways of locating financial assistance that applies to you is to use the Internet. Naturally this means having access to a computer. If you do not yet own a computer, you can check with your local library or ask a friend who has a computer to allow you to use theirs. Also most schools today have computers your child can use.

Free College Aid

It's a little known fact but there are literally billions of dollars in financial aid available to help students pay for their college education. This money is available from thousands of public and private sources. Much of this money is available as outright grants that never has to be repaid. Still more money for college is available through low-cost loans and work-study programs. The first place to check is with the financial aid office of the college of your choice. Counselors will help you locate all the sources of money including scholarships, grant-in-aid, work study programs and low interest government-backed student loans. Next, you will definitely want to use the Internet as a tool to search for financial assistance. In the listings that follow, you'll find the most important sources.

Free Computer Search To Locate College Scholarships And Grants

Are you looking for money for college? The Internet is the very best way to search for the financial aid that is waiting for you. Start your search with this computerized web site which was developed by the nation's financial aid adminis- trators. At this web site you will find a number of great scholarship searches that are entirely free.

What you will do is fill out a detailed questionnaire on your computer screen while you are online. The informa- tion you list about yourself and your background on this questionnaire will be compared to the information in huge databases and you will be notified of the grants, scholar- ships and loans you qualify for. To begin your search go to the web site:

www.finaid.org/finaid

Once you are at the finaid.org web site you will find sev- eral other sites (listed below) where you will find the ques- tionnaires that will begin your search. They will ask you to answer several pages of specific questions about your back- ground and financial situation. Based on the answers to your these questions it will set up a personalized profile that will match your specific skills, needs and interests. It will begin the search through its massive database for all of the money that is available for you. Once the search is completed, it will report to you exactly what assistance you qualify for and exactly how to get it.

And despite the enormous value of this search and the fact that other organizations have charged up to $300 for this service, there is no charge to you for these extensive searches!

• **FastWEB:** A database of more than 300,000 private-sector scholarships, grants, fellowships and loans is the Internet's largest free scholarship search site. Also, FastWEB Classifieds offers a tailored search of employment opportunities across

the U.S. that is available to students absolutely free.
www.fastweb.com

• **SRN Express:** A version of the Scholarship Resource Network (SRN) database with information from several hundred thousand financial aid sources with a special focus on scholarship information. They also have information on student loan forgiveness programs for college graduates who need alternatives for loan repayment.
www.srnexpress.com

Low Cost Loans To Pay for College

Sallie Mae is the leading source of money for college loans. They will be delighted to help you find the money you will need to pay for college.

The College Answer Service. First, they have a toll free hotline where you can speak to a financial aid expert who will answer your questions dealing with paying for college, loans, aid packages, advice on financial aid applications, deadlines, and lots more. You will also learn how to save hundreds of dollars with the lowest cost student loans available. Due to the low interest rates they offer, loans with Sallie Mae can cost a lot less to pay back. Call them Monday through Friday between the hours of 9am to 9pm EST at: **1-800-891-4599.**

Sallie Mae also has a number of helpful booklets including *Paying For College* and *Borrowing For College.*

Paying For College is a comprehensive guidebook which provides thorough advice on planning for a college education. The book addresses key financial aid terms, formulas for calculating the 'Expected Family Contribution', an overview of the federal student loan program and a summary of loan repayment programs ...many of which reward students for on-time payment.

Borrowing For College helps students and their parents choose low-cost student loan lenders in their area. To get free copies call: **1-800-806-3681**

www.sallie.mae.com One visit to their web site and you will see just how valuable it is. You will be able to do a free online search for scholarship money available from over 300,000 sources. Plus you can e-mail your financial aid questions and get quick advice from experts.

Student Loans & Grants

If you're a college student or plan to be one and are short of money to continue your education, be sure to get a free copy of *Funding Your Education* and *The Student Guide.* They are the most comprehensive resources of student financial aid from the U.S. Department of Education. It covers major aid programs including Pell Grants, Stafford Loans and PLUS loans. Contact:

THE U.S. DEPARTMENT OF EDUCATION,
400 MARYLAND AVE. S.W. ROOM 2097
WASHINGTON. D.C. 20202
OR CALL THEIR INFORMATION HOTLINE:
1-800-4-FED-AID

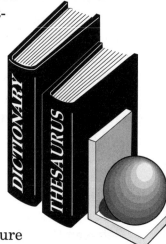

Also, for information on Federal student aid backed by the U.S. Government, be sure to visit the Department of Education's web site at: **www.ed.gov**

Paying For College

With the costs of going to college spiraling out of sight many students are not able to attend college without financial assistance. This guide will help you with all the many questions you have about paying for your college education. Ask for *Meeting College Costs,* free from:

THE COLLEGE BOARD
45 COLUMBUS AVE.
NEW YORK, NY 10023-6992

Free Help Choosing The Right College

Selecting the right college or university can be a challenging and time-consuming task but one that will bring immeasurable rewards for the rest of your life. To help you make the right choice, State Farm Insurance has a fantastic guide from U.S. News and World Report. In its close to 300 pages you will find valuable information about tuition, room and board, financial aid, entrance requirements and lots more on over 1,400 universities and colleges. To get your free copy of this important guide, call State Farm toll-free at:
1-888-733-8368

Comparing College Costs

Computer users can quickly compare the cost of more than 1500 public and private colleges and get an estimate of what it will cost to attend. When you call, ask for *College Savings Plus,* a free computer disk available from John Hancock Mutual Life Insurance Company. After you ask for the free computer disk, a John Hancock agent will likely call to ask if you want help devising a savings plan. Call:
1-800-633-1809

College Planning

T. Rowe Price's College Planning Guide helps parents project what a college education may cost for their young children so you can plan ahead and start saving now. It's free. Call:
1-800-225-5132

$1,500 To Pay For College

Paying for college can be a huge burden, but now there's hope. In fact it's called the 'Hope Scholarship' and actually it's even better than a scholarship because it's an income-tax credit aimed at middle income people. There are no applications to fill out. All you do is when you file your tax return, you subtract the amount of the credit right from the amount you owe. In effect, the government gives you up to $1,500 back per student. Here's how it works:

- The income tax credit equals 100% of the first $1,000 paid in college tuition and fees plus 50% of the next $1,000, for a total of $1,500.

- The credit is for you, your spouse or your dependent children in their first and second academic year as long as they're enrolled at least half time in a 2 year or 4 year college or in a trade school.

- You can claim as many credits as you have qualified students. So for example, if you have two children in their first or second year of college, you get $3,000.

- To qualify for the full credit your adjusted gross income must be under $40,000 if you are single (between $40,000 and $50,000 you still get a partial credit) or $80,000 if you are married (between $80,000 and $100,000 you still get a partial credit.)

- Tuition must be paid in the same year you claim the credit. For example, you must have paid the tuition in 1999 to claim a credit on your 1999 tax return.

- In addition to the Hope Scholarship, there is also the Lifetime Learning credit of $1,000 which can be taken for any student of any age, for any number of years and even for a single adult education course, for example. Right now this credit is worth up to $1,000 (20% of the first $5,000 paid in tuition and fees) and you can take just one credit per tax return no matter how many students you may have in school. While you can't take both credits at once for the same student, you can take the Hope credit for one and the Lifetime Learning credit for another.

If you qualify, these tax credits can be an important source of additional money for college. For more information, ask the IRS or your accountant.

Religion

Free Devotional Reading For Each Day

Our Daily Bread provides inspirational readings from the scriptures for each day of the month. You'll get a new book each month. Ask them to add your name to their mailing list for this devotional guide plus discovery series booklets as well as a campus journal for young people. All free from:
RADIO BIBLE CLASS
P.O. BOX 2222
GRAND RAPIDS, MI 49555

Free Catholic Information

The Knights of Columbus has dozens of booklets available on all aspects of the Catholic religion. The only cost is a nominal postage charge (generally 25¢ per booklet). They also have a 10 part home-study Catholic correspondence course that is free for the asking. The course is for both Catholics and non-Catholics who would like to learn more about Catholicism. It is sent in an unmarked envelope. For a complete listing of publications or to get your free correspondence course write to:
CATHOLIC INFORMATION SERVICE
KNIGHTS OF COLUMBUS
BOX 1971
NEW HAVEN, CT 06521

You Can Make A Difference In This World

News Notes are inspirational brochures published by the Christophers 10 times a year and are free for the asking. The Christophers exist for one purpose: to spread the message that one person can make a difference in this world. Write and ask for information on titles available in any of these categories, *News Notes*, books, videocassettes, they even have Spanish language material. Drop a postcard to :

THE CHRISTOPHERS
12 EAST 48TH ST.
NEW YORK, NY 10017

Inspiration And Prayer

The Lutheran Laymen's League has several religious publications you might like to have. A few of the titles currently available are: *'Escape From Loneliness', 'I Am An Alcoholic,' 'Stress - Problem or Opportunity?'* and *'The Truth About Angels.'* All of them are free from:

INTERNATIONAL LUTHERAN LAYMEN'S LEAGUE
2185 HAMPTON AVE.
ST. LOUIS, MO 63139

Free From The Worldwide Church Of God

The Worldwide Church of God has an excellent series of booklets available without charge (nor will they make any solicitations of any kind). Titles change frequently so drop a card for a current list of books available. Write to:

WORLDWIDE CHURCH OF GOD
PASADENA, CA 91123
OR CALL TOLL-FREE: **1-800-423-4444**

Beautiful Inspiration

Often in our daily lives events become too much to handle. The Salesian Missions have a beautiful series of booklets that are a pleasure to read and provide inspiration to help make our lives more fulfilling. Excellent! Send a postcard and ask for the *free inspirational booklets* from:

SALESIAN MISSIONS
2 LEFEVRES LANE
NEW ROCHELLE, NY 10801

Free Gospel Of Saint John Course

If you would like to learn more about the life of Christ, you can receive a free Gospel of John in English or Spanish (please specify) and a Gospel of John Correspondence Course. Drop a postcard to:

THE POCKET TESTAMENT LEAGUE
PO BOX 800
LITITZ, PA 17543

Free King James Bible

If you would like a 764 page copy of the King James version of the Bible, it's yours free from The Church of Jesus Christ of Latter Day Saints...The Mormons. They may ask if you would like to speak with a church member but that is your option and is not required to receive the free bible. They also have a beautifully produced video called *Lamb of God* that is yours for asking. For a free copy of the *King James Bible* or the *Lamb of God* video (both of which will be sent by mail), call:

1-800-535-1118

Free Bible Reading Guides

For a new understanding of the Bible, you may want to receive the simplified Bible Reading Guides that are yours free from the Real Truth Ministries. To enroll in this bible course, call toll free:
1-800-863-5789

Cars & Drivers

Does Your Car Really Need That Tune-up?

Whether you have a new car or an older one, you want to be prepared for any trouble you may encounter. Most of us are very trusting souls when it comes to a car repair. We rely on the mechanic as the expert. When he tells us the car needs a tune-up or has any other prob-lem, we have him check it out immediately. The Car Coun-cil wants us to be aware of *The Eight Most Common Signs Your Car Needs a Tune-up.* It's full of easy to understand advice on what to look for before it's too late. To get your free copy simply write to:
THE CAR COUNCIL, DEPT. T-M-S
1 GRANDE LAKE DR.
PORT CLINTON, OHIO 43452

Call This Toll-Free Number First If You Bought A Lemon

If you're having problems with your car and can't seem to get satisfaction from the dealer or manufacturer don't de-spair - help is on the way. The Auto Safety Hotline is anx-ious to hear about your complaint so they can get to work on it. They've even set up a toll-free hotline and an Internet

site for you to contact them to report your problem. To report your problem, call toll-free:
1-800-424-9393. Or write to:
National Highway And Traffic Safety Administration
400 7th St., S.W.
Washington, DC 20590
Or visit their Internet site at:
www.nhtsa.dot.gov

If at this point you would just like to gather more information about recalls and auto defect reports, call this toll-free number operated by the Technical Information Services division of NHTSA:
1-800-445-0197

NHTSA does not get involved in individual cases of complaints between the conusmer and the dealer or manufacturer. If you have such a complaint, call the Federal Trade Commission for assistance at:
1-202-326-3128

Car Shopping On The Internet

Thinking of buying a car? Want to negotiate the best deal and save thousands of dollars? The Internet has scores of Web sites with auto information. The most useful ones reveal invoice cost, road-test performance and rebates and incentives. Try these:

For up-to-date information, analyses and columns from auto industry experts, check out the **Car Connection**'s web site at:
www.thecarconnection.com

Use this Web site to go to the **Auto Channel**, which has links to every automaker's Web site for lease help, chat rooms and more.
www.excite.com/autos

Edmund's Vehicle Price Guide. Find out how much the car dealer pays for the car you are thinking of buying. You will also discover how much the "holdback" allowance is. The holdback allowance is an additional profit that the manufacturer later gives back to the dealer after the car is sold. It usually runs about 3 percent of the suggested retail price. The site also has information on rebates and incentive plans.
www.edmunds.com.

The Kelly Blue Book web site can give you a good idea what your trade in is worth, or the real value of a used car you want to buy.
www.kbb.com

Consumer Product Ratings site offers ratings of cars, hotels, restaurants volunteered by online users. (They are not affiliated with Consumer Reports magazine.) You can reach them on the Internet at:
www.consumeratings.com

What Does Consumer Reports Think?

If you would like to see just what Consumer Reports thinks of the car you are thinking of buying, visit their Internet site. You will find evaluations of over 180 makes of new cars. Access to their site costs $2.95 a month but you can visit their *Best of the Best* page for free.
www.consumerreports.org

Save Thousands On Your Next Car Purchase Or Lease

One of the very best ways of saving a lot of money on the

purchase or lease of a vehicle is to use the online vehicle brokers. They have nationwide networks of thousands of dealers of every make of auto or truck.

Consumer Car Club

In addition to offering you online auto insurance quotes, an auto comparison guide and a loan-versus-lease cost comparison, they also offer three ways to buy a car or truck. First, they will refer you to a dealer at no charge. They also offer a factory direct ordering service for $179 and a Personal Shopper service for $179. Visit their site at: **www.carclub.com**

Nationwide Auto Brokers

They will sell you a car and even bring it right to your front door. How's that for convenience! Their advertised prices range from $50 to $125 over dealer invoice. They charge $11.95 for the first price quote on the car of your choice and $9.95 for each additional quote. Check out their Web site at: **www.car-connect.com**

CARS@COST

They offer many models of new cars at dealer invoice plus their fee. Their fees range from $249 to $499 depending upon the car you are buying.
www.carscost.com

Dealer Referral Services

As a smart shopper it's essential to inform yourself fully before you go out to buy your next car. One of the best ways to gather the information you'll need to make an intelligent choice and get the very lowest price is by visiting these online Internet sites where you will not only learn lots of valuable information about cars, but also get referrals to auto dealers in your local area.

AUTO-BY-TEL

With several million customers, this is one of the largest and most useful web sites around. They have links to six car pricing sites, over 2,700 dealers in their referral network and a great reputation to boot. You'll find a lease-buy comparision calculator and even an online finance application. Visit their web site at:
www.autobuytel.com

AUTOWEB.COM

At this site you'll find well organized information that will help you buy a new car, buy or sell a used car, check out insurance rates from State Farm on the car you are thinking of buying, check financing from Nations Bank and find a list of dealers in your area. Visit them on the Internet at:
www.autoweb.com

AUTOBUYER

There's not too much detailed information but this is a great place to visit to get a dealer quote on the car of your choice

without the pressure of a car salesman in the showroom. Their web address is:
www.autobuyer.com

CARSMART

A great consumer buying guide with loads of very useful information on topics like financing, best time to buy a new car, air bags, anti-lock brakes and much more. You can even get insurance and financing quotes, links to dealer and manufacturers' sites and vehicle pricing reports ($4.90 each report).
www.carsmart.com

Microsoft CarPoint

This Online Car Buying web site previews various car models and offers "test drives" of selected cars. You'll find lots of reviews, photos and reports on safety, road tests, and more. You'll also find very useful features like side-by-side comparisons and even an affordability calculator. Check it out before you buy your next car. Their web address is:
www.carpoint.msn.com

For AAA Members

If you're a member of AAA, you should know that they offer an excellent tour service. Contact your local AAA office and tell them the destination you would like to drive to and they'll give you detailed road maps with your route outlined in pencil. Many local offices also offer members a car buying service that can save you thousands of dollars on your next auto purchase or lease.

10 Ways To Slash Auto Insurance Costs

1. MAINTAIN A GOOD DRIVING RECORD. Accidents and speeding tickets are a fast way to drive up your premiums. Drive carefully and defensively. Consider walking or taking other means of transportation or car pooling to reduce your risk of accidents.

2. RAISE YOUR DEDUCTIBLES. This is the amount you must pay for any loss before your insurance kicks in. If your current deductible is $250 or less, raising it to $500 can save you 15%-30%.

3. PROTECT AGAINST THEFT. Security devices like care alarms and even having your serial number etched on the window saves you 15% on your comprehensive auto insurance.

4. ASK ABOUT DISCOUNTS. Insurance companies offer special deals and discounts if you are retired, belong to a business association, have been insured with a company for a number of years, insure all your cars or have your home and car with the same firm.

5. TAKE A DRIVER IMPROVEMENT COURSES to get a discount. For example, AAA has a Driver Improvement Program for people 55 and older that leads to car insurance discounts.

6. REDUCE YOUR COVERAGE OR ELIMINATE COVERAGE YOU DON'T NEED. For example, many new cars now come with towing or road service included. If that's the case you can eliminate that coverage from your auto insurance.

7. MANY INSURERS GIVE DISCOUNTS TO DRIVERS OVER 50 OR THOSE WITH LOW ANNUAL MILEAGE. Others give students with good grades a 5% discount. If your child maintains a B average or better in school or has taken driver's education you may be eligible for discounts. If you child is away at college as long as the car stays home and college

is 100 miles or more away depending on the insurance company, you may also be eligible for discounts.

Rates are also much lower when the teenage driver is considered only an occasional driver of the parent's cars.

8. CHECK INSURANCE RATES *BEFORE* YOU BUY A CAR. The cost of insuring a Porsche is much higher than the cost of insuring an inexpensive family car.

9. SHOP AROUND. Talk to friends and neighbors about their insurance coverage and rates. Get quotes from several companies, compare rates and coverage.

10. GET A CAR WITH ANTI-LOCK BRAKES AND AIR BAGS AND SAVE AN ADDITIONAL 5%.

Should You Buy That Car Or Lease It?

If you can't decide whether to buy or lease a vehicle you need to have this guide...*A Consumer Education Guide to Leasing vs. Buying* free from the National Vehicle Leasing Association. Simply write your name and address on a 3 x 5 card and send it with $1.00 postage & handling to:

HEGGEN & ASSOCIATES INC.
PO Box 5025
EVANSTON, IL 60204-5025

What To Do If You Have A Car Accident

- Write down names and addresses of all persons and all witnesses involved.
- Notify the police immediately
- Get medical attention if needed
- Contact your insurance agent and do not admit liability or discuss your accident with anyone except your insurance representative or the police.

Be A Good Neighbor...
Be A Good Friend

State Farm wants to help give you, your college, civic group or professional organization free *designated driver presentation items*. They're a colorful way to remind your friends and associates of the importance of safe driving. They will send your group a free designated driver kit. It has a presentation guide, video and sample speeches. Write to:

STATE FARM INSURANCE COMPANIES
ACTION NETWORK-PUBLIC AFFAIRS
DESIGNATED DRIVER PROGRAM
ONE STATE FARM PLAZA
BLOOMINGTON, IL 61710

How Safe Are Your Tires?

Did you know that when you keep your tires properly inflated that the air provides a cushion of protection when you hit a pothole? If the tire is under inflated you could damage the wheel. If it is over inlated the tire will be damaged. For the best information around for caring and protecting your tires, send for a free copy of *The Motorist Tire Care and Safety Guide*. Send a long SASE to:

TIRE INDUSTRY SAFETY COUNCIL
PO BOX 3147
MEDINA, OHIO, 44258

A Safer Car

Before you go shopping for your next car, be sure to get a copy of *Injury, Collision and Theft Losses - Shopping For A Safer Car*. This informative booklet will help you make an intelligent choice about which is the safest vehicle for you.

It provides you with an excellent safety and loss comparisons for hundreds of passenger cars, vans, pick ups and utility vehicle models. Write to:

HIGHWAY LOSS DATA INSTITUTE, DEPT R 92-2
1005 N. GLEBE RD., SUITE 800
ARLINGTON, VA 22201

Automobile Hotline Numbers

If you thinking of buying or leasing a car in the near future, be sure you get all the information you need to make an intelligent decision before you go to the dealer showroom. Your first step should be to call the toll-free hotline phone number for the cars you are interested in. The manufacturers will send you beautiful color product information booklets and even video tapes featuring their cars.

ACURA	1-800-TO-ACURA
BMW	1-800-334-4BMW
BUICK	1-800-4-RIVIERA
CADILLAC	1-800-333-4CAD
CHEVY MONTE CARLO & GEO	1-800-950-2438
CHEVY TAHOE	1-800-950-TAHOE
CHRYSLER	1-800-4-A-CHRYSLER
DODGE	1-800-4-A-DODGE
EAGLE VISION TSI	1-800-2-TEST-EAGLE
FORD	1-800-392-3673
GMC SIERRA	1-800-GMC-TRUCK
HONDA	1-800-33-HONDA EXT 435
HYUNDAI	1-800-826-CARS
INFINITI	1-800-950-8074
ISUZU	1-800-726-2700
JAGUAR	1-800-4-JAGUAR
JEEP	1-800-925-JEEP
LAND ROVER	1-800-FINE-4WD

LEXUS	1-800-USA-LEXUS
LINCOLN	1-800-446-8888
MERCEDES	1-800-FOR-MERCEDES
MERCURY	1-800-531-6870
MITSUBISHI	1-800-55-MITSU
NISSAN	1-800-NISSAN-3
OLDSMOBILE	1-800-448-0092
OLDSMOBILE AURORA	1-800-718-7778
PONTIAC	1-800-2-PONTIAC
PORSCHE	1-800-PORSCHE
SAAB	1-800-582-SAAB EXT 201
SUBARU	1-800-WANT-AWD
SUZUKI	1-800-650-4445
TOYOTA	1-800-GO-TOYOTA
VOLKSWAGEN	1-800-DRIVE-VW
VOLVO	1-800-960-9988

Free For Sports Fans

Senior Sports

Healthy eating and exercise are the keys to keeping fit, feeling great and living longer. Keeping active physically also keeps us alert mentally. Whatever your favorite sport Go out and *DO IT!* If you are unable to participate in a fitness program, WALK.

Did you know that there is a Seniors Softball World Championship and a Seniors Softball World Series each year?

Believe it or not Senior Softball was started in 1930 by a hotel owner in Florida who was looking for something for her elderly guests to do. She organized the *'Three-Quarter Century Club.'* Members had to be at least 75 years old. Think about that the next time you're too tired and feel you can't exercise.

For more information on Senior Athletic Competition like Senior Softball, write to:

U.S. NATIONAL SENIOR SPORTS ORGANIZATION
14323 S. OUTER FORTY RD.
ST. LOUIS, MO 63017

And also to:

SENIOR SPORTS INTERNATIONAL, INC.
5726 WILSHIRE BLVD.
LOS ANGELES, CA 90036

Also contact your local senior center, city recreation dept, library or YMCA.

Women: Get Involved With Sports

This organization encourages women to get involved in sports. They will offer your group or school free films of women in sports to help encourage other women to be active and stay active. They also publish a guide listing scholarships to American colleges and universities for women who are into sports. It's a myth that only men get sports scholarships to college. Call them toll-free:
1-800-227-3988
or visit them at their web site:
www.lifetimeTV.com/wosport

Outdoor Sports

L. L. Bean, the outdoor sporting specialists for 67 years, would like to send you a copy of their *catalog*. It features fine quality apparel and footwear for the outdoorsman or woman as well as equipment for camping, fishing, hiking and canoeing. Send a postcard to:
L.L. BEAN
FREEPORT, ME 04033

The Story Of The Olympic Games

The History of The Olympics gives you the complete story of the Olympics starting with the earliest recorded game in 776 B.C. and traces the game's history right up to through the present. For your free copy, write:
U.S. OLYMPIC COMMITTEE
1750 EAST BOULDER ST.
COLORADO SPRINGS, CO 80909

99 Tips For Family Fitness

One of the best ways to stay in shape is by involving the

whole family in a fitness progam. In *99 Tips* you'll find a slew of fun fitness activities for kids and parents alike. You'll also find advice from notable athletes like Troy Aikman. Just send a postcard to:

99 TIPS FOR FAMILY FITNESS
MET-RX FOUNDATION FOR HEALTH ENHANCEMENT
2112 BUSINESS CENTER DRIVE
IRVINE, CA 92715

Free Hockey Cards

If you are a hockey fan, you'll definitely want to send for this freebie. When you request it you will receive 10 free hockey cards. To get your cards, just send a long SASE and 50¢ to:

DANORS, DEPARTMENT H
5721 FUNSTON STREET BAY 14
HOLLYWOOD, FL 33023

Free From Your Favorite Team

Do you love sports? How would you like to receive photos of your favorite teams? Most sports clubs have all kinds of freebies for their loyal fans. These neat freebies often include team photos, souvenir brochures, stickers, fan club information, playing schedules, catalogs and lots more. All you have to do is write to your favorite sports teams at the addresses in this book. Tell them you're a loyal fan and ask them for a "fan package."

Even though it's not always necessary, it's always nice idea to send a long self-addressed-stamped envelope with your name and address written in so they can return your freebie right in your own envelope.

Also, if you have a favorite player on the team, write his name on the envelope.

Sometimes it takes a while to get an answer since most teams are flooded with mail. Just be patient and you'll hear from them.

HOCKEY

National Hockey League
75 International Blvd. Suite 300
Rexdale, Ontario Canada M9W 6L9

Eastern Conference

Boston Bruins
1 Fleet Center, Suite 250
Boston, MA 02114

Buffalo Sabres
Memorial Auditorium
140 Main St
Buffalo, NY 14202

Carolina Hurricanes
5000 Aerial Center
Suite 100
Morrisville, NC 27560

Florida Panthers
Miami Arena
100 NE Third Ave., 10th Fl
Ft. Lauderdale, FL 33301

Montreal Canadians
2313 St. Catherine St. West
Montreal, Quebec,
Canada H3H 1N2

New Jersey Devils
Byrne Meadowlands Arena
PO Box 504
E. Rutherford, NJ 07073

New York Islanders
Nassau Colliseum
Uniondale, NY 11553

New York Rangers
Madison Square Garden
4 Penn Plaza
New York, NY 10001

Ottawa Senators
301 Moodie Dr., Suite 200
Nepean, Ontario, Canada K2H 9C4

Philadelphia Flyers
The Spectrum
Pattison Place
Philadelphia, PA 19148

Pittsburgh Penguins
Civic Arena, Gate No. 9
Pittsburgh, PA 15219

Tampa Bay Lightning
501 E. Kennedy Blvd., Ste 175
Tampa, FL 33602

Washington Capitals
U.S. Air Arena
Landover, MD 20785

Western Conference

Anaheim Mighty Ducks
Arrowhead Pond of Anaheim
2695 Katella Ave
Anaheim, CA 92806

Calgary Flames
Olympic Saddledome
PO Box 1540, Station M
Calgary, Alberta, Canada T2P 3B9

Chicago Blackhawks
1901 W. Madison
Chicago, IL 60612

Colorado Avalanche
1635 Clay St.
Denver, CO 80204

Dallas Stars
211 Cowboys Pkwy
Irving, TX 75063

Detroit Red Wings
Joe Louis Arena
600 Civic Center Dr.
Detroit, MI 48226

Edmonton Oilers
Northland Coliseum
7424-118 Ave
Edmonton, Alberta,
Canada T5B 4M9

Los Angeles Kings
PO Box 17013
Inglewood, CA 90308

St. Louis Blues
PO Box 66792
St. Louis, MO 63166-6792

San Jose Sharks
San Jose Arena
525 W. Santa Clara St.
San Jose, CA 95113

Toronto Maple Leafs
Maple Leaf Gardens
60 Carlton St
Toronto, Ontario,
Canada M5B 1L1

Vancouver Canucks
Pacific Coliseum
100 N. Renfrew St
Vancouver, B.C.,
Canada V5K 3N7

Phoenix Coyotes
2 North Central
Phoenix, AZ 85004

NATIONAL BASKETBALL ASSOCIATION

Atlanta Hawks
1 CNN Center
South Tower, Suite 405
Atlanta, GA 30303

Boston Celtics
151 Merrimac St., 4th Fl.
Boston, MA 02114

Charlotte Hornets Fan Mail
100 Hive Dr.
Charlotte, NC 28217

Chicago Bulls
1901 West Madison
Chicago, IL 6O612-4501

Cleveland Cavaliers
1 Center Court
Cleveland, OH 44115

Dallas Mavericks
Reunion Arena
777 Sports St.
Dallas, TX 75207

Denver Nuggets
1635 Clay St.
Denver, CO 80204

Detroit Pistons
2 Championship Dr.
Auburn Hills, MI 48326

Golden State Warriors
Oakland Coliseum Arena
7000 Coliseum Way
Oakland, CA 94621

Houston Rockets
10 Greenway Plaza
Houston, TX 77046

Indiana Pacers
300 E. Market St.
Indianapolis, IN 46204

Los Angeles Clippers
L.A. Memorial Sports Arena
3939 S. Figueroa
Los Angeles, CA 90037

Los Angeles Lakers
Great Western Forum
P.O. Box 10
Inglewood, CA 90306

Miami Heat
1 Southeast Third Ave.
Miami, FL 33131

Milwaukee Bucks
1001 N. 4th St.
Milwaukee, WI 53203

Minnesota Timberwolves
600 1st Ave. North

Minneapolis, MN 55403

New Jersey Nets
405 Murray Hill Parkway
E. Rutherford, NJ 07073

New York Knicks
Madison Square Garden
2 Penn Plaza
New York, NY 10121

Orlando Magic
P.O. Box 76
Orlando, FL 32802

Philadelphia '76ers
Veteran Stadium
P.O. Box 25040
Philadelphia, PA 19147

Phoenix Suns
P.O. Box 1369
Phoenix, AZ 85001

Portland Trail Blazers
700 N.E. Multnomah St.
Ste 600
Portland, OR 97232

Sacramento Kings
1 Sports Parkway
Sacramento, CA 95834

San Antonio Spurs
100 Montana Street
San Antonio, TX 78203

Seattle Supersonics
P.O. Box C900911
Seattle, WA 98109-9711

Toronto Raptors
20 Bay Street Ste. 702
Toronto, Ontario
Canada M5J 2N8

Utah Jazz
301 W. South Temple
Salt Lake City, UT 84101

Vancouver Grizzlies
General Motors Place
800 Griffith Way
Vancouver, BC
Canada V6B 6G1

Washington Bullets
U.S. Air Arena
Landover, MD 20785

■ ■ ■ ■ ■ ■ ■ ■ ■ ■ ■ ■ ■ ■ ■ ■ ■ ■ ■

FOOTBALL

National Football League
280 Park Ave.
New York, NY 10017
212-450-2500

AMERICAN CONFERENCE FOOTBALL TEAMS

Baltimore Ravens
11001 Owings Mills Blvd.
Owings Mills, MD 21117

Buffalo Bills
1 Bills Dr.
Orchard Park, NY 14127

Cincinnati Bengals
1 Bengals Drive
Cincinnati, OH 45204

Denver Broncos
13655 Broncos Pkwy.
Englewood, CO 80112

Indianapolis Colts
7001 W. 56th St.
Indianapolis, IN 46254

Jacksonville Jaguars
One Stadium Place
Jacksonville, FL 32202

Kansas City Chiefs
1 Arrowhead Dr.
Kansas City, MO 64129

Miami Dolphins
7500 SW 30th St.
Davie, FL 33329

New England Patriots
Foxboro Stadium - Route 1
Foxboro, MA 02035

New York Jets
1000 Fulton Ave.
Hempstead, NY 11550

Oakland Raiders
1220 Harbor Bay Pkwy
Alameda, CA 94502

Pittsburgh Steelers
Three Rivers Stadium
300 Stadium Cir.
Pittsburgh, PA 15212

San Diego Chargers
Qualcomm Stadium
San Diego, CA 92160

Seattle Seahawks
11220 NE 53rd St.
Kirkland, WA 98033

Tennessee Oilers
Baptist Sports Park
7640 Highway 70 S.
Nashville, TN 37221

NATIONAL CONFERENCE FOOTBALL TEAMS

Arizona Cardinals
8701 S. Hardy Drive
Phoenix, AZ 85284

Atlanta Falcons
One Falcon Place
Suwanee, GA 30174

Carolina Panthers
800 South Mint Street
Charlotte, NC 28202

Chicago Bears
1000 Football Drive
Lake Forest, IL 60045

Dallas Cowboys
Cowboys Center
1 Cowboys Pkwy.
Irving, TX 75063

Detroit Lions
1200 Featherstone Rd.
Pontiac, MI 48342

Green Bay Packers
1265 Lombardi Ave.
Green Bay, WI 54307

Minnesota Vikings
9520 Viking Dr.
Eden Prairie, MN 55344

New Orleans Saints
5800 Airline Hwy
New Orleans, LA 70003

New York Giants
Giants Stadium
East Rutherford, NJ 07073

Philadelphia Eagles
3501 South Broad Street
Philadelphia, PA 19148

San Francisco 49ers
4949 Centennial Blvd.
Santa Clara, CA 95054

St. Louis Rams
One Rams Way
St. Louis, MO 63045

Tampa Bay Buccaneers
1 Buccaneer Pl.
Tampa, FL 33607

Washington Redskins
PO Box 17247
Dallas International Airport
Washington, D.C. 20041

BASEBALL
Major League Baseball
350 Park Ave.
New York, NY 10022

AMERICAN LEAGUE BASEBALL TEAMS

Baltimore Orioles
333 W. Camden Street
Baltimore, MD 21201

Boston Red Sox
Fenway Park
Boston, MA 02115

California Angels
P.O. Box 2000
Anaheim, CA 92803

Chicago White Sox
333 W. 35th St.
Chicago, IL 60616

Cleveland Indians
Jacobs Field
2401 Ontario Street
Cleveland, OH 44115

Detroit Tigers
Public Relations
2121 Trumbull Ave.
Detroit, MI 48216

Kansas City Royals
P.O. Box 419969
Kansas City, MO 64141

Milwaukee Brewers
P.O. Box 3099
Milwaukee, WI 53201

Minnesota Twins
501 Chicago Ave. South
Minneapolis, MN 55415

New York Yankees
Yankee Stadium
Bronx, NY 10451

Oakland Athletics
Oakland Coliseum
Oakland, CA 94621

Seattle Mariners
P.O. Box 4100
Seattle, WA 98104

Texas Rangers
P.O. Box 90111
Arlington, TX 76004

Toronto Blue Jays
1 Blue Jay Way
Sky Dome
300 Bremmer Blvd., Suite 3200
Toronto, Ont., Canada MSV 3B3

NATIONAL LEAGUE BASEBALL TEAMS

Atlanta Braves
P.O. Box 4064
Atlanta, GA 30302

Chicago Cubs
Wrigley Field
1060 West Addison St.
Chicago, IL 60613

Cincinnati Reds
100 Riverfront Stadium
Cincinnati, OH 45202

Colorado Rockies
1700 Broadway Ste 2100
Denver, CO 80205

Florida Marlins
Joe Robbie Stadium
2267 NW 199th St.
Miami, FL 33056

Houston Astros
P.O. Box 288
Houston, TX 77001-0288

Los Angeles Dodgers
1000 Elysian Park Ave.
Los Angeles, CA 90012

Montreal Expos
PO Box 500, Station M
Montreal, Quebec, Canada HIV 3P2

New York Mets
Shea Stadium
Flushing, NY 11368

Philadelphia Phillies
Veteran Stadium
P.O. Box 7575
Philadelphia, PA 19101

Pittsburgh Pirates
Three Rivers Stadium
Pittsburgh, PA 15212

St. Louis Cardinals
250 Stadium Plaza
St. Louis, MO 63102

San Diego Padres
P.O. Box 2000
San Diego, CA 92112

San Francisco Giants
Candlestick Park
San Francisco, CA 94124

Money Matters

Do You Need A Financial Planner?

Are you are always having difficulty making ends meet? Maybe you would like to have more money to enjoy your retirement. You might need the help of a financial planner. *When and How to Choose a Financial Planner* is a free booklet available from the National Endowment for Financial Education, that will help you choose a planner. This 12 page guide gives basic information on when you should seek advice, as well as how to go about choosing a financial planner. To get your free copy, write to:

NATIONAL ENDOWMENT FOR FINANCIAL EDUCATION
DEPARTMENT 1778
4695 S. MONACO ST.
DENVER, CO 80237-3403

Finding The Right Financial Adviser

Everybody with assets to protect, regardless of their age, should have a financial advisor. Just remember, you worked hard for your money and now it's time to make your money work harder for you. Oppenheimer Funds has published a guide, *Finding A Financial Adviser Who's Right For You.* It will take you through the process step-by-step of selecting names, conducting interviews, making the final decision, and maintaining a relationship

that will be profitable. This is a must for anyone looking for help in making intelligent financial planning decisions. To order your free copy call:
1-800 525-7048

How To Make Educated Investments

American Century Investments is offering free investor education materials you might find useful. Here are some of the more popular ones:

IRA CHOICES AND CHALLENGES, a 16 page booklet that compares the different types of IRAs created by the 1997 Tax Relief Act

INVESTING WITH A PURPOSE, a 26 page booklet that explains the concepts of diversification and asset allocation, offers four sample portfolios based on your stage in life, and includes a do-it-yourself investor profile questionnaire

COLLEGE PLANNER, a slide-rule calculator for determining college costs

POST-RETIREMENT CALCULATOR, a slide-rule calculator for determining how long your savings will last, depending on how much you spend

FAST TAXFACTS, a laminated card with tax rates and general information on IRA rules and IRA Rollovers and much more.

For your free copy of any or all of these booklets or calculators, call American Century Investments toll-free at:
1-800-345-2021

Tax Saving Investments

If would like to lower your income taxes maybe you should be looking at investments that are completely or partially free of federal, state or local income tax. Lebenthal, one of the nation's leading municipal bond dealers has the *Lebenthal Municipal Bond Information Kit* that will show

you the advantages of investing in tax-exempt bonds. For your kit, call them toll-free at:
1-888-425-6116

Before You Buy A Franchise

Did you ever think of starting your own business maybe by buying one of the thousands of franchises that are available? Before you decide to make your mark as an franchise entrepreneur, you owe it to yourself to learn more about franchising. Some valuable sources to contact are:

The *ACCESS Franchise Directory*, the most comprehensive database of franchise information on the Internet. This site lists more than 2500 franchises at their web address: **www.entremkt.com.**

The Federal Trade Commission, which has an excellent 12 page pamphlet called *A Consumer Guide to Buying a Franchise*. You can download it from the FTC's Web site: **www.ftc.gov.**

Free Help Starting A Business

Service Corps of Retired Executives (SCORE) can give you free advice on starting a small business. This is a group of working and retired executives and business owners who donate their time and expertise to provide individual confidential business counseling and business workshops for aspiring entrepreneurs and small business owners. To find the SCORE office nearest you, call them at:
1-800-634-0245

Money To Start A Business

For some seniors the definition of retiring is to stop doing your usual job and starting up something new. If you've always wanted to start a business, now's your chance. The

U.S. Small Business Administration (SBA) is a great resource you can use for starting that business. They have a variety of programs including a loan guarantee program you might want to use. The SBA has offices throughout the U.S. But to find out more, first call the SBA Answer Desk at:
1-800-827-5722
Or visit the U.S. Small Business Administration web site:
www.SBAonline.SBA.Gov

Searching the Web for the Best Mortgage Loans

Before you shop for a new mortgage, be sure to find out what rates are being charged in your area, find out mortgage trends and use repayment calculators. Even a slightly lower interest rate can often save you thousands of dollars over the repayment period of your loan. Once you've become an informed consumer you can then shop intelligently for a mortgage loan either on the Internet or at your local financial institution. Here are three online sites where you can find up-to-date rate information and lots more. They do not offer mortgages directly but will provide you with all kinds of highly useful information you can use:

FANNIE MAE
www.fanniemae.com/
index.html
Provides all kinds of mortgage and home refinancing information. They also list the co-op, condos and houses that they own due to foreclosures throughout the nation. A great place to shop for a terrifc buy on your next home.

MORTGAGE MARKET INFORMATION SERVICE, INC.
www.interest.com/rates.html
Employs an easy-to-use click-on map to find up-to-date information about mortgage rates and lenders in specific areas around the country.

MICRO SURF
www.microsurf.com
This site is the largest independent source of mortgage information on the Internet. While they are not lenders or brokers, they do allow you to compare the rates offered by 1,300 lenders nationwide who update their rates daily.

Save Thousands By Shopping For Your Mortgage Online

Your home mortgage is the most important financial transaction your family is likely to ever make. But if you have ever shopped for a mortgage you know how long, tedious... and expensive the process can be. Now there may be a better way...online mortgages.

With the application filed out on your home computer and sent electronically, online mortgage applications offers you a combination of speed, convenience and cost savings. Financial experts agree that getting your mortgage online will almost definitely save you money. In fact, sometimes the savings can total tens of thousands of dollars over the term of the mortgage! The reason is that the online mortgage companies deal with lenders throughout the country and they are constantly searching for the very best rates to offer you. Mortgage approval can often be a matter of minutes instead of weeks or even months that it takes the traditional way.

In addition, several of the online mortgage companies offer you a variety of additional services that include help in finding a home, tips on negotiating and inspecting the home you plan to buy and lots more. Here are three of the leading online mortgage companies you can contact directly through their Internet sites:

Intuit Inc.: www.quickenmortgage.com

E-Loan: www.eloan.com

HomeShark: www.homeshark.com

Do You Have Unclaimed Money Waiting For You?

Did you know that there are actually $300 billion dollars in unclaimed funds waiting for their rightful owner to come along? What often happens is that people move and forget to notify everyone of their new address. You may have a bank account from years ago with money that was never withdrawn. Also, there are 3 million stock brokerage accounts with securities that belong to shareholders who are currently lost. If you think there's even a remote possibility that you have funds or securities you have forgotten about, be sure to check at these web sites and see what you have and how you can claim your funds. It's like winning the lottery!

The first Internet website is for a lost funds search company called The CapitaLink. Their web address is: **www.ifast.com**

And, 25 states with web sites have a combined site where you can search by name for unclaimed property they hold. Check out this web site at: **www.unclaimed.org**

Download Coupon Savings

One of the traditional ways of saving money is to clip coupons and use them in your shopping. The trouble is that it takes a lot of time to scour the newspapers to find the coupons you will use. Now there's an easier way of getting those same savings without the hassle...dowloading them from the Internet.

One of the leading companies helping you get these coupons online is called *CoolSavings*. Their electronic method of couponing has met with great success and their web site has quickly become one of the most visited Internet sites. The way it works is that you go to their web site and fill out a brief online questionnaire, select the coupons you want, download them into your computer and print them out. You'll find a vast array of companies at their web site including everything from local pizza delivery stores to national chains like J.C. Penney, Toys 'R Us and McDonalds. To check out their free web site go to:
www.coolsavings.com

IRA - Roth IRA – What's The Difference?

You probably know that Individual Retirement Accounts commonly known at 'IRA's' are allowed to help you save tax sheltered money for retirement. But do you know what the difference is between an IRA and a ROTH IRA? To help taxpayers learn more about all kinds of IRA's and so you can determine which is right for you, the IRS has updated its 'Publication 590' that focuses on these types of accounts. Call them at:
1-800-829-3676
Or visit their website at: www.irs.ustreas.gov

How To Avoid Phone Scams

Be careful…unscrupulous individuals and companies have a phone scheme that preys on consumers and especially on seniors. Without your knowledge they 'slam' or 'cram' your phone.

'Slamming' means switching your phone service to their company without your permission.

'Cramming' is the practice of charging you for services you never ordered.

Here are tips from the National Fraud Information Center, on how to avoid slamming and cramming, and what to do if you think you've been defrauded.

Check every page of your phone bill as soon as you get it for unauthorized charges. If you find something that is unclear call your local phone company.

Read the fine print before filling out any contest form or coupon offer.

Take care when calling 800 or 900 numbers. Be especially wary of following instructions that say, "enter activation code numbers or of answering 'yes' to questions that may result in your authorizing unwanted telephone services. Here's what to do once you feel you have been defrauded:

• Call the National Fraud Information Center at:
1-800-876-7060

• Send a letter describing what happened and enclose a copy of your bill to the
FEDERAL COMMUNICATIONS COMMISSION
CONSUMER PROTECTION BRANCH
MAIL STOP 1600A2
WASHINGTON, DC 20554

• File a complaint with your local attorney general and telephone regulators.

Planning For Retirement

Whether you are just starting to invest or already have a plan, Charles Schwab has a free source book that will help you with those important financial decisions. *The Essential Investor* will help you plan for a more secure financial future. It includes a checklist of investing essentials to get you started as well as sample portfolios and even a quick retirement planner. Ask for *The Essential Investor* when you call: **1-800-924-0868**

Women and Money

The *Money Minded* web site is designed specifically for women. It addresses questions about saving, family goals, and investing mostly from a woman's perspective. On the site you'll find featured entrepreneurs and financial risk-takers who offer their great advice and important information for women and their money. Their web address is: **www/.moneyminded.com/index.htm**

The Best Online Broker

The financial newspaper, Barrons, rates Discover Brokerage as the #1 overall online broker. If you buy or sell securities on the Internet and would like to get important financial information about Discover's brokerage services, call: **1-800-58-INVEST**
Or visit their web site: www.discoverbrokerage.com

Understanding Mutual Funds

A Guide to Understanding Mutual Funds is available free from the Investment Company Institute, the mutual fund industry's principal trade group. This guide describes the various types of funds and explains the risks involved, discusses how funds are structured, and how to set up an in-

vestment plan. They also discuss important tax considerations and give you a guide to finding and analyzing information on funds yourself. To get your free copy, call:
202-326-5800

Mutual Fund Report Card

Are you holding the right mutual funds? Charles Schwab
has a series of report cards for different mutual funds that
give you their ratings, performance and growth records. You
can request up to three reports for any mutual funds even if
they're not available through Schwab. There's no cost or obligation. Call them toll-free at:
1-800-540-8117
Or visit their web site at www.schwab.com

Mutual Fund Info

Waterhouse Securities, Inc. will send you the *Top Perform-
ing Mutual Funds Guide* and the *Mutual Funds Information and Comparison Guide*. If you invest in mutual funds
or are thinking of investing, you'll definitely want these free
guides. Call toll-free:
1-800-708-9283
Or visit them at their web site: www.waterhouse.com

Getting Your Budget In Shape

To help you keep your budget in shape, the Internet has a
number of helpful sites that will help you:

SMART CALC:
You'll find a number of very useful calculators at this web
site that will help you budget your spending, determine how
much your mortgage payments will be… and lots more.
www.smartcalc.com

HEALTHY CASH

Are you an overspender? Are there things you can do to avoid the devastating effects of this habit? To discover your 'Spending Personality,' take a self-test online at *Healthy Cash* which is at the Health World Online Web site at:
www.healthy.net/library/articles/cash/assessment/ assessment.htm

THE MONEY WISE HOME GUIDE:
www.mpicture.com/homeguide/financial/debt.htm

Tips To Get Financially Fit

- Pay off your credit card debt to reduce interest expenses. Start with the credit cards that have the highest finance charge. If possible pay off your balance every month.
- Switch to using credit cards with no annual fees.
- Be a smart shopper and always shop around before you buy something especially big ticket items.
- If you do find it necessary to carry balances on your credit card, be certain you are not using a card that charges a high percentage rate on unpaid balances. Remember, you can get the interest rate lowered with most credit cards just by asking for a lower rate. Tell them you are thinking of dropping their card and using another one that charges a lower interest rate. You'll be amazed at how often they will offer you a substantially lower rate rather than lose you as a customer.
- Join a credit union if you're eligible. Credit unions generally charge lower fees than banks especially if you maintain only small balances in your checking and savings accounts.

Money Facts

The Federal Reserve Bank of Atlanta has a free fascinating booklet that describes how currency is designed, printed,

circulated and eventully destroyed. There's even a section on how to redeem bills that might have been damaged in a fire or chewed up by the family dog. Ask for *Fundamental Facts About U.S. Money.* Write to:
FEDERAL RESERVE BANK OF ATLANTA
PUBLIC AFFAIRS DEPT.
ATLANTA, GA. 30303

Fast Banking

The American Bankers Association's free brochure on *A Dozen Ways to Save Time and Money at the Bank* offers a variety of tips on money management. It will help you take charge of your finances. For a free copy, write to:
ATTENTION: *'A DOZEN TIPS.'*
THE AMERICAN BANKERS ASSOCIATION
1120 CONNECTICUT AVE. N.W.
WASHINGTON, D.C. 20036

Choosing The Mortgage That's Right For You

Are you ready to shop for a mortgage? This easy to read 40 page guide can help. It walks you through the mortgage shopping process in three easy steps. Discover how big a mortgage loan you can afford, how to choose the mortgage that's right for you, and how to compare terms commonly used among lenders. This guide is free from:
FANNIE MAE
PO BOX 27463
RICHMOND, VA 23286-8999
OR CALL 1-800 688-HOME

Tax Do's & Don'ts For Mutual Fund Investors

This helpful 20 page booklet, *Tax Do's & Don'ts For Mutual*

Fund Investors, lists 13 points to consider about the tax aspects of mutual fund investing. For example , it warns you *not* to assume that all fund distributions are the same, that you owe no taxes on reinvested dividends or that you owe no tax if you exchange shares from one fund for shares of another in mutual fund 'families.' For a copy of the free booklet, write to:
ICI
1401 H St. N.W., Suite 1200
Washington, D.C. 2005

Investing For Retirement

IRA Transfers is a free brochure that explains tax-sheltered retirement investing. It can help you get the most from your investments. It is published by the AARP Investment Program from Scudder, Stevens & Clark - a group of no-load mutual funds designed for members of the AARP, but open to investors of any age. (No-load means there is no sales commission.) For free a copy, call:
1-800-322 2282, Ext. 8271

The State Tax Laws: A Guide for Investors Aged 50 and Over is another free publication from AARP. Scudder prepared this 112 page guide in conjunction with the National Conference of State Legislatures. For a copy call:
1-800-322-2282, Ext 8254

Finding The Right Tax Professional

When tax time comes around it's always an excellent idea to have a tax pro help you. To help you through the difficult process of choosing the right tax pro, you might want to start by getting the names of professionals in your area and interviewing a number of them. For the names of tax experts in your area, call the National Association of Enrolled Agents at: **1-800 424-4339**

Before You Go Into Business

If you've ever thought of going into business and starting a new corporation, here's a booklet you will definitely want to get. *Starting Your Own Corporation* will answer many of the questions you may have regarding setting up the right kind of corporation. For your free copy, call the 'Corporation Company' at:
1-800-542-2677.

Personal Finance Helplines

If you are not sure where to turn for good advice regarding your personal finances, here are several toll-free hotlines you can turn to for help. They will either provide you with the information you need or they will tell you where you can go for further assistance.

Financial Planning

THE INSTITUTE OF CERTIFIED FINANCIAL PLANNERS - FOR BROCHURES & REFERRALS, CALL: **1-800-282-7526**

THE AMERICAN INSTITUTE OF CERTIFIED PUBLIC ACCOUNTANTS' PERSONAL FINANCIAL PLANNING DIVISION CALL: **1-800-862- 4272**

THE INTERNATIONAL ASSOCIATION FOR FINANCIAL PLANNING CALL: **1-404-395-1605**

THE NATIONAL ASSOCIATION OF PERSONAL FINANCIAL ADVISERS. CALL: **1-800 366-2732**

THE AMERICAN SOCIETY OF CLU AND ChFC. CALL: **1-800-392-6900**

Choosing The Right Stock Broker

The best way to find a good stockbroker is to ask for referrals from friends, professional acquaintances or from your

family. If you have any questions and would like to check on a particular broker's background, call:
THE NATIONAL ASSOCIATION OF SECURITIES DEALERS:
1-800-289-9999

Savings Bond Redemption

Did you know that all Series E Savings Bond issued since 1941 are still earning interest? If you own any bonds tucked away in a safety deposit box and would like to know exactly how much they're worth today, write for *Tables of Redemption Values For Savings Bonds* from:
BUREAU OF PUBLIC DEBT
SAVING BOND OPERATIONS
200 THIRD AVE.
PARKERSBURG, WV 26101-1328
OR VISIT THEIR WEB SITE: **www.savingbonds.gov**

Buying U.S. Government Securities

Americans have been buying Series E Savings bonds for many years. But few people know they can also buy Treasury Bonds and Bills that pay even higher interest. For more information on how you can get in on this no-risk, high-yield investment, write for *U.S. Securities Available to Investors.* From:
PUBLIC DEBT INFORMATION
U.S. DEPARTMENT OF THE TREASURY
WASHINGTON, D.C. 20226

Recovering Lost Money

Did your dog chew up some money you left on the table? Did it get partially destroyed in a fire? Well the U.S. Department of Treasury can help get that money back for you. Drop them a line with a plausible detailed explanation. Once the claim is processsed and verified, the actual payment is made by federal check. For more information write:

U.S. Department of the Treasury
Office of Currency Standards
15th Street & Pennsylvania Ave., N.W.
Washington, D.C. 20220
or call: 1-202-622-2000

Getting A New Mortgage

If you are looking for a new mortgage either to buy a new house or to take advantage of lower mortagage rates, it is important that you learn how to evaluate the type of mortgage that is best for you. As a first step you might call First Financial Equity on their toll-free number for more information and for answers to your mortgage questions. Call: 1-800-454-0505

Evaluating Your Investments

Before you make any significant investment, learn what to look for to find the one that's best for you. Also discover how to evaluate your investment and determine how well it meets your objectives. The first step is to ask for *Evaluating Investment Performance,* when you contact:

Neuberger & Berman
Individual Asset Management Group
605 Third Ave.
New York, NY 10158
or call 800-234-9840

Savings Just Because You're Over 50

Now that an ever growing part of the population is over 50 years old, there are lots of bargains and discounts available just for the asking. Remember if you don't ask you'll never know. In any store you shop in always check to see if there are certain days or certain times when seniors are offered discounts or specials. Many hotels offer discounts on their

rooms as well as discounts if you eat in their restaurants. You can also apply for a travel club card if you are a member of AARP...The American Association of Retired Persons. Their toll-free phone number is:
1-800-424-3410.

Learning About Mutual Funds

If you would like to learn all about mutual funds and find out which are the best ones for you, check out the Strong Equity Performers from Dreyfus. Call them toll-free at:
1-800 THE LION EXT 4043
Or visit a Dreyfus Financial Center via the Internet at:
www.dreyfus.com/funds

Global Utilities Fund

Basic utilities such as water and electricity are always in demand and telecommunications is growing in all countries. That's why the Franklin Global Utilities Fund might be a growth fund for you. They will manage a portfolio especially designed for you. If this sounds like something you would consider, call today for a free brochure and prospectus:
1-800 342-FUND   OR WRITE:
FRANKLIN FUNDS
777 MARINERS ISLAND BOULEVARD
SAN MATEO, CA 94404-1585

The Lowest Cost Life Insurance - Guaranteed!

If you are looking for the maximum life insurance coverage at the lowest cost...this one's for you. A company called Quotesmith actually guarantees they will find the lowest term life rates in America or they'll send you $500.00! That's quite a claim but it's worth checking them out.

What they do when you request a quote by calling their

toll-free number is scan the 350 insurance companies in their database and give you the lowest price quotes that that search comes up with. There is no charge for their service so you may want to give them a try. It could save you a bundle. You can call them at:
1-800-431-1147

Fund Raising Kit

If your school or organization needs money, this *free fund-raising kit* will teach you how. This kit will help show your group how to collect member's recipes and publish them into a great cookbook. Write for your free kit to:
FUNDCRAFT
410 HIGHWAY 72 WEST
BOX 340
COLLIERVILLE, TN 38017

Lower Your Insurance Premiums

Did you know that if you're in the market for Medicare and Medigap policies for health insurance for yourself or a parent, your premiums will be lowest if you enroll between three months before, to four months after your 65th birthday? After that the premiums may grow by 10 percent each year you wait. For more information, ask for The Social Security Administration's free *Guide to Health Insurance for People with Medicare.* Contact:
THE HEALTH INSURANCE ASSOCIATION OF AMERICA
PUBLICATION OFFICE
555 13TH ST. NW SUITE 600-E
WASHINGTON, D.C. 20004
OR CALL TOLL-FREE: **1-800-772-1213**

Mutual Funds For Investors Over 50

You've worked hard to save money for your retirement and to help it grow, now you must be sure you do everything you

can to preserve and protect that important investment. *Understanding Mutual Funds: A Guide for Investors Aged 50 and Over*, defines the basics to help older individuals choose funds appropriate for their needs. It's your free! Contact:
AARP INVESTMENT PROGRAM
SCUDDER PROCESSING CENTER
BOX 5014
JANESVILLE, **WI 53547.**
OR CALL: **800-322-2282,** EXT **4884**

Check Out Money Market Funds

If you want higher interest than you will get in a bank but still want instant access to your money, be sure to check out the money market funds. To find out more about money market funds, contact one or more of these large funds and ask for their *prospectus and information package:*
DREYFUS SERVICE CORP.
600 MADISON AVE.
NEW YORK, **NY 10022**
1-800-645-6561

FIDELITY CASH RESERVES
P.O. BOX 832
BOSTON, **MA 02103.**
CALL: **1-800-225-6190.**

IDS CASH MANAGEMENT FUND
P.O. BOX 369
MINNEAPOLIS, **MN 55440.**
CALL: **1-800-437-4332**

Tax-Free Income Fund

If you are in a high tax bracket and would like to lower your tax bite, did you know you can start earning tax-free income with as little as $1,000 with instant liquidity and no sales or redemption fee? For more information on tax-free investing, call:
1-800-638-5660

IRS Or H&R Block?

Few people realize that the IRS is committed to giving tax-payers every legitimate deduction they're entitled to. The IRS has toll-free numbers throughout the country you can call for assistance and/or forms. As a start, for answers to your income tax questions, call The Internal Revenue Service's tax hotline toll-free:
1-800-829-1040

The IRS also has a series of helpful publications such as *Federal Income Tax* available free of charge. Call the toll-free number for this publication or a list of the others available.

The IRS also has a toll-free number to assist deaf/hearing-impaired taxpayers who have access to TV-Phone/Teletype-writer equipment (800-428-4732; In Indiana: 1-800-382-4059).

"Congratulations! You've Just Won...."

Even though the world is full of people who would never think of doing anything dishonest, there are still plenty of people out there who wouldn't give a second thought to con-ning you out of your life savings. One of the most common scams is calling elderly people with an exciting announce-ment such as... *"Congratulations, Mr. Jones, you're name has been selected as the winner of an exciting cruise. Isn't that great? All you need to do to claim your prize is to put up a good faith deposit by sending us a check for $$$$$$."*

Hang up the phone right there. One rule you must always follow is:

Never...EVER buy anything or pay money to claim your *'free prize.'* No reputable company will ever ask you to send them money to get a 'free' prize.

For more information on these scams and what you can

do to keep from falling prey to one, get your free copy of *Telemarketing Travel Fraud.* It's your free from:
PUBLIC REFERENCE
FEDERAL TRADE COMMISSION
ROOM 130
WASHINGTON, DC 20580
202-326-2222

Be Your Own Broker

If you have a computer and like to make your own invest-ment decisions without the help of a stockbroker, this one may be for you. Charles Schwab has free computer software you can use to buy and sell securities over the Internet for just $29.95 for up to 1,000 shares. The software also allows you to do your own research using various Internet data-bases, track the stocks you are interested in and lots more. For more information call: **1-800-E-SCHWAB.**

For a listing of online brokers that allow you to trade for a small fraction of what it would cost you from a full service broker, see the listings at the end of this section.

Six Ways To Protect Your Family With Estate Planning

1. **CREATE A WILL**

    The will is an essential part of your estate plan. It should detail how and when to distribute your assets and who will manage your estate upon your death. If your kids are minors, under age 18, you also should appoint legal guardians in case both you and your spouse die. In the event that you don't name a guardian, the court will select one for your kids. In addition, if family members fight over custody, your estate pays the legal fees. Also, if you die without a will the court chooses an executor to distribute your assets. In many cases, a court administrator is chosen and he or she gets paid from your estate. The court, regardless of your intentions, may divide your assets between your surviving spouse and children, even if your spouse needs the children's share to meet day-to-day expenses.

2. **TAKE ADVANTAGE OF TAX EXEMPTIONS**

    With the proper planning, you can structure your estate plan to take advantage of valuable tax exemptions. There has recently been a change in the tax laws that will allow an increasing amount of your estate to pass tax exempt to your heirs. Starting in 1999, the first $650,000 of your assets is exempt from federal estate and gift tax. After that a marital deduction will allow you to transfer an unlimited amount of property tax-free to your spouse. When your spouse dies, $650,000 of assets in the estate is shielded from estate taxes and amounts over $650,000 are taxed at rates ranging from 37-55 percent. Couples with modest estates can plan ahead and minimize their taxes by dividing their assets. This way, each spouse owns no more than $650,000 in assets.

3. **USE TRUSTS TO REDUCE YOUR TAXABLE ESTATE.**

   If you have more than $650,000 in assets, a By-Pass Trust allows you to pass more assets directly to your heirs. A typical Bypass Trust enables the surviving spouse to receive income from the trust. At his or her death, the principal would then pass to the heirs. Since the assets are in a trust, they are not included in the taxable estate of your spouse.

4. **CONSIDER GIFTING.**

   If your assets far exceed any possible use you may have for them in your lifetime, you might consider giving portions of your assets to those you would want to have them.

5. **UNDERSTAND THE VALUE OF YOUR ESTATE.**

   Simply put, your estate includes everything you own. Most of us don't realize how quickly your assets add up. Make a personal financial statement that totals up the value of your home, any other real estate, stocks, bonds and investment interests, even the value of your life insurance policies, as well as any valuables you may own.

6. **SPEAK TO A PROFESSINAL**

   Tax laws are confusing and change periodically. Before you decide on any estate plan you may be considering, be sure to consult with an accountant or attorney who specializes in tax law.

Save Hundreds of Dollars On Every Stock Trade By Trading Online

22 ONLINE BROKERS CHARGING $20 PER TRADE OR LESS

If you are an active trader or investor in stocks and make all of your own buying and selling decisions without the advice of a broker, you can save a lot of money on your trades by using an online broker.

Here are stock brokerage firms that charge $20.00 per transaction or less for online trades. Some, like Ameritrade, Datek, and Suretrade, even charge less than $10 for trades that would cost several hundred dollars at a full-service firm! The services they offer, speed of execution and investor financial requirements vary from one firm to the next. Most firms also let you trade using their toll-free phone number but they generally charge somewhat more for these trades than those you make online. To find out more, check out their Internet sites at the web addresses listed here or call their toll-free phone numbers.

BROKER	INTERNET ADDRESS	TOLL-FREE
Ameritrade	www.ameritrade.com	800-669-3900
Brown & Co.	www.brownco.com	800-965-1191
Bull & Bear Securities	www.bullbear.com	800-847-4200
Burke, Christensen & Lewis Securities	www.bclnet.com	800-821-6756
Datek	www.datek.com	800-922-5966
Discover Brokerage Direct	www.discoverbrokerage.com	800-688-6896
DLJ Direct	www.dljdirect.com	800-825-5723
E*trade	www.etrade.com	800-786-2575
Fidelity Investments	http://personal.fidelity.com/brokerage	800-544-3902
Freedom Investments	www.freedominvestments.com	800-944-4033
Investex Securities Group	www.investexpress.com	800-392-7192
JB Oxford & Co.	www.jboxford.com	800-656-1776
National Discount Brokers	www.ndb.com	800-888-3999
Pacific Brokerage Services	www.tradepbs.com	800-421-8395
Preferred Technology	www.preftech.com	888-778-7799
Quick & Reilly	www.quick-reilly.com	800-368-0446
Scottsdale Securities	www.discountbroker.com	800-619-7283
Sunlogic Securities	www.sunlogic.com	800-556-4600
Wall Street Electronica	www.wallstreete.com	888-925-5783
WaterhouseSecurities Inc.	www.waterhouse.com	800-934-4479
WIT Capital	www.witcapital.com	888-494-8227
Ziegler Thrift Trading	www.ziegler-thrift.com	800-342-8941

Traveling Free Or At Huge Savings

The Four Best Ways To Get Free Travel

Most people don't know it but there are lots of ways you can get free or almost free travel. Here are a few of the best...

If you have a unique skill or hobby, many cruise lines will give you a free trip in exchange for giving a lecture about your specialty on one of their cruises. They often have theme cruises you might fit in with. For example, if you are a fitness specialist, they often look for people to teach aerobics on board. So if you have a unique skill...let's say you're an amateur magician or perhaps a financial advisor, the cruise line will often give you a free trip just for spending an hour a day instructing others while on the cruise. Check the travel section of your local newspaper or check the toll-free directory for the phone numbers of the cruise lines. If you have a computer, you can also reach the cruise lines via the Internet. See the Internet listings at the end of this section.

There are some courier services that will ask you to carry a package anywhere in the world they travel to. With that you get a free trip for carrying the parcel. Sometimes you can get to stay a few extra days as long as you can catch their plane on the return flight. For more information, contact the International Association of Air Travel Couriers at: **561-582-8320** or on the Internet at: **www.courier.org**

A common practice of all airlines is to overbook their flights since they know from experience that a certain percentage of people do not show up for their flight and the airline wants to leave with a full plane. When too many passengers show up the the airlines will offer free tickets to anywhere they fly just for changing your flight. One great method of getting free airline tickets is as soon as you get to the airport for your next trip, volunteer to take the next flight out if they are overbooked in exchange for a free ticket on a future flight. (See the following report: *10 Tips On Getting Free Travel When Your Plane Is Overbooked.*)

Frequent flyer programs are still a good deal that costs you nothing. Many charge cards will give you frequent flyer miles just for using their cards. Check with your charge card company. Also, make sure you are a member of the airline's frequent flyer club if you plan on doing any airline travel. They usually don't put a time restriction on them.

When they travel, some families look for housesitters. In return for watching their home, you get a free place to live. If you like to travel, you can even trade apartments and homes with people in other parts of the country (or the world) through different real estate exchanges. Check the classified section of your local newspaper.

Adventure Tours For Seniors

A great number of seniors who are in fairly good physical condition want trips that involve challenges and cultural learning experiences. These seniors are looking for new adventures and also want to learn about local culture and nature in such places as Africa and South Africa. Elder Treks specializes in senior adventure tours to 30 different countries including Africa and South Africa. If you are looking for that adventurous tour call Elder Treks at:
1-800-741-7956
Or visit their web site: www.eldertreks.com

10 Tips On Getting Free Travel When Your Plane Is Overbooked

A lot of plane flights are overbooked. That means that the airline has sold more tickets than there are seats on the plane. The reason they overbook is that often people do not show up for their flights and the airline wants to fly with as full a passenger load as possible. When a flight is overbooked, the airline must offer inducements to passengers to voluntarily take a later flight. The inducement generally will be a voucher for free plane tickets on their airline. If the flight is very overbooked, you might be able to get an even better deal that might include vouchers for more than one flight, upgrade to first-class on their next flight, overnight hotel stay if there are no more flights until the next day and even cash. Here are ten useful tips:

1. Volunteer *before* airline representatives offer vouchers, if you think your flight may be oversold.

2. Make an informed decision. Ask how long it will be until the next flight leaves for your destination.

3. If there are no takers after a voucher is announced for a low amount and it's a popular flight don't raise your hand. The voucher value is likely to increase.

4. Use the voucher immediately. Most expire within a year and are not replaceable if lost or stolen.

5. Ask for a meal voucher.

6. When using a travel voucher, plan in advance. In some cases, limited seating may make it more difficult to redeem your free or discounted travel exactly when you want to.

7. If you have a travel agent, show him or her the front and back of your voucher to determine whether it qualifies for a particular flight.

8. Read the fine print. Some vouchers may not be used on certain days and holidays.

9. Many vouchers themselves are not transferable. But the recipient generally can buy a ticket for someone else,.

10. Be polite but don't be afraid to ask for more...for example, in addition to travel vouchers you might ask for an upgrade to first class on the next fight out. Remember, they *must* get people off the overbooked flight and will offer whatever it takes.

Travel Bargains For Seniors

One of the great benefits of becoming a senior are those discounts on just about everything from 'senior day' at your local retail store to movies, theater, restaurants and best of all...travel.

Next time you plan to venture out on any trip, be absolutely sure to ask about senior discounts.

There are a number of ways for seniors to get discount travel. For example, the airlines offer discount booklets you can purchase for substantial savings on your air fare.

Next, don't forget to become a member of AARP... The American Association of Retired Persons. (No, you don't have to be retired but you or your spouse must be 50 years of age or older.) For a membership fee of $8 per year, (including your spouse) you'll receive a magazine, *Modern Maturity*, newspaper updates and a membership card that gets you discounts on just about everything (hotels, insurance, drugs and more.) Once you're a member, to get your discounts you simply show your membership card or call their member services toll-free phone number: **1-800-424-3410**
Or visit them on the Internet at:
www.aarp.org

Most of the airlines offer special programs for seniors. Before you book your plane reservation, check with the airline you are planning to travel on to be sure they offer at least 10% discount for seniors 62 and older. They also have programs where you can purchase coupon booklets or passport programs that allow you to travel domestically and internationally at substantial discounts.

CONTINENTAL AIRLINES has a Freedom trip booklet and Senior passport program that allows you to enjoy discounted domestic and international travel.
Call them from 6:30 am to 10 pm Central time.at:
1-800 441-1135 or **1-800-248-8996**

DELTA AIRLINES has a discount program for domestic and international for seniors 62 and older. Call: **1-800-221-1212**

For information on AMERICAN AIRLINES SENIOR DISCOUNT program, call them at: **1-800-237-7981**

TWA has a senior coupon book you can purchase for domestic travel plus they will include a coupon for 20% off international travel. Anyone 62 or older can take advantage of these great money savings programs. Call them toll-free at: **1-800-221-2000**

Lowest Air Fares

While planning your next trip, be sure you are getting the best fares to and from the cities you will be visiting. There are a number of companies that specialize in getting you the lowest fares available. They check constantly with the various airlines and track their prices to insure that when you contact them you will get the best fare. For example, recently Global

Discount Travel Services had fares from New York to San Francisco of just $111 one way. While fares change constantly, similar savings are available to and from many other major cities both within the U.S. and on international flights. To check their fares, call them at:
**1-888-777-2222 OR VISIT THEIR WEB SITE AT:
www.lowestfare.com**

Also check the following web site where you can actually 'name your own price' for hotels and airfare:
**www.priceline.com
OR CALL THEM AT: 1-800-PRICELINE**

Airline Coupons For Seniors

As a senior citizen you're now eligible to purchase *Senior Citizen Airline Coupons*. With Senior Citizen coupons you can fly anywhere an airline flies within the 48 states for no more than $298 round trip currently or even less on some airlines. Airlines that go to the U.S. Virgin Islands, Puerto Rico and the Bahamas, and several that fly to Canada even throw in those destinations for the same low price.

The coupons are usually sold in a book of four one-way flights. Price change but currently on American, United and Delta the books cost $596; On Continental or U.S. Airways: $579; On America West or TWA: $548; and on Northwest: $540. Continental also sells a book of eight coupons for $1079.

Each coupon is good for a one-way fare, and while some airlines require a 14 day advance reservation, you can also use them to fly standby. You don't have to travel round trip, so there's no minimum stay. *Senior Coupon* travel also earns you frequent flier miles. With most airlines a couple cannot share a coupon book.

TWA is the only airline that sells coupon books for companions of any age for $648. To use the coupons you must travel with a qualifying senior.

America West and US Air both allow a senior to share a

coupon book with a child aged 2-11.

Also, don't forget to check with all the airlines for special seniors' clubs and senior discounts. For example, American, Delta and United run senior clubs that offer zoned fares ranging from $98-$298, round trip, for travel within the lower 48 states, depending on distance. In other words, you pay no more than the usual senior-coupon price for a long trip, and get an even better price on shorter trips. Those clubs also offer discounted international travel that isn't available with the regular coupons. Remember as a senior you get at least a 10% discount but check with the airline for an even bigger discount and the best travel deal.

50% Discount On Hotels

Want to save a lot of money the next time you book a hotel reservation in a large city? Try using a 'hotel broker'.

Just like airline-ticket consolidators, hotel brokers are outlets through which hotels rent some of their vacant rooms... *cheap*.

Hotel brokers are given blocks of discounted rooms by big city hotels. They in turn pass the bulk of the savings onto you. They concentrate mainly on big cities...Boston, Chicago, Los Angeles, New York, San Francisco, Washington, and more. A few even handle larger cities overseas, such as London, Sydney, Paris and Hong Kong. Where they operate, these consolidators can cut your hotel costs by as much as 50%. The brokers are classified into two groups.

BOOKING-AGENT BROKERS:
Some brokers make a reservation for you at the discounted rate. Once you have your confirmed discounted reservation you simply check in at the hotel as you ordinarily would and pay the discounted amount when you check out.

PREPAY BROKERS:
Other brokers are like tour operators. They sell hotel rooms at the same reduced rates they would in package tours. Here

you must prepay for your entire stay in order to get the best rate, and the broker sends you a voucher, which you use to pay upon arriving at the hotel.

When comparing the two types of brokers just keep in mind that with the first method where you pay at the check-out, you don't have to worry if you are forced to cancel or reschedule your trip.

The largest PREPAY-VOUCHER BROKER is Hotel Reservations Network, or HRN.
HOTEL RESERVATIONS NETWORK: 1-800-964-6835
Or visit their web site at: www.180096hotel.com
(You'll also find a link to HRN on many other discount-travel Web sites.)

The largest BOOKING-AGENT BROKER is:
QUICKBOOK
You can call them toll-free at: **800-789-9887**
Or visit their Web site at: www.quikbook.com

Another BOOKING-AGENT BROKER is Express Reservations which specializes only in New York and Los Angeles hotel bookings:
EXPRESS RESERVATION:
Call them toll-free at: **1-800-356-1123**
Or visit them on the Internet at: www.express-res.com

If you plan to travel to Florida and would like to save money on hotels, be sure to check with the Florida Tourist Bureau, Inc. Despite the official sounding name they are not a state agency but rather a private travel company that specializes in saving you up to 50% on your hotel accomodations throughout Florida. They work on the pre-paid voucher system where you book your room and pay in advance in exchange for a very substantial discount at the

best hotels and motels. Call them toll-free at:
1-888-246-8728

Half-Price Hotels

Many people have found that membership in a discount club is an excellent way to save money on their travel. If you spend more than a few nights a year in hotels, the annual price of membership in a good hotel discount club can be a good investment.

Most clubs promise 50% discounts off rack rate, subject to availability and the occupancy level the hotel expects. Here are some of the largest discount programs:

ENTERTAINMENT PUBLICATIONS: **1-800-445-5137**

GREAT AMERICAN TRAVELER: **1-800-548-2812**

ENCORE: **1-800-638-8976**.

15% Senior Savings On Amtrak

For seniors who prefer to travel by train, Amtrak offers year-round discounts for anyone 62 and older. These discounts include 15% off regular fares, special one way fares, Explore America Fares and special group fares. They also have beautiful brochures describing their fun vacation packages. Call Amtrak toll-free at:

1-800-USA-RAIL (THAT'S **1-800-872-7245**)
Or visit the web site: www.amtrak.com

Jet Vacations

If you plan to travel to France and want to save money on everything... quality air travel, hotels, car rental, ski packages, sightseeing, call Jet Vacations This company specializes in

trips to Paris, France and to the Riviera. Plan your trip early and save. Call them toll-free and learn how you can enjoy France 3,435 different ways. Call *Jet Vacations* at:
1-800-538-0999

Before You Travel

Planning a trip? Before you go you'll want to get a copy of *Lightening The Travel Load Travel Tips*. This handy booklet is filled with "how-to" materials on selecting, packing, traveling and caring for luggage. Send a postcard to:
SAMSONITE TRAVELER ADVISORY SERVICE
11200 E. 45TH AVE.
DENVER, CO 80239

Importing A Car

Can you save money by buying a foreign car on your next trip abroad? What are the customs requirements? What should you know about emission standards on a car you import yourself? For answers, send a postcard asking for *Importing A Car* and also *U.S. Customs Pocket Hints*. It's yours free from:
U.S. CUSTOMS SERVICE
WASHINGTON, DC 20229

Travelodge Directory

There's a *free directory* of the more than 500 TraveLodge motels and motor hotels waiting for you. It lists location, room rates and a map for each TraveLodge. You'll also find information on their new group rates, family plan and bargain break weekends. Contact:
TRAVELODGE INTERNATIONAL
250 TRAVELODGE DR.
EL CAJON, CA 92090
1-800-578-7878

Days Inn Directory

Quality accommodations for the American traveler at economical rates has been the motto of Days Inn since its founding in 1970. For a *free directory* of the 301 Inns and 229 Tasty World Restaurants with their rates, maps, toll free numbers and more, call: **1-800-325-2525**

Holiday Inn Directory

For a complete listing of all Holiday Inns both in the U.S. and worldwide, request a free copy of their huge directory. In seconds you can locate any of the thousands of Holiday Inns with room rates, list of recreation activities, even a map for each hotel. Call toll free:
1-800-238-8000. OR WRITE:
HOLIDAY INN
3 RAVINIA DR. SUITE 2000
ATLANTA, GA 38195

Enjoy A Club Med Vacation

Club Med's unique vacation resorts have delighted thousands of people tired of 'the same old thing'. If you're interested in a fun vacation that really is something different, send for the free color *travel booklet*. Club Med offers seniors 55 and older a $100 discount on stays of 7 nights or more. To get your free booklet or for more information on their clubs, contact them at:
CLUB MED, INC.
3 E. 54TH ST.
NEW YORK, NY 10019
OR CALL: **1-800-CLUB-MED (**THAT'S **1-800-258-2633)**
Or visit their web site at: www.clubmed.com

Barefoot Adventure Cruise

Are you ready for something different? For a vacation un-

like any you've ever been on, consider sailing a tall ship to a small island in the Caribbean. The full color *Barefoot Adventure* will tell you all about 'Barefoot' shipboard adventures aboard schooners that once belonged to Onassis, Vanderbilt and the Duke of Westminster. Call toll free: **1-800-327-2600. OR SEND A POSTCARD TO:**
WINDJAMMER BAREFOOT CRUISES
BOX 120
MIAMI BEACH, FL 33119

Safety Guide

Did you ever wonder if you should be concerned about your health and safety when you travel to foreign destinations? Travel Medicine has a free *Travel Safety Guide* that offers practical quick tips on insect protection, medical kits, mosquito nets, protective clothing and water filters and more. Before you venture out on your next travel adventure, make sure you send for this free guide. Write to:
TRAVEL MEDICINE INC.
351 PLEASANT ST., SUITE 312
NORTHAMPTON, MA 01060

Foreign Exchange

If you plan to travel abroad, did you know that you can now buy francs, pounds or yen over the Internet? This service can be useful for travelers who want to have small amounts of currency upon arrival in a foreign country. At their web site, International Currency Exchange lists rates at which they sell foreign currency. If you decide to buy, you can pay by check or credit card and receive currency in 2-4 days via express mail. You can call them toll-free at:
1-877-630-8100
Or visit their web site:
www.foreignmoney.com

A Diet For Jet Lag?

Do you travel frequently and find that you suffer from jet lag? If so this free wallet size card should help. It summarizes the amounts and types of food you should eat and tells you the best times to eat to reduce the effects of jet lag. Ask for *The Anti-Jet Lag Diet.* To get a copy, send a long SASE to:

ARGONNE NATIONAL LABORATORY
JET LAG DIET
9700 S. CASS AVE.
ARGONNE, IL 60439

Volunteer For A Free Vacation

Regardless of how young or old you are, one of the most fascinating ways to enjoy a wilderness experience in a national park is by being a volunteer.

A variety of government agencies including the U.S. Forest Service, The National Park Service, U.S. Army Corps of Engineers, plus individual state park systems welcome volunteers to serve as campground hosts in exchange for a free stay. Every year hundreds of thousands of people who love the outdoors volunteer their services for anywhere from one day to a full year.

In addition to acting as hosts, volunteers also help as caretakers, researchers, ranger assistants, trail repair crews, plumbers and carpenters. This reflects the growing interest in 'doing vacations' or educational travel. In exchange for their services, volunteers may receive free camping and other recreational privileges that often include cabins, house trailers or bunkroom accommodations at no cost. While some volunteers are given an expense allowance, most should expect to pay for food and transportation costs.

If this sounds like a vacation you might be interested in, you can contact the park, forest, refuge, fish hatchery or other facility that you are interested in or check with the following:

NATIONAL PARK SERVICE,
They are looking for 95,000 volunteers a year who are interested in a stay of up to one or three months in one of the nation's 369 parklands to help with trail projects, species control and campground hosts. To get a brochure listing all of the parks in the U.S. along with an application, send a postcard to the address below.
NATIONAL PARK SERVICE,
VOLUNTEERS IN PARKS COORDINATOR
1849 C ST. N.W. SUITE 7312
WASHINGTON, DC 20240
OR VISIT THEIR WEB SITE AT: WWW.NPS.GOV/VOLUNTEER

U.S. FOREST SERVICE
Check in your local telephone operator or in the phone book blue pages for the phone number of the nearest U.S. Forest Service office. In their *Volunteers in the National Forests Program* they have up to 100,000 volunteers every year to serve in one of the nation's 155 national forests or 20 national grasslands.
The U.S. Forest Service also has a program called *Passports In Time*. This program welcomes families for one day to one week stays that focuses on archaeological digs and historical restorations. Call them toll-free at:
1-800-281-9176

BUREAU OF LAND MANAGEMENT
ENVIRONMENTAL EDUCATION AND VOLUNTEER PROGRAM
1849 C ST., N.W. LS-1275
WASHINGTON, DC 20240
1-202-452-5078
They need roughly 20,000 volunteers a year for their National Volunteer Program. Volunteers will be restoring watersheds, building trails, staffing visitor centers, patrolling cultural sites, writing brochures and conducting educational programs in federal lands, mostly in the West.

U.S. FISH AND WILDLIFE SERVICE
DIVISION OF REFUGES
NATIONAL VOLUNTEER COORDINATOR OFFICE
4401 NORTH FAIRFAX DR., ROOM 22203
ARLINGTON, VA 22203

This service oversees hundreds of wildlife refuges and fish hatcheries throughout the nation. Volunteers are needed to help with raising fish, banding birds, restoring fragile habitats, and conducting tours of the habitats and fisheries.

To get a visitors guide and map with all of the national wildlife refuges, call:
1-800-344-9453

U.S. ARMY CORPS OF ENGINEERS
1-800-865-8337

They manage 460 lakes throughout the country. Volunteers are needed to help with a variety of programs that include archaeological digs, pest control and campground hosts.

ALASKA DIVISION OF PARKS AND OUTDOOR RECREATION
ALASKA STATE PARKS VOLUNTEER COORDINATOR
3601 C STREET, SUITE 1200
ANCHORAGE, AK 99503-5921
1-907-269-8708

Alaska has one of the most extensive summer volunteer programs to help out as archaeological assistants, back-country ranger assistants, researchers and trail crew members. They will pay transportation expenses from Anchorage plus a small expense allowance for commitments of two weeks to three months.

To volunteer closer to home, try checking your local phone directory for your state's Department of Parks and Recreation and ask about their parks volunteer programs.

Healthy Travel To Foreign Lands

If you are on medication and plan to travel abroad be sure to get this free booklet. Put out by the International Society of Travel Medicine, it lists over 500 medicine clinics in 44 countries (including the U.S.). You'll also find answers to questions you may have about health risks in the countries you are visiting, what shots are needed, which medicines to pack and how to get medical assistance while you are there. Ask for the *Travel Medicine Clinics booklet.* Free from:

ISTM CLINIC DIRECTORY
c/o IMODIUM A-D DRAWER D
1675 BROADWAY, 33RD FLOOR
NEW YORK, NY 10019

Before you travel, you may also want to check with the following organizations for updates on illnesses in the countries you will be visiting:

THE WORLD HEALTH ORGANIZATION
1-202-974-3000

THE CENTERS FOR DISEASE CONTROL & PREVENTION
1-404-332-4559

INTERNATIONAL ASSOCIATION FOR MEDICAL ASSISTANCE TO TRAVELERS
Links travelers to doctors in 130 countries
1-716-754-4883

Internet Sites For Travelers

Surfing the worldwide web is one of the easiest and most convenient ways to simplify your travel planning and to save money. If you are planning to travel and have access to the Internet either at home, at work or at your public library, here are a number of sites you will want to visit.

TRAVELOCITY
www.travelocity.com

If you would like to quickly check for the lowest plane fares from any major city to any other major city in the U.S., be sure to check out this site. Updated on a daily basis, you will find a listing of the lowest air fares at that time. You will also find several other features of interest including:

• **PRICESHOPPER** - great buys on vacation and cruise packages in the U.S. and abroad.

• **HOT DEALS** - for steals, deals and all round great travel bargains worldwide.

• **FLIGHT PAGING** - Keeps you informed of changes to your flight's departure or arrival times and gate assignments - all sent to your alphanumeric pager.

• **FARE WATCHER E-MAIL** - Sends low fare updates directly to your e-mail quickly and reliably.

• **SHOP SAFE GUARANTEE** - They protect every credit card transaction you make on Travelocity

• **REVIEWS** - for independent, non-biased reviews of vacation choices.

• **WEATHER FORECASTS** - Complete updated weather forecasts for cities around the world.

Looking for the best fares to the world's big cities? While at the TRAVELOCITY'S web site, if you enter a multiple airport city code, www.Travelocity.com will search for the lowest fare available at all metropolitan airports. Here are a few cities where this feature is valid:

New York City (NYC)

Washington, DC (WAS)

Chicago (CHI)

London (LON)

Paris (PAR)

Dallas (QDF)

Houston (QHO)

In addition, you may enjoy significant savings if you are

willing to fly into nearby airports. For example, when traveling to Los Angeles (LAX), you may want to consider flying into the Burbank (BUR), Orange County (SNA) or Ontario (ONT) airports.

Similarly, the cost of a trip to San Francisco (SFO) might be reduced by flying into San Jose (SJC) or Oakland (OAK), while travel to Miami (MIA) may be less expensive if you fly into Ft. Lauderdale, FL.

■ ■ ■ ■ ■ ■ ■ ■ ■ ■ ■ ■ ■ ■ ■ ■ ■ ■ ■ ■

www.weather.com

What's the weather like in the city you are about to fly to? Are there any flight delays due to bad weather? For answers, go to this web site, a service of the Weather Channel. Before your next trip check to see what weather's in store for you.

■ ■ ■ ■ ■ ■ ■ ■ ■ ■ ■ ■ ■ ■ ■ ■ ■ ■ ■ ■

www.biztravel.com

If you travel by plane a lot, you know how frequent flyer miles can add up quickly. To track just how many frequent flyer and frequent stay credits you have accumulated with various accounts, visit this site. Companies that participate in this program include United Mileage Plus, American AAdvantage, Delta SkyMiles, Continental OnePass, Northwest WorldPerks, Marriott Honored Guest Awards, Marriott Miles, Hilton Honors, and ITT Sheraton Club.

■ ■ ■ ■ ■ ■ ■ ■ ■ ■ ■ ■ ■ ■ ■ ■ ■ ■ ■ ■

www.delta-air.com/womenexecs

As a result of a partnership between American Express and Delta Airlines, the woman executive can now enjoy The Executive Woman's Travel Network™. It will provide you with fight upgrades, companion fares of just $99 and savings of $30 to $100 on air fares. Plus you'll be kept informed of special offers and exclusive airfares.

■ ■ ■ ■ ■ ■ ■ ■ ■ ■ ■ ■ ■ ■ ■ ■ ■ ■ ■ ■

www.thetrip.com

This site is designed to save the money for small business travelers. You can book airline tickets, hotel rooms and car rentals at lower rates. To help you save money 'thetrip' will automatically search for flights from alternate airports and for connecting flights. You will also find Frommer City Guides with restaurant and hotel reviews plus maps with point-to-point directions from anywhere in the U.S. to anywhere else.

■ ■

www.reservation.com

This is the web site for Preview Travel. It allows you to make airline and rental car reservation online.

■ ■

www.expedia.com

This is Microsoft's travel web site. While it is primarily geared toward leisure travelers, business travelers will find a number of useful features including city maps and restaurant listing. Another nice feature is expedia's low-fare tracker that will alert you to discount fares for cities you select.

■ ■

www.webflyer.com

The ultimate site for the frequent flyer. You will find all kinds of special bonus mileage offers and exclusive discount fares available only online. It's best feature is the fact that it tracks all airline, hotel and car rental discounts by city and saves you time by listing them all at one site.

■ ■

www.quikbook.com

This web site has been called one of the web's best sites for hotel discounts by *Consumer Reports Travel Letter*. At this site you will find out where you can get big hotel discounts of up to 60% in major cities like New York, Atlanta, Los Angeles, Boston to name a few.

■■■■■■■■■■■■■■■■■■■■

www.vicinity.com
Vicinity provides a variety of services for the business traveler including
- BUSINESS FINDER - find the nearest businesses, hotels, travel destinations or other points of interest in any city. Includes interactive maps and driving directions.
- MAPBLAST. With this free service you can generate interactive maps of residences of businesses that you can use or e-mail to associates.
- YELLOW PAGES - dynamic local listings of 16 million businesses nationwide.

■■■■■■■■■■■■■■■■■■■■

City.Net: www.city.net
Epicurious: www.epicurious.com (Gourmet Magazine & Conde Nast Web site)

The Travel Channel: www.travelchannel.com
Yahoo: www.yahoo.com/recreation/travel

■■■■■■■■■■■■■■■■■■■■

Cruise Lines Web Sites

If you are thinking of taking a cruise and aren't sure which cruise is right for you, before you book, be sure to check out the web sites of the cruise lines you are considering. Here's a selection of web sites of cruise lines:
American Hawaii Cruises: www.cruisehawaii.com

The Big Red Boat: www.bigredboat.com

Carnival Cruise Lines: www.carnival.com/

Celebrity Cruises: www.celebrity-cruises.com/

Clipper Cruise Line: www.clippercruise.com/

Cunard Lines: www.cunardline.com

The Delta Queen Steamboat Co.: www.deltaqueen.com

Holland America Line: www.hollandamerica.com/intro.html

KD River Cruises of Europe: www.rivercruises.com

Norwegian Cruise Lines: www.ncl.com/ncl

Premier Cruise Lines: www.asource.com/dolphin/

Radisson Seven Seas Cruises: www.regalcruises.com/

Renaissance Cruises: www.rencruises.com/

Royal Caribbean International: www.royalcaribbean.com

Royal Olympic Cruises: www.epirotiki.com

Silversea Cruises: www.asource.com/silversea/

Spice Island Cruises: www.indo.com/cruises/spice island/

Tall Ship Adventures: www.asource.com/tallship/

Windjammer Barefoot Cruises: www.windjammer.com

Windstar Cruises: www.windstarcruises.com

World Explorer Cruises: www.wecruise.com/

5 Tips To Save Money On Plane Travel

www.travelocity.com

Finding the lowest fare isn't always easy. Discount fares typically have restrictions that can be difficult, sometimes frustrating, to interpret. If you're looking for the cheapest price, here are a few suggestions that will help.

1. Make your reservation early. Many discount fares require that you make a reservation 7, 14 or 21 days before your trip depending on the fare. The best international fares often require a reservation 30 days in advance. Making a reservation as soon as you know your travel dates increases your chances of finding a fare you can live with.

2. Flying on a weekday usually costs less. Flights on Tuesday, Wednesday and Thursday usually offer the lowest fares. Fares are sometimes (but not always) higher on Monday and Friday than on other weekdays. Saturday flights occasionally have discount fares, but as a rule it's more expensive to fly on a weekend than a weekday.

3. Stay over a Saturday night. Most low fares require that you stay over at least one Saturday night before your return flight. However, some fares may only require you to stay a minimum of 3 or 4 days.

4. One airline is better than two. It's almost always less expensive to use only one airline for the entire trip instead of two. In fact booking two airlines can, in some cases, cost hundreds of dollars more. Airlines sell only a limited number of seats at the lowest fares. When those seats sell out, the price goes up. If you don't at first succeed, try an earlier or later flight. To get the lowest roundtrip fare, that fare must be available on both the departing and return flights you select. If the fare is sold out on either of these, the price you end up with will be much higher.

5. Try an earlier or later flight if you can't find the fare you want or if possible, consider flying on another day.

Traveling The USA

Planning ahead can make all the difference in the world between having great fun and having a run-of-the mill trip.

One of the very best sources of information are the tourist offices for the states you plan to visit. These offices are set up to provide maps, brochures and other information about the tourist attractions, climate, restaurants and hotels for their states.

If you plan to tour any part of the U.S.A., call the tourist offices of each of the 50 states you intend to visit. When you call them, tell them which areas of the state you plan to visit and indicate any special sight-seeing interests you may have. Often they can provide you with additional materials on the areas that interest you most.

The following is a list of state tourism offices. Where a toll-free number or web site is available, it is given.

ALABAMA
Bureau of Tourism & Travel
1-800-ALABAMA
www.touralabama.org

ALASKA
907-465 2010
www.commerce.state.ak.us/
tourism/

ARIZONA
602-230-7733
www.arizonaguide.com

ARKANSAS
1-800-NATURAL
(that's 1-800-628-8725)
www.arkansas.com

CALIFORNIA
1-800-TO-CALIF
(that's 1-800-862-2543)
http://gocalif.ca.gov

COLORADO
1-800-433-2656
www.colorado.com

CONNECTICUT
1-800-CT-BOUND
(that's 1-800-282-6863)
www.state.ct/ustourism.htm

DELAWARE
1-800-441-8846
www.state.de.us

DISTRICT OF COLUMBIA
1-800-635-6338
www.washington.org

FLORIDA
1-888-735-2872
www.flausa.com

GEORGIA
1-800 VISIT-GA
(that's 1-800-847-4842)
www.gomm.com

HAWAII
1-800-464-2924
www.gohawaii.com

IDAHO
1-800-635-7820
www.visitid.org

ILLINOIS
1-800-487-2446
www.enjoyillinois.com

INDIANA
1-800-289-6646
www.indianatourism.com

IOWA
1-800 345-IOWA
www.state.ia.us

KANSAS
1-800-2-KANSAS
www.kansascommerce.com

KENTUCKY
1-800-225-TRIP
www.kentuckytourism.com

LOUISIANA
1-800-964-7321
www.louisianatravel.com

MAINE
207-535-9595

MARYLAND
1-800-MD-IS-FUN
www.mdisfun.org

MASSACHUSETTS
1-800-447-MASS
www.mass-vacation.com

MICHIGAN
1-800-5432-YES
www.michigan.org

MINNESOTA
1-800-657-3700
www.exploreminnesota.com

MISSISSIPPI
1-800-WARMEST
www.mississippi.org

MISSOURI
800-877-1234
www.missouritourism.org

MONTANA
1-800-VISIT-MT
www.visitmt.com

NEBRASKA
1-800-228-4307
www.visitmebraska.org

NEVADA
1 800-NEVADA-8
(that's 1-800-638-2328)

NEW HAMPSHIRE
1-800-FUN-IN-NH Ext. 159

NEW JERSEY
1-800-JERSEY-7
www.state.nj.us

NEW MEXICO
1-800 545-2040
www.newmexico.org/

NEW YORK
1-800-CALL-NYS (that's 1-800-225-5697)
www.iloveny.state.ny.us

NORTH CAROLINA
1-800-VISIT-NC
www.visitnc.com

NORTH DAKOTA
1-800-HELLO-ND
www.ndtourism.com

OHIO
1-800-BUCKEYE
www.ohiotourism.com

OKLAHOMA
1-800-652-6552
www.travelok.com

OREGON
1-800-547-7842
www.traveloregon.com

PENNSYLVANIA
1-800-VISIT-PA
www.state.pa.us

RHODE ISLAND
1-800-556-2484
www.visitrhodeisland.com

SOUTH CAROLINA
1-800-872-3505
www.travesc.com

SOUTH DAKOTA
1-800-SDAKOTA
(1-800-732-5682)
www.statesd.us

TENNESSEE
1-800-836-6200
www.state.tn.us/tourdev

TEXAS
1-800-8888-TEX
www.travelTex.com

UTAH
1-800-200-1160
www.utah.com

VERMONT
1-800-VERMONT
(that's 1-800-837-6668)
www.travel-vermont.com/

tourism/vermont.htm

VIRGINIA
1-800-VISIT-VA
www.virginia.org

WASHINGTON
1-800-544-1800
www.tourism.wa.gov

WASHINGTON, D.C.
See District of Columbia

WEST VIRGINIA
1-800-CALL-WVA
(that's 1-800-225-5982
www.state.wv.us/tourism/
default.htm

WISCONSIN
1-800-432-TRIP
www.tourism.state.wi.us/

WYOMING
1-800-225-5996
www.commerce.state.wy.us/
west/

U.S. TERRITORIES

AMERICAN SAMOA
1-684-633-1093

GUAM
1-800-US-3-GUAM

PUERTO RICO
Find out why Puerto rico is
called "the complete island".
There is something here for
everyone — sightseeing, sports,
night life, casinos and lots more.
1-800-223-6530

U.S. VIRGIN ISLANDS

For great duty-free shopping consider the U.S. Virgin Islands for your next vacation. No passports are needed, their language is English and they use U.S. currency. For full travel information contact:

**U.S. Virgin Islands Tourism
1270 Avenue of the Americas
New York, NY 10020
1-800-372-8784**

NATIONAL PARKS

Enjoy the great outdoors. Get back to nature. Visit our beautiful national parks. There's a series of interesting guides to the 7 most popular national parks free for the asking. Send for any (or all) guides you'd like:

• Rocky Mountain National Park, Colorado
• Mt. McKinley National Park, Alaska
• Mesa Verde National Park Colorado
• Hot Springs National Park, Arkansas
• Hawaii National Park
• Yellowstone National Park
• Carlsbad Caverns, New Mexico

You might also want the free map of the National Park System. Request by name the guides you would like. Write to:
**Dept. of the Interior
National Park Service
Washington, DC 20240**

INTERNATIONAL VACATIONLAND— 1000 ISLANDS

The 1000 Islands region features the best of two countries — U.S. and Canada. Some of the many attractions include fishing, golf, tennis, biking, hiking, houseboat rentals, shopping and recreational sports in all seasons. Three tour packages are available for the asking:

1. Write: 1000 Islands, Box 428 Alexandria Bay, NY 13607. **(In Canada write: 1000 Islands, Box 10, Landsdoune, Ontario KOE ILO.**

2. Write: Kingston Bureau of Tourism, Box 486, 209 Ontario St., Kingston, Ontario K7L 2ZI.

3. Write: Rideau Lakes Thousand Islands, P.O. Box 125 Perth, Ontario K7H 3E3

CHOCOLATE TOWN USA

If you are looking for a really fun time, why not try a special theme weekend at the fun Hershey Park in Hershey, Pennsylvania. For more detailed information, call:

1-800-HERSHEY

Foreign Travel

Before you travel abroad be sure to contact the tourist office for the countries you plan to visit. They are delighted to send you a beautiful package of travel brochures, places to visit and a whole lot more.

ANTIGUA & BARBUDA
Antigua & Barbuda Dept of Tourism, 610 Fifth Avenue, Suite 311, New York, NY 10020

ARGENTINA
For maps and color brochures describing Argentina drop a card to: **Argentina Embassy, 1600 New Hampshire Ave., Washington, DC 20009**

ARUBA
Go sailing, scuba diving in the turquoise Caribbean, casinos, discos and lots more. Ask for "Sun Worshippers" with hotel rates and tourist information. Write: **Aruba Tourist Office, 1000 Harbor Boulevard, Weehawken, NJ 07087**

AUSTRIA
Write for the *"Austrian Information package"* and you'll receive a beautiful assortment of travel guides and student education opportunities. Drop a card to: **Austrian National Tourist Office; 500 Fifth Ave., New York. NY 10110**

BAHAMAS
Bahamas Tourist Office: call toll-free 1-800-422-4262

BARBADOS
Discover the many sides of Barbados that make it a luscious vacation spot. A nice tow *package* including several huge wall posters are yours for the asking. Write: **Barbados Board of Tourism, 800 Second Ave., New York, NY 10017**

BELIZE
Belize Tourist Board, 83 North Front Street, PO Box 325, Belize City Belize, Central America

BRAZIL
Brazil Reservations, 1050 Edison St. Suite C2, Santa Yorez, CA 93460. Or call: 1-800-544-5503

BRITISH VIRGIN ISLANDS
British Tourist Board, 370 Lexington Avenue, New York, NY 10017

BRITAIN
There's always something new to discover in England, Wales, Scotland & Ireland. Drop a card requesting the *Britain Information package* and you'll receive a beautiful color magazine, photos, maps, tours, etc. Send to: **British Tourist Authority, 551 Fifth Ave., New York, NY. Or call: 1-800-462-2748**

BRITAIN BY RAIL
Tour scenic Britain by rail. BritRail offers unlimited travel on most rail, bus & ferry routes. For a free guide travel hints as well as bargain ticket rates write to: **BritRail. Travel International, 1500 Broadway, New York, NY 10017**

BERMUDA
Thinking of traveling to Bermuda? Don't go without this information *package.* It includes travel tips, a map, hotel rates, and more. Write to: **Bermuda Dept. of Tourism. PO Box 77050, Woodside, NY 11377**

CANADA
"Touring Canada" is a big guide to 54 exciting tours of Canada. You'll learn where to go, what to see, what clothes to bring and much more. You'll find there's more to do in 'our neighbor to the north' than you had ever imagined. Write to: **Canadian Government Office of Tourism Ottawa, Canada KIA OH6**

CANCUN & COZUMEL
Cancun & Cozumel Tourist Office, 405 Park Avenue, Suite 1401 New York, NY 10022

CARIBBEAN SUN FUN
Discover the fun and excitement each of the Caribbean islands has to offer. Ask for the *travel package* free from: **Caribbean Tourism Assn., 20 E. 46th St., New York, NY 10017**

CAYMAN ISLANDS
Cayman Islands Tourism, 420 Lexington Avenue, #2733, New York, NY 10170

CHINA - TAIWAN
Taiwan Visitors Association, One World Trade Center, New York, NY

CURACAO
Curacao Tourist Board, 475 Park Ave. South Suite 2000, New York, NY 10016

EGYPT
Travel back in time to the cradle of civilization. Explore the pyramids and discover the old and new wonders of Egypt. Ask for the *Egypt Information package.* Write to: **Egyptian Government Travel Office, 630 Fifth Ave., New York, NY 10111**

FRANCE
The *France Information package* is a mini-tour of France with a large full color tour book plus Paris on a budget, a tour of Paris, hotels and motels in France off-season packages, and more. Contact: **French Government Tourist Office, 444 Madison Ave., New York, NY 10022. Or call: 1-212-838-7800**

GERMANY
"Welcome To Germany" is a beautiful guide full of color photos that are absolutely breathtaking. This is just part of the Germany Tour package free from: **Lufthansa German Airlines, 1640 Hempstead Turnpike, East Meadow, NY 11554**

GERMANY TRAIN TRAVEL
If you're planning a trip to Germany one of the best ways to tour the country is by train. With German Rail you will have unlimited travel plus discounts on many bus and boat routes. For free information write: **GermanRail, 747 Third Ave., New York, NY 10017**

BERLIN
This city is the Gateway to Continental Europe. You can experience the mix of Berlin's dynamic culture, historic sights and non- stop nightlife. Call for your free *Berlin Travel kit* today. Call **1-800-248-9539**

GREECE
To help you make your trip to Greece more enjoyable, here's a large packet of brochures, maps and booklets on the beautiful Greek Islands. Request the *Greece Tour package* from: **Greek National Tourist Organization, Olympic Tower, 645 Fifth Ave., New York, NY 10022**

GRENADA
Grenada Board of Tourism, 820 Second Avenue, Suite 900 D New York, NY 10017

GUYANA
Guyana Tourism, c/o Caribbean Tourism Organization 80 East Broad Street Suite 3200, New York, NY 10004

HUNGARY
Like beautiful picture post cards, the color illustrations in this package will take you for a tour of the sights and attractions of Hungary. Ask for the *Hungary Travel package* which includes a map of the country. Send a card to: **Consulate General of Hungary, 223 East 52nd St., New York, NY 10022**
Or call: 212-752-0661

INDIA
Dozens of scenic color photos of India are included in the *India Tour Kit* yours free from: **Information Service of India, Embassy of India, Washington, DC 20008**

INDONESIA
For facts on the Indonesia archipelago including their history, geography, culture, maps, and more drop a card requesting their *information package*. Write to: **Consulate General of Indonesia, Information Section, 5 E. 68th St., New York, NY 10022**

IRELAND
Call: **1-800-SHAMROCK** or write to: **Irish Tourist Board, 345 Park Ave., New York, NY 10154**

ISRAEL
If you enjoyed the book you'll love the country. For a nice collection of *guide books and maps* of Israel and the Holy Land write to: **Israel Government Tourist Office, 350 Fifth Ave., New York, NY 10118**

ITALY
A beautiful arm chair tour of Italy is in store for you. Write for *"A Trip To Italy tour package"* with road maps and marvelous full color guide books. It's yours free from: **Italian Government Travel Office, 630 Fifth Ave., New York, NY 10111.**

IVORY COAST
Learn about the rites of Panther Men and the fascinating culture of the Agri Kingdom. All this and much more in the travel kit from: **Ivory Coast Embassy, 2424 Massachusetts Ave. N.W., Washington, DC 20008**

JAMAICA
Soft beaches, jungle waterfalls, hot discos and sailing in the sunshine—it's all in a beautiful full color book that features 56 great vacations. Ask for the free *"Jamaica Vacation Book"* from: **Jamaica Tourist Board, 8237 NW 66th St, Miami, FL 33160**

JAPAN
The *Japan Tour package is* an impressive collection of travel booklets in full color with marvelous illustrations. You'll receive a mini tour of Japan chuck full of facts about Japan's history with travel tips and many fascinating tid bits. For all this write to: **Japan Travel Bureau, 810 Seventh Ave. 34th Floor, New York NY 10019. Or call: 212-698-4900**

MARTINIQUE
Martinique Dept. of Tourism, 610 Fifth Avenue New York, NY 10020

MEXICO
For a set of over a dozen color brochures showing the sights and tourist attractions of Mexico, drop a post card to: **Mexican National Tourist Council, 405 Park Ave., New York, NY 10022**

MONTSERRAT
Montserrat Tourism Information, 485 Fifth Avenue New York, NY 10017

MOROCCO
Exotic Morocco has some of the most magnificent scenery in the world. For a kit of *travel information and tour packages* to this ancient kingdom drop a card to: **Royal Air Maroc, 55 East 59th St., New York, NY**

PORTUGAL
Discover all the beauty of Portugal— its beaches, entertainment and hotels — all in this package of full color brochures. Call: **TAP Air at 1-800-221-7370.**

RUSSIA
Write to: **Embassy of The Russian Federation, 1125 16th St. N.W., Washington, D.C. 20036**

ST. MAARTEN
For beautiful travel brochures of the island of St. Maarten call: **1-800-ST-MAARTEN**

SCOTLAND
For colorful brochures on Scotland, call toll-free: **1-800-343-SCOT**

SINGAPORE
Singapore's the place where all Asia comes together. Here's a beautiful color package of things to do and see plus a map and even a recipe booklet with delightful meals of Singapore. Write to: **Embassy of Republic of Singapore, 1824 'R' St. N.W., Washington, D.C. 20009**

SOUTH AFRICA
Write to: **Embassy of South Africa, 3501 Massachusetts Ave. N.W., Washington, D.C. 20008**

SPAIN
Write to: **Spain Office of Tourism, 666 Fifth Ave, New York, NY 10103**

SWITZERLAND
For a mini-tour of the Alps send a postcard for the *Swiss Tour package*. You'll receive beautifully illustrated booklets, maps, travel tips, recipes and more. All of this comes to you free from: **Swiss National Tourist Office, 608 Fifth Ave., New York, NY 10020**

THAILAND
Come to Thailand and enjoy its dazzling scenery, incredible shopping bargains and the special joy of sharing the Thai people have. Drop a postcard to: **Tourism Authority of Thailand, 3440 Wilshire Blvd., Suite 1101, Los Angeles, CA 90010.** Or: **Tourism Authority of Thailand, 5 World Trade Center, Suite 2449, New York, NY 10048**

ZAMBIAN SAFARI
Zambia has a big package of travel & tourist information waiting for you. The beautiful color brochures are a mini-safari through the African bush. Write to: **Zambia National Tourist Board, 800 Second Ave., New York, NY 10017. Or call: 212-949-0133**

PERU AND NATURE
Here are colorful maps, charts and pictures of native birds, flowers and animals. You'll also find a listing of national parks and reserves, as well as interesting archaeological and historical highlights. Write to: **Explorations, Inc., 27655 Kent Rd., Bonita Springs, FL 33923**

HONG KONG TOURIST INFORMATION
If you are over 60 years old and are thinking of going on a shopping trip to Hong Kong, there's a free discount booklet that will save you money on your shopping. Write to: **Hong Kong Tourist Information, 590 Fifth Ave., New York, NY 10036**

NOVA SCOTIA, CANADA
"Nova Scotia Holiday" is a beautiful color book that tells all about things to see, history, legends, customs crafts and more. Call toll-free: **800-341-6096** or write to: **Nova Scotia Information. P.O. Box 130 Halifax. Nova Scotia, Canada B3J 2M7**

Free From The Government

The U.S. Government Toll-Free Helpline

Have you ever tried to find an answer to a simple question about the Federal Government and ended up on a merry-go-round of referrals. Or you may have had a question about the Federal Government that was so difficult you had no idea where to begin. Well relax! Now there's one toll-free number you can call for assistance. It's called the *Federal Information Center* and it's a clearinghouse of all government agencies. It is designed to help the average person find the information they need quickly and effortlessly.

They will also refer you to the government agency that deals with the type of problem or question they may have. Their Information Specialists are extraordinary when it comes to finding the exact place you should contact for help. Some of the things they can help you with are... who you

can contact for help with your social security benefits, sales & auctions of siezed properties, consumer complaints, veteran's benefits, offices of the aging and virtually all other branches of the government. Their hours of operation are 9 a.m. to 5 p.m EST.
Call them toll-free at:
1-800-688-9889
(Disabled individuals using text phones [TDD/TTY] may call toll-free anywhere in the U.S. by dialing 1-800-326-2996).
If you have access to the Internet you can also find help on all government related questions by going to:
www.info.gov

Exactly How Much Social Security Will You Get?

If you've ever wondered exactly how much money your Social Security benefits will be once you retire, there's an easy way to find out...get your Personal Earnings and Benefit Estimate Statement. For an estimate of what your retirement benefits might be call the toll-free phone number and ask for an *'earnings estimate request'* to fill out and return.

The Social Security Administration will then do a free search of their records and send you a detailed printout of how much has been contributed each year and how much your benefits will if you retire at different ages. Find out what disability benefits you qualify for... and how the value of your benefits compares with the amount of Social Security taxes you have paid over the years. This statement is yours free from the Social Security Administration.

At the same toll-free number they are also happy to answer any other questions you may have relating to your Social Security. Call:
1-800-772-1213
You can also access them on the Internet at:
www.ssa.gov

Do You Need Extra Money From Social Security?

Many low income seniors never realize it but even if they don't qualify for regular Social Security benefits, they may still qualify for thousands of dollars in extra income.

If you are over 65 and find that you have difficulty meeting your normal living expenses, or if you are blind or disabled at any age, you may qualify for a program called Supplemental Security Income (SSI).

This program was established to help seniors over the age of 65 who have too little income to pay for their basic needs and to help those who are not able to work because they are disabled regardless of their age.

To qualify you must meet a maximum asset and monthly income qualification but studies have shown that as many as half of the seniors who do qualify never receive SSI benefits because they don't realize that they are eligible for this extra income. However, once you do qualify for SSI, you will also automatically qualify for both Medicaid and Food Stamps.

To find out if you qualify, either contact your local Social Security office or call their toll-free helpline: 1-800-772-1213

Free Food For Seniors

When you live on a limited budget you learn to cut corners wherever you can. But one of the areas you should never cut corners on is in eating properly. If you are living on a limited budget even if you are living with someone else, you may qualify for food stamps that will save you thousands of dollars. And as a senior, if you are not able to travel to the social services agency to apply for the food stamps, they may visit your home or take the application right over the phone. Check the blue pages of you local phone book for a social services agency in your area. You can also get the address and phone number by calling the OFFICE OF THE AGING in your area. (See listings at the back of this book).

Locating A Missing Person

If you have a problem of trying to locate a missing relative or friend, a letter to the Social Security Administration may help. When you write be sure to include as much information as you can about the missing person including their last address and date of birth. Write to:

PUBLIC INQUIRIES
SOCIAL SECURITY ADMINISTRATION
6501 SECURITY BLVD.
BALTIMORE, MD 20235

Free Books & Magazines

Did you know that the National Library Service has a large collection of books , magazines, journals, music materials in Braille, large type and recorded format for those who have temporary or permanent vision loss or physical limitations? Special playback equipment is available on a loan basis from the Library of Congress, and cassettes and CD's are available from over 155 participating libraries. And if you are unable to hold a book or have a serious visual handicap, you can borrow these materials postage-free. They will even pay the postage in sending the materials back to them. Contact them at the address and phone number below or ask your local library to find out what's available to you.

HANDICAPPED READERS REFERENCE SECTION
NATIONAL LIBRARY SERVICE FOR THE BLIND AND PHYSICALLY HANDICAPPED
LIBRARY OF CONGRESS
WASHINGTON, DC 20542
800-424-9100

Or access them on the web:
www.loc.gov/nls

A Boat For $100.00?

Yes you can really own a boat, luxury car, fancy gems even a house with all its treasures for just a tiny fraction of its true value. All these treasures are confiscated from drug raids or other illegal activities. The government has no use for these goods and can't store them all so they have contracted with private companies to auction off these goods.

At these auctions you have an excellent chance of getting goods for practically nothing. You can get a free copy of the *National Sellers List* which lists the local sellers of the Marshall Services goods. To get that list you must reach them either by fax or at their Internet site or from the Consumer Information Catalog:

THEIR FAX NUMBER IS: **202-307-9777**

Their Internet address is:
www.usdoj.gov/marshals/

The IRS also has auctions throughout the country of property of every kind ...everything from houses to cars, jewelry and lots more...all seized for non-payment of taxes. For a list of sales and auctions for properties siezed by the IRS, request the list from:

TREASURY SALES & AUCTIONS
EG&G SERVICES, INC
37 PENDER DRIVE
FAIRFAX, VA 22030
OR CALL THEM AT: **703-273-7373**

Striking It Rich

Did you know that the U.S. Government will let you prospect on public lands? If you would like to find out how to strike it rich on government lands, send a card to the Forest Service. Ask for *A Guide To Your National Forests*. Write to:

MINERALS AND GEOLOGY STAFF
FOREST SERVICE, DOA
BOX 2417
WASHINGTON, DC 20013

Free Firewood

Did you know that in most of the 154 National Forests, firewood for your own personal use is free. To find out how you can get free firewood and also how to select, purchase and use firewood ask for the *Firewood Information package*. Free from:

FIREWOOD #559,
FOREST SERVICE
BOX 2417
WASHINGTON, DC 20013

Buying U.S. Government Surplus

Every year the federal government buys billions of dollars of every kind of merchandise imagineable. Much of this is never used and eventually the U.S. Government must sell all this surplus property on a regular basis. To find out how to buy everything from binoculars to autos at super low bargain prices, write to:

SURPLUS SALES CENTER
WASHINGTON NAVY YARD
WASHINGTON, DC 20408

You're Paying Too Much Income Tax

Wouldn't that be a welcome notice to receive from the IRS? Believe it or not many seniors really *are* paying a lot more income tax than they should be. The reason is that they just aren't aware of all the deductions and exemptions they are entitled to. To be sure you're not paying more taxes than you should, ask for a free copy of *Protecting Older Americans Against Overpayment of Income Taxes..* Contact:

SPECIAL COMMITTEE ON AGING
U.S. SENATE
WASHINGTON, D.C. 20410
202-224-5364

You're Also Paying Too Much Real Estate Tax

Throughout the nation, states and local governments are recognizing that seniors deserve a break when it comes to the real estate taxes they pay on their home. After all by the time they are 65 years old most seniors no longer have children in public school. And yet they're still paying school taxes on their real estate.

For example, New York State recently instituted what it calls the 'STAR' program. Under this program, seniors aged 65 or older who own a home are entitled to a whopping 40% reduction in the school taxes they pay as part of their real estate tax. This reduction is not based upon low income or financial need. It is available to *all* seniors in NYS who ask for it. But they will not get the reduction unless they ask. What that means is that you must check with your local town or county tax assessor's office to see if they offer a senior citizen tax reduction. Until you apply you could be paying thousands of dollars too much in real estate tax.

What **Else** Does The Secret Service Do?

Did you know that the Secret Service does more than protect the President? It was originally created to suppress counterfeiting - a job they still perform. To learn more, ask for *"Counterfeiting and Forgery"* which shows how to detect a counterfeit bill. Write to:

U.S. SECRET SERVICE
1800 'G' ST. N.W., ROOM 941
WASHINGTON, DC 20223

Just How Secure Is Your Home?

The F.B.I. would like every family to feel more secure. Learn how to better protect your family against crime. *A Way to*

Protect Your Family Against Crime offers tips you and your family can safely use to take a bite out of crime. Ask for the free *Crime Resistance booklet.* You might also want a copy of the *Abridged History of the F.B.I.* All free from:
F.B.I. PUBLIC AFFAIRS DEPT.
10TH & PENNSYLVANIA AVE.
WASHINGTON, DC 20535

Pension & Retirement Hotline

If you have tax questions dealing with your pension or retirement plans, now you can ask the tax attorneys at the IRS for help. These attorneys specialize in tax law dealing specifically with pension and retirement plans. Now you can get expert tax advice right from the source...for free! Call them between 1:30 pm and 3:30 pm EST, Monday through Thursday. Call:
1-202-622-6074.

"You're Too Old...You're Fired!!"

No you aren't likely to hear these exact words but that doesn't mean you won't be discriminated against because of your age. Just remember that if you are over 40 years old, the law is clear. It is against the law to discriminate against anyone because of their age when it comes to hiring, firing, pay, promotions and other conditions of employment. And to insure that an employer will not discriminate against you on the basis of your age, sex, race, or disability and get away with it, the government has set up The Equal Employment Opportunity Commission. If you feel that you have been a victim of discrimination by an employer (or potential employer), be sure to contact:
THE EQUAL EMPLOYMENT OPPORTUNITY COMMISSION
1801 L STREET NW
WASHINGTON, DC 20507
AND TO BE CONNECTED TO THE EEOC OFFICE NEAREST YOU JUST DIAL:
1-800-669-4000

Free Help Getting A New Job

With all the downsizing and early retirements, many older American's find themselves in a situation where they can't afford to live on just their Social Security and yet unable to find a new job because of their age or because they need new skills. Well now thanks to government programs aimed specifically at seniors, there is help. This help comes in the form of free job training programs, counseling, as well as financial and tax incentives for companies to hire graduates of these training programs. For more information on programs available in your area, refer to the listing in the back of this book under *"Job Training Programs for Seniors.*

Golden Passport To Fun

Did you know that as a senior you can buy a lifetime entrance to national parks, monuments, historic sites, recreation areas and national refuges for a one time fee of just $10.00! This also entitles you to a whopping 50% discount on fees for things like camping, swimming, parking, boat launching and cave tours. It's called the Federal Golden Age Passport and it could be worth its weight in gold. And for the blind and disabled there's the Federal Golden Access Passport which is completely free. To get your passport, call the National Park Service at:
202-208-4747

$10,000 To Fix Up Your Home

Is your home in bad need of repair but you just can't afford the money to fix it up? Well now there's help in the form of grants of anywhere from $1,000 to as much as $10,000 with money coming from the U.S.D.A. Rural Housing Service.

Right now there are more than 2.5 million substandard homes across the nation. The federal government is helping remedy this situation by giving money to local non-profit groups who must use this money to make low-interest loans and out-right grants that never have to be repaid. This money is for low-income homeowners aged 62 and older who otherwise would have to live in homes that are a safety or health risk.

To apply for a loan or grant, check the blue pages of your phone book under 'federal government' for your local *'U.S. Department of Agriculture – Rural Development'* office. If you can't find it in your local phone book, you can contact:
U.S.D.A. Rural Housing Service
Stop 0700 1400 Independence Ave S.W.
Washington, DC 20250-0780
202-720-8732
You can also check on the Internet at: http://rdinit.usda.gov

Free Legal Services

If you've ever needed the services of an attorney you already know just how expensive legal help can be. But did you know that you can get legal help worth thousands of dollars - all paid for with money from the federal government or from legal services donated by attorneys who volunteer for "pro bono" (free) service to help those who can not afford legal representation.

See the back of this book for the *Free Legal Services Directory* which lists hundreds of legal service and pro bono attorney offices across the country. Find the office nearest you and call them the next time you need the services of an attorney.

Valuable Information From The U.S. Government

The U.S. Government offers thousands of special programs and services that your tax dollars have already paid for. But to benefit from them you must know they are there.

To keep you informed about these programs and to help you with a wide range of problems you may have, the government has hundreds of highly informative booklets that are yours free or practically free. These booklets are distributed through an agency called...

Consumer Information in Pueblo CO 81002

All of the publications listed here are either free or are available for a very nominal charge. You can order up to 25 free publications by simply enclosing $2.00 as a processing fee. (See more complete ordering details at the end of this section.)

RETIREMENT PLANNING

ANNUITIES.
Detailed information on the different types of annuities that can accumulate and generate retirement income. Includes a helpful quiz and questions to ask. 11 pp. **# 588F. Free.**

FROM HERE TO SECURITY.
Provides specific advice and actions to take for each of five different steps to financial security from setting goals and choosing investment products to checking your progress. 8 pp. **# 359F. 50¢.**

LUMP SUM DISTRIBUTION.
Before you take out the money built up in a pension plan, consider the tax and investment benefits and risks of your options. 14 pp. **# 589F. Free.**

A PREDICTABLE, SECURE PENSION FOR LIFE: DEFINED BENEFIT PENSIONS.
Describes traditional benefit pension plans, how they operate, and the rights and options of the workers covered by them. 24 pp. **# 590F. Free.**

TOP 10 WAYS TO BEAT THE CLOCK AND PREPARE FOR RETIREMENT.
Gives practical tips to help build your retirement savings and resources for more information. 2 pp. **# 591F. Free.**

WOMEN AND PENSIONS.
Provides a checklist of questions to ask about retirement benefits, including plan type, eligibility, penalties, spousal benefits, and more. 6 pp. **# 592F. Free.**

MONEY

BEING AN EXECUTOR.
Explains what an executor is and does in order to settle an estate. Includes a checklist and resources for more help if you are named an executor. 8 pp. **# 579F. Free.**

FEDERAL CREDIT UNIONS.
Explains what benefits and services are offered and how to become a member. 2 pp. **# 345F. 50¢.**

MAKING A WILL.
Explains why a will is important, how to prepare one, what to include, and how to keep it current. 12 pp. **# 580F. Free.**

PLANNING YOUR ESTATE.
How to estimate the size of your estate, minimize taxation, and provide for your heirs. 10 pp. **# 581F. Free.**

SWINDLERS ARE CALLING.
Eight things you should know about telemarketing fraud, nine tip-offs that a caller could be a crook, and ten ways to avoid becoming a victim. 4 pp. **# 346F. 50¢.**

WHAT YOU SHOULD KNOW ABOUT BUYING LIFE INSURANCE.
Describes various types with tips on choosing a company and agent, and making sure a policy meets your needs. 23 pp. **# 582F. Free.**

CREDIT

CONSUMER HANDBOOK TO CREDIT PROTECTION LAWS.
Explains how consumer credit laws can help you apply for credit, keep up a good credit standing, and complain about an unfair deal. 44 pp. **# 347F. 50¢.**

CREDIT AND DIVORCE.
Compares the benefits and disadvantages of individual, joint and "user" accounts. Steps to take if you divorce or separate. 2 pp. **# 348F. 50¢.**

FAIR CREDIT REPORTING.
How to find the credit bureau that has your report, how to dispute information, who can get a copy of your report, and what investigative consumer reports are. 8 pp. **# 349F. 50¢.**

FAIR DEBT COLLECTION.
Describes what debt collectors may and may not do if you owe money. How and where to complain if you are harassed, threatened, or abused. 2 pp. **# 350F. 50¢.**

HOW TO DISPUTE CREDIT REPORT ERRORS.
Gives tips on correcting errors, registering a dispute, and adding information to your file. 2 pp. **# 351F. 50¢.**

MANAGING YOUR DEBTS: HOW TO REGAIN FINANCIAL HEALTH.
Learn where to begin - what you can do for yourself, how counseling can help, facts about bankruptcy, and more. 2 pp. **# 352F. 50¢.**

SHOP...THE CARD YOU PICK CAN SAVE YOU MONEY.
Use the helpful chart of major credit card issuers to compare annual percentage rates, annual fees, and other features, and select the best card for you. 18 pp. **# 353F. 50¢.**

WHAT SAVVY CONSUMERS NEED TO KNOW ABOUT DEBIT CARDS.
Explains how debit cards work and what to do if your debit card is lost or stolen. Includes 10 tips on how to protect your card and a special form to keep track of card numbers. 7 pp. **# 583F. Free.**

SAVING & INVESTING
66 Ways to Save Money. Practical ways to cut everyday costs on transportation, insurance, banking, credit, housing, utilities, food, and more. 4 pp. **# 354F. 50¢.**

THE CONSUMER'S ALMANAC.
Organize your daily expenses, save and invest for the future, and manage your credit with monthly calendars and worksheets. Also includes helpful charts, checklists, and seasonal tips. 32 pp. **# 355F. 50¢.**

AN INTRODUCTION TO MUTUAL FUNDS.
Explains what they are, how to compare them, what factors to consider before investing, and how to avoid common pitfalls. 15 pp. **# 356F. 50¢.**

INVEST WISELY.
Basic tips to help you select a brokerage firm, make and monitor an investment, questions to ask, and signs of problems. 14 pp. **# 357F. 50¢.**

INVESTMENT SWINDLES: HOW THEY WORK AND HOW TO AVOID THEM.
Protect against illegal, yet legitimate-sounding, telemarketing and direct mail offers. 22 pp. **# 584F. Free.**

INVESTORS' BILL OF RIGHTS.
Tips to help you make informed investment decisions. 7 pp. **# 585F. Free.**

PLANNING FINANCIAL SECURITY.
Explains a wide variety of savings and investment options to achieve short-term and long-term goals. Includes a monthly budget worksheet, an investment risk tolerance quiz, and more. 12 pp. **# 586F. Free.**

TEN QUESTIONS TO ASK WHEN CHOOSING A FINANCIAL PLANNER...COVERING CREDENTIALS, COSTS AND SERVICES.
Includes an interview checklist and resources to contact for more information. 12 pp. **# 587F. Free.**

U.S. SAVINGS BONDS INVESTOR INFORMATION.
Detailed information on savings bond purchase, interest, maturity, replacement, redemption, exchange, and taxes. 14 pp. **# 358F. 50¢.**

INFORMATION ABOUT FEDERAL PROGRAMS

THE AMERICANS WITH DISABILITIES ACT: QUESTIONS AND ANSWERS
Explains how the civil rights of persons with disabilities are protected at work and in public places. 32 pp. **# 520F. Free.**

ARE THERE ANY PUBLIC LANDS FOR SALE?
Describes the federal program to sell excess undeveloped public land and why there is no more available for homesteading. 12 pp. **# 110F. $1.00.**

FEDERAL INFORMATION CENTER.
Lists where and when to call when you need assistance from the federal government. 1 pp. **# 521F. Free.**

A GUIDE TO DISABILITY RIGHTS LAWS.
Describes your rights regarding fair housing, public accommodations, telecommunications, education, and employment. 14 pp. **# 522F. Free.**

GUIDE TO FEDERAL GOVERNMENT SALES.
We've all heard about the thousands of cars and homes the government has to sell, but how can you get a good deal? Learn more about how to buy homes, cars and other property from 17 federal sales programs. 19 pp. **# 111F. $2.00.**

HOW YOU CAN BUY USED FEDERAL PERSONAL PROPERTY.
Describes used equipment and industrial items sold by the government, how it is sold, and where to call for more information. 5 pp. **# 322F. 50¢.**

NATIONAL SELLERS LIST.
The government sells real estate and personal property that has been forfeited by law. Here's a list of dealers who sell items plus their addresses and phone numbers. 8 pp. **# 323F. 50¢.**

U.S. REAL PROPERTY SALES LIST.
Lists government real estate properties for sale that are sold by auction or sealed bid often at very low prices. It tells how to get more information on specific properties. 5 pp. **# 523F. Free.**

YOUR RIGHT TO FEDERAL RECORDS.
Now you can use the Freedom of Information Act and the Privacy Act to obtain records from the federal government. Answers questions and has a sample request letter. 26 pp. **# 324F. 50¢.**

YOUR SOCIAL SECURITY NUMBER.
Explains why we have social security numbers, when and how to get one, and how to protect its privacy. 2 pp. **# 524F. Free.**

BENEFITS

BASIC FACTS ON SOCIAL SECURITY.
Explains the different kinds of Social Security benefits, who receives them, and how they're financed. 17 pp. **# 525F. Free.**

FEDERAL BENEFITS FOR VETERANS AND DEPENDENTS.
Explains disability compensation, pension, health care, education and housing loans, and other benefit programs for veterans and their families. 95 pp. **# 112F. $3.75.**

MEDICARE MANAGED CARE.
Compares the benefits and disadvantages of managed care vs. fee-for-service plans. 19 pp. **# 526F. Free.**

REQUEST FOR EARNINGS AND BENEFIT ESTIMATE STATEMENT.
A form to complete and return to Social Security to get your earnings history and an estimate of future benefits. 3 pp. **# 527F. Free.**

SOCIAL SECURITY: UNDERSTANDING THE BENEFITS.
Explains retirement, disability, survivor's benefits, Medicare coverage, Supplemental Security Income, and more. 40 pp. **# 528F. Free.**

SOCIAL SECURITY: WHAT EVERY WOMAN SHOULD KNOW
...About benefits upon retirement, disability, widowhood, or divorce. 19 pp. **# 529F. Free.**

YOUR MEDICARE HANDBOOK.
Summarizes Medicare benefits, rights and obligations, with information about managed care plans and Medigap insurance. Includes a listing by state of organizations to contact for assistance. 40 pp. **# 113F. $3.50.**

SMALL BUSINESS

AMERICANS WITH DISABILITIES ACT: GUIDE FOR SMALL BUSINESSES.
Discusses basic requirements businesses must follow to ensure that facilities are accessible. Includes toll-free sources for more assistance. 15 pp. **# 593F. Free.**

COPYRIGHT BASICS.
Covers what can be copyrighted, who can apply, what forms to use, and much more. 12 pp. **# 360F. 50¢.**

RESOURCE DIRECTORY FOR SMALL BUSINESS MANAGEMENT.
Going out on your own and starting a business is a big decision.
It can also be intimidating. Here's some help. This guide offers a
listing of useful publications and videotapes to help you get off
the ground. 6 pp. **# 361F. 50¢.**

SBA BORROWER'S GUIDE.
Explains SBA's loan programs, including maximum amounts
available, interest rates, eligibility, etc. Includes a reference chart
covering 10 loan programs and a loan repayment guide. 29 pp.
 # 594F. Free.

SBA PROGRAMS & SERVICES.
Discusses how SBA can help you start or expand a business.
Lists phone numbers, on-line information, business counseling
and training, lending programs, and much more. 23 pp.
 # 595F. Free.

CARS

AIR BAGS & ON-OFF SWITCHES.
Discusses when using air bags is unsafe and specific steps to
take to reduce the risk. Describes on-off switches and who should
consider installing them. Includes the required
form to request an on-off switch. 10 pp.
 # 301F. 50¢.

BUYING A NEW CAR.
Discusses pricing terms, financing options,
and various contracts. Includes a worksheet
to help you bargain. 2 pp. **# 302F. 50¢.**

BUYING A USED CAR.
Learn about your limited rights when buying from an individual
and about the "Buyer's Guide" sticker required by law on all
used cars sold by a dealer. 9 pp. **# 303F. 50¢.**

GLOVE BOX TIPS.
Five booklets to help you get your car ready for summer and
winter driving, choose the right repair shop, and get the best
work from your mechanic. 10 pp. **# 305F. 50¢.**

HOW TO FIND YOUR WAY UNDER THE HOOD & AROUND THE CAR.
Instructions for 14 preventative maintenance services you can
perform on your car. 2 pp. **# 306F. 50¢.**

How to Get a Great Deal On a New Car.
Step-by-step instructions for a proven negotiation technique that you can use to save money on your next car. 4 pp. **# 307F. 50¢.**

Keys to Vehicle Leasing.
Explains the differences between leasing and buying a car. Sample form explains all the information that is required on a lease agreement, as well as your rights and responsibilities. 6 pp. **# 308F. 50¢.**

Nine Ways to Lower Your Auto Insurance Costs.
Tips on what to do to lower your expenses. Includes a chart to compare discounts. 6 pp. **# 309F. 50¢.**

Underhood Tips to Help You Keep Your Cool.
Learn how non-Freon air conditioners affect you and the environment. 2 pp. **# 501F. Free.**

EMPLOYMENT

Changing Your Job.
Lists important questions to consider about your career plans, financial position, pension, industry outlook, skills and interests before you make a move. 12 pp. **# 517F. Free.**

Handy Reference Guide to the Fair Labor Standards Act.
Explains the federal laws on minimum wage, overtime pay, child labor, and more. 18 pp. **# 317F. 50¢.**

Health Benefits Under COBRA (Consolidated Omnibus Budget Reconciliation Act).
How to keep or buy coverage for yourself and family after a job loss, reduced work hours, divorce, or death. 24 pp. **# 318F. 50¢.**

Help Wanted & Finding a Job.
Describes both private companies and government agencies that offer consumers help in finding a job. Lists precautions to take when contacting an employment service firm. 8 pp. **# 319F. 50¢.**

High Earning Workers Who Don't Have a Bachelor's Degree.
Lists more than 100 occupations requiring less than a college degree. 8 pp. **# 104F. $1.00.**

How to File a Claim for Your Benefits.
What to do if your claim or appeal for health, disability, or severance benefits is denied. 2 pp. **# 320F. 50¢.**

OSHA: Employee Workplace Rights.
What to do if you question the safety of, or hazards in your workplace. Lists addresses and phone numbers for more information. 28 pp. # **518F. Free.**

Resumes, Application Forms, Cover Letters, and Interviews.
Tips on tailoring your resume for specific jobs and sample interview questions. 8 pp. # **106F. $1.25.**

Sales Occupations.
If you're interested in going into sales, this guide will help. It offers information on different types of sales positions and gives details on each specific position. 21 pp. # **107F. $2.25.**

Tips for Finding the Right Job.
Learn how to assess your skills and interests, prepare a resume, write cover letters, and interview for a job. 28 pp. # **108F. $1.75.**

What You Should Know About Your Pension Rights.
Explains your rights, benefits, payment schedules, protections, and more. 48 pp. # **321F. 50¢.**

Your Guaranteed Pension.
Answers 19 frequently asked questions about the security of private pension plans, including benefits and plan termination. 11 pp. # **519F. Free.**

FOOD & NUTRITION

Action Guide for Healthy Eating.
Eating healthy foods may require you to make only a few minor changes in your lifestyle. This guide gives helpful hints to help you include more low fat, high-fiber foods in your diet.16 pp. # **530F. Free.**

Bulking Up Fiber's Healthful Reputation.
Explains how fiber is associated with a reduced risk of certain cancers, diabetes, digestive disorders, and heart disease and lists recommended sources. 5 pp. # **531F. Free.**

Can Your Kitchen Pass the Food Safety Test?
Take the 10-point quiz on food storage, handling, and cooking to protect your family from foodborne illnesses. 4 pp. # **532F. Free.**

CRITICAL STEPS TOWARD SAFER SEAFOOD.
Discusses how the FDA helps keep seafood safe and gives tips on safe food handling practices and selecting wholesome seafood. 5 pp. # 533F. **Free.**

DIETARY GUIDELINES FOR AMERICANS.
How to choose a diet that will taste good, be nutritious, and reduce chronic disease risks. 43 pp. # 325F. **50¢.**

EAT RIGHT TO HELP LOWER YOUR HIGH BLOOD PRESSURE.
Lists menu ideas and recipes to help you control your weight and high blood pressure. 30 pp. # 114F. **$2.75.**

EATING FOR LIFE.
Eating right may reduce your risk of developing cardiovascular disease and cancer. This booklet helps you learn to make healthy, appetizing food choices. 23 pp. # 115F. **$1.25.**

FIGHT BACK ! FOUR SIMPLE STEPS TO FOOD SAFETY
...gives advice on how to handle food safely so you, your family and friends don't become ill. 5 pp. # 534F. **Free.**

THE FOOD GUIDE PYRAMID.
Use this easy guide to get the nutrients you need (without too many calories) and to reduce the fat, cholesterol, sugar, sodium, or alcohol in your diet. 29 pp. # 116F. **$1.00.**

A FRESH LOOK AT FOOD PRESERVATIVES.
Describes how and why food preservatives are used and what safety standards are followed. 5 pp. # 535F. **Free.**

FRUITS AND VEGETABLES: EATING YOUR WAY TO 5 A DAY.
Eating fruits and vegetables cuts calories and reduces the risk of heart disease and cancer. Gives ideas to help you meet the 5 A Day goal with a chart showing the best nutrient sources. 8 pp. # 536F. **Free.**

HOW TO HELP AVOID FOODBORNE ILLNESS IN THE HOME.
Easy but essential tips that will keep your food free from the four most common and dangerous bacteria. 8 pp. # 537F. **Free.**

IRRADIATION: A SAFE MEASURE FOR SAFER FOOD.
Learn how irradiation helps control foodborne illnesses without making food radioactive. 6 pp. # 538F. **Free.**

A PINCH OF CONTROVERSY SHAKES UP DIETARY SALT.
Discusses the effects of hidden salt in your diet and gives tips on reducing salt intake to prevent the risk of high blood pressure. 6 pp. **# 539F. Free.**

SNACK SMART FOR HEALTHY TEETH.
Tips on choosing the right snacks to prevent tooth decay and promote healthy eating, with a list of suggested items from the five basic food groups. 4 pp. **# 326F. 50¢.**

HEALTH

CLEARING UP COSMETIC CONFUSION.
Learn what the terms on cosmetic labels mean, what products are prohibited, and how to protect yourself against hazardous misuse. 5 pp. **# 540F. Free.**

THE SUN, UV, AND YOU.
Explains what the UV (ultraviolet radiation) index is and how to avoid skin cancer, cataracts, and premature aging of the skin. Gives special information for children. 12 pp. **# 541F. Free.**

WATER ON TAP: A CONSUMER'S GUIDE TO THE NATION'S DRINKING WATER.
Explains where it comes from and how it's treated, what contaminants are, and what to do in case of a problem with either your public or private water supply. 22 pp. **# 542F. Free.**

DRUGS & HEALTH AIDS

A GUIDE TO CONTRACEPTIVE CHOICES.
Compares 13 methods of birth control according to effectiveness, health risks, availability, convenience, and how well they protect you from sexually transmitted diseases. 8 pp. **# 543F. Free.**

FDA'S TIPS FOR TAKING MEDICINES.
Prescription and over the counter drugs can be sensitive and may react in strange ways to different things. Learn more about the do's and don'ts of medicine with this publication. 4 pp. **# 544F. Free.**

HOMEOPATHY: REAL MEDICINE OR EMPTY PROMISES?
Learn about this method of treating disease, including its history, current practices, and how it's regulated. 5 pp. **# 545F. Free.**

It's Quittin' Time.
Describes the benefits and side effects of five stop-smoking aids: the nicotine patch and gum, nasal spray, inhaler, and an anti-smoking pill. Gives suggestions on creating a plan to stop smoking with resources for more help. 5 pp. **# 546F. Free.**

Keeping an Eye on Contact Lenses.
Wish you could trade in your glasses for contacts? Want to change your eye color? This informative booklet looks at the different types of contact lenses available and if they are right for you. 5 pp. **# 547F. Free.**

Nonprescription Medicines: What's Right for You?
Advice on choosing over-the-counter (OTC) medicines and avoiding harmful interactions. 12 pp. **# 548F. Free.**

Taming Tummy Turmoil.
Lists over-the-counter medications (and their possible side effects) for motion sickness, heartburn, indigestion, and overindulgence. 4 pp. **# 549F. Free.**

Unproven Medical Treatments Lure Elderly.
Americans spend nearly $20 billion each year on unproven medical treatments. Learn why these can be dangerous and how to avoid fraud. 5 pp. **# 550F. Free.**

DIET & EXERCISE

Dieter's Brews Make Tea Time a Dangerous Affair.
Many dieter's teas contain stimulant laxatives, which can cause serious side effects. Learn how to check labels and recognize dangerous symptoms. 5 pp. **# 551F. Free.**

Helping Your Overweight Child.
If you are the parent of an overweight child, or are concerned about your child's eating habits, this guide can help put you and your family on the path to good nutrition and health. 15 pp. **# 327F. 50¢.**

Keep Active.
How older people can use exercise and sports to help lower the risk of common diseases, relieve arthritis pain, and recover faster from illness.

Includes an activity log to track progress and lists practical tips to prevent injury. 5 pp. **# 328F. 50¢.**

Physical Activity and Nutrition: A Win-Win Situation.
3 booklets cover the most frequently-asked questions about sports and nutrition. Includes a nutrient content chart for selected foods and how to participate in the Presidential Sports Award program. 17 pp. **# 552F. Free.**

Should You Go On a Diet?
Discusses the risks of fad diets and diet pills for teenagers, and gives healthy tips for anyone trying to lose weight. 3 pp. **# 553F. Free.**

Walking for Exercise and Pleasure.
Includes illustrated warm-up exercises and advice on how far, how fast, and how often to walk for best results. 14 pp. **# 117F. $1.00.**

Ways to Win at Weight Loss.
How to create a successful weight loss plan, including over-the-counter medications, prescription drugs and diet and exercise programs. 7 pp. **# 554F. Free.**

Weight Loss for Life.
Always following the latest diet fads? Quick fixes may not always be the best answer. This guide will help you learn how to lose weight safely and stay healthy. 20 pp. **# 329F. 50¢.**

Medical Problems
Alzheimer's Disease...is a group of diseases that lead to the loss of mental and physical functions. Learn how Alzheimer's is diagnosed, possible causes, and current treatments. 36 pp. **# 555F. Free.**

Bipolar Disorder (Manic-Depressive Illness).
Learn signs and symptoms, available treatments, and how to get help. 12 pp. **# 556F. Free.**

Boning Up on Osteoporosis.
Osteoporosis is a silent thief. It drains away bone over many years without warning to the patient or doctor. Learn more about this condition and how to prevent it. 6 pp. **# 557F. Free.**

BREAST CANCER AND MAMMOGRAMS.
Describes who is at risk for breast cancer, what you can do, and how a mammogram can help. 5 pp. **# 558F. Free.**

COLDS & FLU.
Explains the differences between a cold and the flu. Suggests ways to avoid viruses; and reviews over-the-counter medications, the flu shot, and home remedies. 4 pp. **# 559F. Free.**

CONTROLLING ASTHMA.
Discusses what triggers an asthma attack, possible causes, and medications to prevent attacks and relieve symptoms. 5 pp. **# 560F. Free.**

COPING WITH ARTHRITIS IN ITS MANY FORMS.
Describes symptoms and treatments for the 7 most common types of arthritis, and how to avoid being a target for fraudulent "cures." 5 pp. **# 561F. Free.**

DIABETES DEMANDS A TRIAD OF TREATMENTS.
With a variety of treatments, it is now possible for diabetics to control their disease. This pamphlet explores the different treatments for diabetes and how they can improve diabetics' lives. 5 pp. **# 562F. Free.**

DON'T LOSE SIGHT OF GLAUCOMA.
Find out who is most likely to develop glaucoma, its symptoms, and how it is treated. 2 pp. **# 330F. 50¢.**

FEVER BLISTERS & CANKER SORES.
Discusses causes, treatments, and research on these mouth infections. 12 pp. **# 331F. 50¢.**

GALLSTONES.
Explains what gallstones are, who's at risk, symptoms, and how they're diagnosed and treated. 6 pp. **# 332F. 50¢.**

GETTING RID OF YEAST INFECTIONS.
There are a variety of drugs available to fight yeast infections. Learn more about this illness and which drugs may work best for you. 2 pp. **# 563F. Free.**

HEADACHES.
Tests and treatments for headaches, including migraines, and when adults and children should see a doctor. 36 pp. **# 118F. $2.25.**

High Blood Pressure: Treat it for Life.
High blood pressure can lead to heart failure, kidney failure and stroke. Fortunately, you can treat this condition through a few simple lifestyle changes. Learn how you can control it through diet, exercise and medication with this guide. 52 pp. **# 119F. $4.00.**

Laser Eye Surgery & Is It Worth Looking Into?
Interested in the new eye surgeries that you keep hearing about on the news? Will they rid you of your glasses and contacts forever? Maybe not. Learn more about corrective eye surgery for near-sightedness and whether it is appropriate for you. 5 pp. **# 566F. Free.**

New Attitudes Towards Menopause.
Provides information about symptoms and treatments, including the benefits and risks of estrogen replacement therapy. Also lists resources for more information and assistance. 4 pp. **# 564F. Free.**

New Ways to Prevent and Treat AIDS.
Describes new home-use testing kits, drug treatments, and other advances in preventing and treating AIDS. 4 pp. **# 565F. Free.**

Noninsulin-Dependent Diabetes.
Discusses who is at risk, the symptoms, causes, and treatments for this disease that maybe hard to identify at first. 35 pp. **# 333F. 50¢.**

Panic Disorder.
What to do when anxiety or sudden fear seems too much to handle. Lists symptoms, treatments, and where to get help. 2 pp. **# 567F. Free.**

Preventing Stroke.
Discusses what a stroke is, warning signs, and risk factors. Includes a chart to estimate your stroke risk. 8 pp. **# 334F. 50¢.**

Prostate Cancer...is the second most common cancer in men.
Learn how it is detected, what treatments are available, and where to get more information. 5 pp. **# 568F. Free.**

So You Have High Blood Cholesterol.
Guidelines for lowering your blood cholesterol through diet, medication, and exercise. 36 pp. **# 120F. $1.75.**

SPREAD THE WORD ABOUT CANCER: A GUIDE FOR BLACK AMERICANS.
Learn what you can do to reduce your chances of getting cancer.
12 pp. **# 569F. Free.**

TIME TO SPRING INTO ACTION AGAINST SEASONAL ALLERGIES.
Explains how to treat chronic allergies, including medication,
nasal sprays and allergy shots. Discusses common questions regarding over-the-counter medications. 5 pp. **# 570F. Free.**

VARICOSE VEIN TREATMENTS.
Explains treatments, risks, and side effects; questions to ask your
doctor; and more. 2 pp. **# 335F. 50¢**

WHAT TO DO WHEN A FRIEND IS DEPRESSED.
Depression is a serious disease that affects people of all ages,
even teenagers. But with this group it is usually mistaken for
growing pains. This guide helps teens understand the myths
about depression and tells where to get help. 3 pp. **# 571F. Free.**

HOUSING

SALES & FINANCING

**BUYING YOUR HOME: SETTLEMENT COSTS AND HELPFUL
INFORMATION.**
Describes the home buying, financing, and settlement (closing)
process. Helpful tips on shopping for a loan with worksheets to
calculate and compare closing costs. 35 pp. **# 121F. $1.75.**

A CONSUMER'S GUIDE TO MORTGAGE LOCK-INS.
Basic information to help you obtain the terms of credit you really want. Lists questions to ask when shopping for a mortgage.
14 pp. **# 336F. 50¢.**

A CONSUMER'S GUIDE TO MORTGAGE REFINANCINGS.
Is refinancing beneficial to you? Learn the costs and how to tell
if the time is right. 8 pp. **# 337F. 50¢.**

HOW TO BUY A HOME WITH A LOW DOWN PAYMENT.
There are private and federal options for obtaining a mortgage.
Learn how to qualify, determine what you can afford, and more.
12 pp. **# 572F. Free.**

HOW TO BUY A MANUFACTURED (MOBILE) HOME.
Tips on selection and placement, warranties, site preparation,
transportation, installation, and more. 22 pp. **# 338F. 50¢.**

THE HUD HOMEBUYING GUIDE.
Here are step-by-step instructions for finding and financing a HUD home. Includes charts to help you estimate mortgage payments. 11 pp. **# 573F. Free.**

TWELVE WAYS TO LOWER YOUR HOMEOWNERS INSURANCE COSTS.
Practical tips to help reduce your expenses. Lists phone numbers of state insurance departments for more information. 4 pp. **# 339F. 50¢.**

HOME MAINTENANCE

AM I COVERED?
Answers 15 common questions regarding homeowners insurance and explains what is covered in a standard policy. 9 pp. **# 340F. 50¢.**

AUTOMATIC AND PROGRAMMABLE THERMOSTATS.
How to choose which of the five basic types will help you save the most money and energy. 4 pp. **# 122F. $1.00.**

BACKYARD BIRD PROBLEMS.
How to control common problems such as destruction of garden plants, nesting in gutters and chimneys, and damage to your home's exterior. 27 pp. **# 574F. Free.**

COOLING YOUR HOME NATURALLY.
Suggests how to save electricity and keep your home cool with landscaping, roof treatments, and more. 8 pp. **# 123F. $1.00.**

ENERGY-EFFICIENT WINDOWS.
Describes how to reduce your home's heating, cooling and lighting costs using properly selected and installed windows. 6 pp. **# 124F. $1.00.**

ENERGY SAVERS: TIPS ON SAVING ENERGY & MONEY AT HOME.
A practical guide on how to reduce your home energy use, with tips on insulation, weatherization, heating and cooling, lighting, landscaping, and much more. 36 pp. **# 341F. 50¢.**

FIXING UP YOUR HOME AND HOW TO FINANCE IT.
Information about hiring a contractor, doing the work yourself, and the HUD Title 1 home improvement loan program. 2 pp. **# 342F. 50¢.**

HEALTHY LAWN, HEALTHY ENVIRONMENT.
Tips on soil preparation, grasses, watering, mowing, pesticides, choosing a lawn care service, and more. 19 pp. **# 343F. 50¢.**

A HOME ELECTRICAL SAFETY CHECK.
Lists symptoms of potential electrical hazards, discusses do's and don'ts, and poses questions to help you keep your home safe. 17 pp. **# 344F. 50¢.**

HOW TO PRUNE TREES.
Illustrated guide shows what to do, what not to do, and what tools to use and when, for healthy, strong trees. 30 pp. **# 125F. $1.50.**

INDOOR AIR HAZARDS EVERY HOMEOWNER SHOULD KNOW ABOUT.
How to identify and reduce the hazards of indoor air pollutants such as asbestos, radon, lead, molds and more. 13 pp. **# 575F. Free.**

KEEPING YOUR HOME SAFE.
Use the crime-stoppers' checklist and other practical tips to protect your home from fire and theft. 13 pp. **# 576F. Free.**

MANAGING THE JAPANESE BEETLE: A HOMEOWNER'S HANDBOOK.
Discusses how to detect and control Japanese beetles, and choose plants that resist Japanese beetle feeding. 16 pp. **# 126F. $2.00.**

NEVER SAY NEVER.
90% of all U.S. natural disasters involve flooding. Learn how to obtain the insurance coverage you should have. 5 pp. **# 577F. Free.**

PROTECT YOUR FAMILY FROM LEAD IN YOUR HOME.
Exposure to lead is dangerous, especially to young children. Learn how to check your home and reduce the hazards. 15 pp. **# 578F. Free.**

SELECTING A NEW WATER HEATER.
Describes how different types of water heaters work and important features to consider when buying. 6 pp. **# 127F. $1.00.**

SHOULD YOU HAVE THE AIR DUCTS IN YOUR HOME CLEANED?
How to decide if your ducts need cleaning, how to choose a cleaning service and evaluate health claims, and how to keep ducts clean. 20 pp. **# 128F. $2.00.**

TRAVEL

DISCOVER AMERICA: A LISTING OF STATE TOURISM OFFICES OF THE U.S.
Use this list to order free vacation information including maps, calendars of events, travel guides, and more. 4 pp. **# 362F. 50¢.**

FLY-RIGHTS.
Advice for travelers on getting the best fares, what to do when faced with lost tickets and baggage, canceled or overbooked flights, and much more. 58 pp. **# 129F. $1.75.**

FLY SMART.
Lists more than 30 steps you can take to help make your flight a safe one. Includes a passenger checklist. 2 pp. **# 596F. Free.**

FOREIGN ENTRY REQUIREMENTS.
Lists 200 embassy and consulate addresses and phone numbers where visas may be obtained. 20 pp. **# 363F. 50¢.**

LESSER KNOWN AREAS OF THE NATIONAL PARK SYSTEM.
Listing by state of more than 170 national parks, their accommodations, locations, and historical significance. 49 pp. **# 130F. $2.50.**

NATIONAL PARK SYSTEM MAP AND GUIDE.
Full color map lists activities at more than 300 parks, monuments, and historic sites. **# 131F. $1.25.**

NATIONAL TRAILS SYSTEM MAP AND GUIDE.
Full color map describes eight national scenic trails and nine national historic trails. **# 132F. $1.25.**

PASSPORTS: APPLYING FOR THEM THE EASY WAY.
How, when, and where to apply for U.S. passports. Includes information on fees. 2 pp. **# 364F. 50¢.**

A SAFE TRIP ABROAD.
How to take precautions against robbery, terrorism, or other dangers. What to do if you find yourself in trouble. 20 pp. **# 133F. $1.25.**

MISCELLANEOUS

1998-99 CONSUMER'S RESOURCE HANDBOOK.
This helpful guide provides assistance with consumer problems and complaints. Lists consumer contacts at hundreds of companies and trade associations, state and federal government agencies, local and national consumer organizations, and much more. 144 pp. **#597F. Free.**

ALL THAT GLITTERS...THE JIVE ON JEWELRY.
Explains terms commonly used in buying gold, platinum, silver, diamonds, and more. Includes a jewelry shopper's checklist. 10 pp. **# 365F. 50¢.**

BUYING A COMPUTER.
Practical advice on how to buy a computer that fits your needs. Gives tips on protecting your computer and data, defines common computer terms, and provides a helpful checklist to use when shopping for a computer. 10 pp. **# 598F. Free.**

CIVIL WAR AT A GLANCE.
This color map illustrates and briefly describes major Civil War battle campaigns. **# 134F. $1.25.**

THE DUCK STAMP STORY.
Help preserve wetlands and wildlife refuges by becoming a collector of these unique stamps. 8 pp. **# 599F. Free.**

FOR THE BIRDS.
How to attract different species of birds, feed them, and build or buy suitable homes. 50 pp. **# 366F. 50¢.**

FUNERALS: A CONSUMER GUIDE.
Tells what costs and services a funeral provider is required to give you when you inquire in person or by phone. 4 pp. **# 367F. 50¢.**

SITE-SEEING ON THE INTERNET.
Like any major trip, traveling the Internet can be both fun and overwhelming. This guide can help you navigate the Internet, learn the local customs and lingo and learn about what to avoid during your travels. 11 pp. **# 368F. 50¢.**

TROUBLE @ THE IN-BOX.
How to avoid junk, bulk and possibly fraudulent unsolicited e-mail messages. 2 pp. **# 369F. 50¢.**

THE U.S. AND THE METRIC SYSTEM.
Explains how to use metric in everyday life. Includes metric conversion charts and more. 10 pp. **# 370F. 50¢.**

WHERE TO WRITE AWAY FOR VITAL RECORDS.
This useful guide offers listings for each state on how to obtain birth, death, marriage and divorce certificates. 32 pp. **# 135F. $2.25.**

WHY SAVE ENDANGERED SPECIES?
Ways to get involved in saving plants and animals. 10 pp. **# 600F. Free.**

YEAR 2000 AND YOU.
Describes some of the possible effects if computers cannot read the year 2000 (Y2K), and how this could disrupt the workplace, services and equipment you use. 2 pp. **# 601F. Free.**

YOUR FAMILY DISASTER SUPPLIES KIT.
Lists kinds of food, first aid supplies, tools, and other items you should stock for an emergency. 4 pp. **# 371F. 50¢.**

COLLEGE PLANNING

ALL ABOUT DIRECT LOANS.
Discusses four types of direct student education loans, how much you can borrow, how to apply, how you'll be paid, repayment, and more. 34 pp. **# 513F. Free.**

DIRECT STUDENT LOAN CONSOLIDATION...COULD BENEFIT YOU FINANCIALLY.
Learn how to consolidate your federal loans into a single account, and much more. 16 pp. **# 514F. Free.**

THE GED DIPLOMA.
Learn what the General Educational Development Diploma tests cover, how to prepare, and where to get more information. 16 pp. **# 515F. Free.**

NONTRADITIONAL EDUCATION: ALTERNATIVE WAYS TO EARN YOUR CREDENTIALS.
Get high school or college credit through the GED program, the National External Diploma program, correspondence and distance study, and standardized tests. 16 pp. **# 101F. $1.75.**

PLANNING FOR COLLEGE.
Strategies to help you plan for tuition and fees along with helpful charts for estimating future costs. 10 pp. # **516F. Free.**

Ordering Free Booklets

While there is no charge for individual free publications, there is a $2.00 service fee to help defray program costs. For that $2.00, you may order up to 25 different free booklets. Payment can be made by check or money order made payable to the "Superintendent of Documents" or charged to your VISA, MasterCard or Discover card. Priority handling is available at an extra charge when you place your order by phone .

Ordering Information

IF YOU ORDER ONLY FREE BOOKLETS, MAIL YOUR ORDER TO:
S. JAMES
CONSUMER INFORMATION CENTER - 9A
P.O. BOX 100
PUEBLO, COLORADO 81002

FOR ALL OTHER ORDERS, MAIL YOUR ORDER TO:
R. WOODS
CONSUMER INFORMATION CENTER - 9A
P.O. BOX 100
PUEBLO, COLORADO 81002

TO ORDER BY PHONE, CALL: **1-888-8-PUEBLO** (THAT'S **1-888-878-3256**)

You can also get these booklets online, along with other consumer news, updates, and information. Use your modem or Internet connection to access this information electronically. Internet address:
www.pueblo.gsa.gov

Free Help For Seniors From Your State's Office of The Aging

Every state in the nation has an agency dedicated to providing seniors with a full range of services they may need. These services will vary from state to state but they include:

- Food Stamps
- Home delivered meals
- Transportation to and from doctor's offices
- In-Home care and assistance where needed
- Job Training programs for older workers wanting to get back into the workforce
- Health insurance counseling & assistance programs to help the elderly get all the health care they need.
- Free prescription drug programs

To find out exactly what services are available to you, contact your state's office of the aging directly. Here is a directory of the offices of the aging for all 50 states plus the District of Columbia, Puerto Rico and the Pacific Islands

National Offices
Administration on Aging - Washington D.C.
U.S. Administration on Aging Office of Management and Policy
330 Independence Avenue, S.W.
Washington, DC 20201
202-619-0641

National Association of Area Agencies on Aging
1112 16th Street N.W., Suite 100
Washington, DC 20036-4823
202-296-8130

State Offices

Alabama
Alabama Commission on Aging
770 Washington Avenue
Montgomery, AL 36104-3816
334-242-5743
Web: http://
webserver.dsmd.state.al.us/coa

Alaska
Alaska Commission on Aging
P.O. Box 110209
Juneau, AK 99811-0209
907-465-3250

Arizona
Arizona Aging and Adult
Administration
1789 W. Jefferson, #950A
Phoenix, AZ 85007
602-542-4446

Arkansas
Arkansas Division of Aging and Adult
Services
7th and Main Street
P.O. Box 1437, Slot 1412
Little Rock, AR 72203-1412
501-682-2441
800-482-8049 In Arkansas

California
California Department on Aging
1600 K Street
Sacramento, CA 95814
916-324-5290
916-324-1903

Colorado
Colorado Division of Aging and Adult
Services
110 16th Street, 2nd floor
Denver, CO 80202-1714
303-620-4147

Connecticut
Connecticut Dept. of Social
Services

25 Sigourney Street, 10th floor
Hartford, CT 06106-5033
860-424-5577

Delaware
Delaware Division of Services for
Aging & Adults
1901 N. Dupont Highway
New Castle, DE 19720
302-577-4791

District of Columbia
District of Columbia Office on Aging
441 4th Street N.W., Suite 900
Washington, DC 20001
202-724-5622

Florida
Florida Department of Elder Affairs
4040 Esplanade Way
Tallahassee, FL 32399-0700
850-414-2000
Web Address: http://fcn.state.fl.us/
doea/doea.html

Georgia
Georgia Office of Aging
2 Peachtree Street N.W., Suite 18-
403
Atlanta, GA 30303-3176
404-657-5258

Hawaii
Hawaii Executive Office on Aging
250 South Hotel Street, Room 109
Honolulu, HI 96813
808-586-0100

Idaho
Idaho State Office on Aging
Statehouse, Room 108
Boise, ID 83720
208-334-3833

Illinois
Illinois Dept. on Aging
421 E. Capital Avenue, #100
Springfield, IL 62701-1789
217-785-2870

Indiana
Indiana Bureau of Aging and In-Home Services
402 W. Washington Street, #E-431
P.O. Box 7083
Indianapolis, IN 46207
317-232-7020

Iowa
Iowa Department of Elder Affairs
200 Tenth St., Suite 300
Des Moines, IA 50309
515-281-5187

Kansas
Kansas Dept. on Aging
915 S.W. Harrison
Topeka, KS 66612-1500
913-296-4986

Kentucky
Kentucky Division of Aging Services
275 E. Main Street, 5W-A
Frankfort, KY 40621
502-564-6930

Louisiana
Louisiana Governor's Office of Elderly Affairs
412 North 4th Street
Baton Rouge, LA 70802
504-342-7098

Maine
Maine Bureau of Elder and Adult Services
35 Anthony Avenue
State House, Station #11
Augusta, ME 04333
207-624-5335

Maryland
Maryland Office on Aging
301 W. Preston Street, 10th floor
Baltimore, MD 21201
410-767-1100

Massachusetts
Massachusetts Executive Office of Elder Affairs
1 Ashburton Place, 5th floor
Boston, MA 02108
617-727-7750

Michigan
Michigan Office of Services to the Aging
611 W. Ottawa
P.O. Box 30026
Lansing, MI 48909
517-373-8230

Minnesota
Minnesota Board on Aging
444 Lafayette Road
St. Paul, MN 55155-3843
612-296-2770

Mississippi
Mississippi Council on Aging
750 N. State Street
Jackson, MS 39202
601-359-4929

Missouri
Missouri Division on Aging
615 Howerton Court
P.O. Box 1337
Jefferson City, MO 65102
573-751-3082

Montana
Montana Governor's Office on Aging
Capitol Station, Room 219
PO Box 8005
Helena, MT 59604-8005
406-444-7787

Nebraska
Nebraska Division on Aging
301 Centennial Mall S.
P.O. Box 95044
Lincoln, NE 68509-5044
402-471-2306

Nevada
Nevada Division for Aging Services
340 N. 11th St., Ste. 203
Las Vegas, NV 89101
702-486-3545

New Hampshire
New Hampshire Division of Elderly
Services
115 Pleasant St,. Annex Bldg. #1
Concord, NH 03301
603-271-4680

New Jersey
New Jersey Division on Aging
S. Broad & Front Streets
Trenton, NJ 08625-0807
609-984-3982

New Mexico
New Mexico State Agency on Aging
224 E. Palace Avenue, 4th floor
Santa Fe, NM 87501
505-827-7640

New York
New York Office for the Aging
Agency Building #2
Albany, NY 12223
800-342-9871
WebAddress:
  http://aging.state.ny.us/nysofa/
Elderly Prescription Insurance
Coverage (EPIC) Hotline:
1-800-332-3742

North Carolina
North Carolina Division of Aging
693 Palmer Drive
Raleigh, NC 27626-0531
919-733-3983

North Dakota
North Dakota Aging Services
Division
600 South Second Street, Suite 1C
Bismarck, ND 58504
701-328-8910

Ohio
Ohio Department of Aging
50 W. Broad Street, 9th floor
Columbus, OH 43215
614-466-5500

Oklahoma
Oklahoma Aging Services Division
312 N.E. 28th Street
P.O. BOx 25352
Oklahoma City, OK 73125
405-521-2327

Oregon
Oregon Senior & Disabled Services
Division
500 Summer Street N.E., 2nd floor
Salem, OR 97310-1015
503-945-5811

Pennsylvania
Pennsylvania Department of Aging
555 Walnut Street, Fifth floor
Harrisburg, PA 17101-1919
717-783-6207

Pacific Islands-Agana
Guam Division of Senior Citizens
P.O. Box 2816
Agana, GU 96910
(011) 671-632-4141

Puerto Rico
Governor's Office for Elderly Affairs
Ponce De Leon Avenue #1603
U.M. Office C
Santurce, PR 00908
787-721-5710

Rhode Island
Rhode Island Dept. of Elderly Affairs
160 Pine Street
Providence, RI 02903-3708
401-222-2858

South Carolina
South Carolina Division on Aging
202 Arbor Lake Drive, Suite 301

PO Box 8206
Columbia, SC 29223
803-253-6177

South Dakota
South Dakota Office of Adult
Services and Aging
700 Governors Drive
Pierre, SD 57501
605-773-3656
Web: www.state.sd.us/asa

Tennessee
Tennessee Commission on Aging
500 Deaderick Street, 9th Floor
Nashville, TN 37243-0860
615-741-2056

Texas
Texas Department on Aging
1949 Interstate Highway 35 S.
P.O. Box 12786 Capitol Station
Austin, TX 78741-3702
512-424-6840
Web: www.state.tx.us/agency/
340.html

Utah
Utah Division of Aging and Adult
Services
120 North 200 West, Room 401
Box 45500
Salt Lake City, UT 84103
801-538-3910

Vermont
Vermont Dept. of Aging and
Disabilities
103 S. Main Street
Waterbury, VT 05671-2301
802-241-2400
Web: www.dad.state.vt.us

Virginia
Virginia Department For The Aging
1600 Forest Avenue, Suite 102
Richmond, VA 23229
804-662-9333

Washington
Washington Aging & Adult Services
Administration
P.O. Box 45050
Olympia, WA 98504-5050
360-586-3768

West Virginia
West Virginia Office of Aging
Holly Grove-Building 10,
1900 Kanawha Blvd. E.
Charleston, WV 25305-0160
304-558-3317

Wisconsin
Wisconsin Bureau of Aging
217 S. Hamilton Street, Suite 300
Madison, WI 53707
608-266-2536

Wyoming
Wyoming Department of Health,
Division on Aging
139 Hathaway Building
Cheyenne, WY 82002
307-777-7986

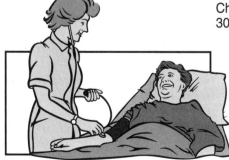

State Pharmaceutical Programs

Free Medication For Seniors

If you're a senior living on a fixed income in one of the following eleven states and you do not have Medicare or private insurance, you could be getting all of your prescription drugs free or for as little as a dollar or two. All you do is make a phone call to your state's office at the numbers listed. If you live in a state not listed here, check with your state's *Office Of The Aging* listed in a directory at the back of this book. Also check out the *Directory of Free Prescription Drugs Programs* that follows the listings below.

Connecticut

CONN PACE Program
PO Box 5011
Hartford, CT 06102
860-832-9265
800-423-5026 (in CT)
• State resident for at least 6 months
• Must be 65 or older or receive Social Security
• Income must not exceed $14,000 (single) or $17,000 (married)
• No Medicaid or private insurance that covers medications
You pay a one time fee of $25 to register. You pay $12 for each prescription and must use generic drugs wherever available unless your physician writes 'brand drug only'.

Delaware

IN WILMINGTON COUNTY
Nemours Health Clinic Program
1801 Rockland Road
Wilmington, DE 19803
302-651-4400   800-292-9538 (in DE only)

IN KENT OR SUFFEX COUNTIES
Nemours Health Clinic Program

915 N. Dupont Blvd.
Milford, DE 19963
302-424-5420   800-763-9326 (in DE only)
• For Delaware residents only
• Age 65 or older
• Can not earn more than 12,500 if single or $17,125 if married
This privately funded prgram covers four areas of health needs: dental, eye, hearing and medicines. In the Kent & Suffex office the coverage is for eye and hearing problems only.

Illinois

Pharmaceutical Assistance Program
PO Box 19021
Springfield, IL 62794
217-524-0435 800-624-2459 (IL only)
• Must be a resident of Illinois
• Must be 65or older or over 16 and totally disabled or a
   widow or widower who turned 63 before spouses death
• Income of $16,000 or less
• You must purchase a Pharmaceutical Assistance card that
   will cost you either $40 or $80 depending upon income.
• Your monthly deductible is $15 if you have a $40 card or $25
   with an $80 card.
• You must use a generic brand where available unless you
   are willing to pay the difference.
• Covers medications for your heart, blood pressure, diabetes
   or arthritis.
• Program pays 100% of the first $800 in medication each year
   and 80% of any costs that are over $800.

Maine

Elderly Low-Cost Drug Program
State House Station 24
Augusta, ME 04332
207-626-8475
• Must be a Maine resident
• Must be 62 or older or if disabled, 55 or older
• Your income must not exceed $10,600 (single) or $13,100
   (married)
• Drug will cost you $2.00 or 20% of the price allowed by the
   Department of Human Services whichever is greater.

Maryland

Maryland Pharmacy Assistance Program
PO Box 386
Baltimore, MD 21203
410-767-5397   800-492-1974
• Must be a Maryland resident
• Program is for anyone in the state who can not afford their medications. Call for income requirements.

Michigan

Michigan Emergency Pharmaceutial Program For Seniors (MEPPS)
PO Box 30676
Lansing, MI 48909
517-373-8230
• Must be a resident of Michigan
• You must be 65 or older
• You must earn no more than 150% of the federal poverty guidelines
• Must spend 10% or more of your monthly income on drugs
• Must use generic drugs unless your doctor specifies otherwise

Here are other programs you will want to check out if you are a Michigan resident.

Medicare and Medicaid Assistance Progam, call: 1-800-803-7174

Michigan Legal Hotline For Seniors, call: 1-800-347-5297

The Michigan Dental Association has a dental program for seniors. For information, call them toll-free at: 1-800-589-2632

New Jersey

Pharmaceutical Assistance to the Aged and Disabled (PAAD)
Special Benefit Programs
PO Box 715
Trenton, NJ 08625
609-588-7049   800-792-9745
• Must be New Jersey resident and purchase the medications in the state.
• Must be 65 or older; if on social Security disability you may be as young as 18
• Must earn no more than $17,918 if single or $21,870 is married

- Copay of $5 per prescription. PAAD will collect payments on your behalf from any insurance or other program you may have that covers prescription drugs.

New York

New York State Elderly Pharmaceutical Insurance Coverage (EPIC)
PO Box 15018
Albany, NY 12212
518-452-3773   800-332-3742
- Must be New York State resident
- Must be 65 or older
- Your income must not exceed $18,500 if single or $24,400 if married.
- You must not be eligible for Medicaid benefits
- There are two EPIC plans. You can qualify right away by paying an annual fee that will range from $20 to $75 depending upon your income. There is also the EPIC Deductible plan where you pay no fee but you pay full price for the medications until you spend the deductible amount of $468 to $638 depending upon your income.

Pennsylvania

Pennsylvania Pharmaceutical Assistance Contract For The
    Elderly
555 Walnut Street 5th Floor
Harrisburg, PA 17101
717-787-7313   800-225-7223
- Must be a state resident for at least 90 days and purchase the medications in the state.
- Must be 65 or older
- Your income can not exceed $16,000 if single or $17,200 if married
- There is also the PACE NET program that allows you to earn more and still qualify. With this program there is a $500 prescription deductible each year.
- You pay an $8.00 co-payment ($6.00 for generic drugs)

Rhode Island

Rhode Island Pharmaceutical Assistance To The Elderly (RIPAE)
Rhode Island Department of Elderly Affairs
160 Pine St
Providence, RI 02903
401-222-3330   800-322-2880 (in RI)

- You must be a Rhode Island resident
- Must be 65 or older
- Must have no other prescription drug doverage
- Your income must not exceed $15,358 is single or $19,199 if married
- You pay 40% copay for certain prescription drugs
- Program covers drugs needed for the following illnesses: high blood pressure; heart disease; cholesterol; asthma; cancer; Parkinson; glaucoma; diabetes; Alzheimers; and circulatory insufficiency

Vermont

VSCRIPT Program
State Pharmaceutical Assistance Program For Elderly & Disabled
103 S. Main St
Waterbury, VT 05671
802-241-2880   800-250-8427

- Must be a Vermont resident
- Must be 65 or older
- Your income can not exceed $12,084 if single or $16,284 if married.
- You may not be in a health insurance plan that pays all or part of your prescription drugs.
- You have a copay of $1 for drugs costing up to $30 and $2.00 for drugs costing over $30.

Directory Of Free Prescription Drugs Programs

It's a little known fact but the pharmaceutical industry has had a long tradition of providing prescription medicines free of charge to people who might not otherwise be able to afford to have medicines they need. This directory lists the drug companies with programs that provide prescription medicine for those people. The programs are listed alphabetically by company. Check with the individual manufacturer for the specific requirements to qualify for their free prescription drug program.

Common Questions

Q. I need medication but can not afford to pay for it. Why hasn't my doctor told me about these programs?

A. Believe it or not even many doctors themselves don't know about these programs until you mention it to them.

Q. What are the steps I should take if I need a medication and can't afford it?

A. First, find out from your doctor the name of the drug you need and the manufacturer. Next, go through this directory and find the listing for the manufacturer. If they list the medication you need as one that they offer free for needy patients, have your physician contact the company and request any forms needed to enroll you in their program. As a general rule, the application for free medication must be filled out and returned by your doctor.

Q. Who determines whether a medication is covered?

A. The individual pharmaceutical company determines which drugs are covered.

Q. Who is eligible for the program? How do you apply?

A. Once again each company makes the determination as to who is eligible for its program. Often they will rely on the doctor's opinion as to whether he/she feels you are needy enough to qualify for free medication.

Just because you don't see a drug company listed here doesn't mean they don't have a program that covers the medicine you need. For numbers of companies not listed here, ask your doctor to consult a Physician's Desk Reference (PDR) for the company's phone number.

Alza Pharmaceuticals

Contact:
Indigent Patient Assistance Program
c/o Comprehensive Reimbursement Consultants
8990 Springbrook Drive, Suite 200
Minneapolis, MN 55433
(800) 577-3788
Product(s) Covered By Program
Bicitra, Ditropan, Elmiron, Mycelex, Neutra-Phos, Neutra-Phos-K Ocusert, PolyCitra, PolyCitra-K, Progestasert, Testoderm
Other Information:
Eligibility if based on patient's income level and insurance status. Physician must request the application from Alza

Amgen, Inc.

NAME OF PROGRAM
Amgen SAFETY NET19 Program for EPOGEN®
Contact: (800) 272-9376
Product Covered By Program: EP0GEN®
Other Information:
The program for dialysis patients who are uninsured or underinsured and is based on patient's income level. Phone-in or written applications are acceptable.

NAME OF PROGRAM
Amgen SAFETY NET Program for INFERGEN®
Contact: (888) 508-8088
Products Covered By Program: INFERGEN19
Other Information:
This program is for patients with chronic hepatitis C only.
Eligibility is based on insurance status and income level of the patient.

NAME OF PROGRAM
Amgen SAFETY NET® Program for Neupogen®
Contact: (800) 272-9376
Product Covered By Program: Neopogen® (Filgrastim)
Other Information:
For medically indigent patients. To enroll a patient, provider should call 1-800-272-9376

Astra Merck, Inc.

Contact:
Astra Merck Patient Assistance Program
(800) 355-6044
Product(s) Covered By Program:
Lexxel™, Plendil®, Prilosec®, and Tionocard®
Other Information:
Health care provider must apply on behalf of the patient who has a medical need but who has a financial hardship that would prevent the patient from filling his/her prescription. Physician should contact Astra Merck's Patient Assistance Program. An application will be sent to the physician's office for their signature. Once approved, medication will be sent to physician's office in 2 to 4 weeks.

Astra U.S.A., Inc.

NAME OF PROGRAM
Foscavir@ Assistance and Information on Reimbursement (FA.I.R.)
Contact:
State and Federal Associates
1101 King Street

Alexandria, Virginia 22314
(800) 488-FAIR (3247)
(703) 683-2239 (fax)
Product Covered By Program: Foscavir® Injection
Other Information:
If the patient is not covered by private insurance or public
coverage and has an income below a level selected by the
company, medication will be provided. Patient does not have to
be poor but retail drug purchase would cause financial
hardship. Company determines eligibility based upon income
information provided by the physician.

Athena Neurosciences, Inc.

Contact:
Athena Indigent Patient Program
Athena Neurosciences, Inc.
800 Gateway Boulevard South
San Francisco, California 94080
Product(s) Covered By Program
Permax®, Zanaflex®, Diastat®
Other Information:
Patient must have a net worth of less than $30,000 and no
third party insurance coverage to qualify. Physician must
provide patient's financial information to the company along
with a request for the medication on his/her letterhead. Upon
approval, three month's supply of the medication will be sent
to physician's office

Bayer Corporation
Pharmaceutical Division

Contact:
Bayer Indigent Program
PO. Box 29209 Phoenix
Arizona 85038-9209
(800) 998-9180
Product(s) Covered By Program
Most Bayer pharmaceutical prescription medications used as
recommended in prescribing information
Other Information:
Patient must be a U.S. resident, not covered by insurance and
have an income below the federal poverty-level guidelines.

Physician must monitor medication usage throughout the therapy. Patient/physician can qualify over the phone with approval or denial given immediately.

Biogen, Inc.

Contact:
Avonexm Support Line
(800) 456-2255
Product Covered By Program: Avonex®
Other Information:
Eligiblity is based on patient's insurance status and income.

Boehringer Ingelheim Pharmaceuticals, Inc.

Contact::
Partners in Health
Boehringer Ingelheim Pharmaceuticals, Inc. (BIPI)
P.O. Box 368
Ridgefield, Connecticut 06877-0368
(800) 556-8317 (for information and form)
Product(s) Covered By Program
Alupent® MDI; Atrovent®; Catapres-TTS; Combivent®; Flomax®; Mexitil®, Serentil® for FDA approved indications only.
Other Information:
Patient must be a U.S. citizen who meets established financial criteria who is ineligible for prescription assistance from public or private sources. A maximum of 3 months supply of medication will be supplied per request.

Bristol-Myers Squibb Company

Contact:
Bristol-Myers Squibb
Patient Assistance Program
PO. Box 4500
Princeton, New Jersey 08543-4500
Mailcode P25-31
(800) 332-2056;
Fax: (609) 897-6859

Product(s) Covered By Program
Many Bristol-Myers Squibb pharmaceutical products
Other Information:
Medications will be supplied free of charge to patients with a
financial hardship and without prescription coverage from
other sources.

Ciba Pharmaceuticals

(See Novartis Pharmaceuticals)

Dupont Merck Pharmaceutical Company

Contact:
DuPont Merck Pharmaceutical Company
Patient Assistance Program
PO. Box 80723
Wilmington, Delaware 19880-0723
(800) 474-2762
Product(s) Covered By Program
All marketed non-controlled prescription products
Other Information:
Physician should request the application by calling the toll-
free number above. Patient must have a financial need and
have exhausted all third party insurance and other available
programs. Patient and physician must complete the
application which will be supplied by the company.

Eisai, Inc.

Contact:
The Aricept® Patient Assistance Program
(800) 226-2072
Product(s) Covered By Program: Aricept®
Other Information:
Eisai, Inc. and Pfizer, Inc. have developed this program for U.S.
residents with no insurance or other coverage and whose
income falls within predetermined guidelines. Patient must
have been diagnosed by the physician as having mild or
moderate dementa of the Alzheimer's type.

Fujisawa U.S.A., Inc.

NAME OF PROGRAM
NebuPent® Indigent Patient Program
Contact:
Fujisawa USA, Inc.
3 Parkway North Center
Deerfield, Illinois 60015-2548
(847) 317-8874, (847) 317-5941 (fax)
Product Covered By Program:: NebuPent®
This program is designed to provide NebuPent® to AIDS
patients who would not otherwise be able to afford this
treatment. All questions can be directed to:
Indigent Patient Coordinator at: (847) 317-8874 or (847) 317-8617

NAME OF PROGRAM
Prograf™ Patient Assistance Program
c/o Medical Technology Hotlines
PO. Box 7710
Washington, DC 20044-7710
(800) 4-PROGRAF
(800) 477-6472, or
(202) 393-5563 in the Washington, DC area
Product(s) Covered By Program:
Prograf™ capsules
Eligibility
Please call the **Prograf™ Reimbursement Hotline (800-4-PROGRAF)** for an application or for information about
eligibility. Once you describe the patient's insurance and
financial situation a member of the program staff can
determine whether patient is likely to quality.

Genentech, Inc.

Contact
Uninsured Patient Assistance Program
Genentech, Inc.
P. O. Box 2586
Mail Stop #13
S. San Francisco, CA 94083-2586
(800) 879-4747, (415) 225-1366 (fax)
Product(s) Covered By Program
Actimmune®, Activase®, Protropin®, Nutropin®, Nutropin

AQ™, Rituxan™
Other Information:
An application must be submitted with patient's medical,
financial and insurance information. To be eligible, patient
must have an annual income of less than $25,000 and must
not be eligible for public or private insurance reimbursement.
Medication will be sent to physician's office.

Genetics Institute, Inc.

NAME OF PROGRAM
The BENEFIX Reimbursement and Information Program
Contact: (888) 999-2349
Product(s) Covered By Program:
Benefix™ Coagulation Factor IX (recombinant)
Other Information:
This program is designed to provide temporary assistance to
patients who meet the financial and insurance criteria.
Patients must reapply every 90 days. Application forms must
be signed by the patient and physician prior to returning to
the program at:
1101 King Street, Suite 600
Alexandria, VA 22314.

NAME OF PROGRAM
The Neumega ® Access Program
(888)-NEUMEGA (638-6342)
Product Covered By Program: Neumega®
Other Information:
This program is for uninsured and underinsured patients with
limited financial resources.

Genzyme Corp.

NAME OF PROGRAM
Ceredase®/Cerezyme ® Access Program (CAP Program)
Contact:
Wytske Kingma, M.D.
Medical Affairs
Genzyme Corp.
One Kendall Square

Cambridge, MA 01239-1562
(800) 745-4447, ext. 7808
Product(s) Covered By Program
Ceredase®, Cerexyme®
Other Information:
Eligibility is based on financial and medical need. The patient
must be uninsured and lack the financial means to purchase
the drug. In order to maintain eligibility, patient is expected to
continue to explore alternative funding options with the
Genzyme Case Management Specialist.

Gilead Sciences, Inc.

Contact:
Gilead Sciences Support Services
1-800-Gilead 5 (445-3235)
or fax 1-713-760-0049
(9:00 a.m. to 5:30 p.m. EST)
Product Covered By Program:: VISTIDE ®, for the
treatment of cytomegalovirus (CMV) retinitis in patients with
AIDS
Other Information:
To determine eligibility, the patient or physician may request
a Patient Assistance Program application and mail or fax the
completed application to Gilead Sciences Support Services.

Glaxo Wellcome, Inc.

Contact:
Glaxo Wellcome Inc.
Patient Assistance Program
PO Box 52185
Phoenix, Arizona 85072-2185
(800) 722-9294
(800) 750-9832 (fax)
Additional information can be found at: www.Helix.com
Program materials may also be ordered by health
professionals through this website.
Product(s) Covered By Program:
All marketed Glaxo Wellcome prescription products
Other Information:
Glaxo Wellcome is dedicated to assuring that no one is denied
access to their prescription drugs as a result of their inability
to pay. This program is designed for financial disadvantaged

patients who do not qualify for or have drug benefits through private or government-funded programs. Income eligibility is based on multiples of the poverty level which is then adjusted for household size. The program is available only to patients treated in an outpatient setting.

Hoechst Marion Roussel, Inc.

Contact:
Indigent Patient Program
Hoechst Marion Roussel, Inc.
PO Box 9950
Kansas City, Missouri 64134-0950
(800) 221-4025
Product(s) Covered By Program:
All prescription products manufactured by Hoechst Marion Roussel, except Rifadin, Rifamate, Rifater, Tenuate
Other Information:
Eligibility is determined by the physician based on the patient's income level and lack of insurance. Physicians are encouraged to participate in the spirit of the program by also providing their services without charge.

NAME OF PROGRAM
Anzement Patient Assistance Program
c/o Comprehensive Reimbursement Consultants (CRC)
8990 Springbrook Drive, Suite 200
Minneapolis, Minnesota 55433
(888) 259-2219
Product(s) Covered By Program: Anzement

Janssen Pharmaceutica

Contact:
Janssen Patient Assistance Program
1800 Robert Fulton Drive
Reston, Virginia 22091-4346
(800) 544-2987
Product(s) Covered By Program:
Janssen's medical prescription products including Duragesic®, Ergamisol®, Hismanal®, Imodium®, Nizoral® Cream, Nizoral® Shampoo, Nizoral® Tablet, Propulsid®, Sporanox®, Vermox®

Other Information:
Medications will be provided free of charge to patients who lack the financial resources and third-party insurance necessary to obtain treatment. Janssen requests that physician not charge patients beyond insurance coverage for their professional services.

NAME OF PROGRAM
Janssen Cares
The Risperdal Patient Assistance Program
4828 Parkway Plaza Blvd., Suite 120
Charlotte, North Carolina 28217-1969
(800) 652-6227, Monday through Friday
(9:00 a.m. to 5:00 p.m. E.T.)
Fax: (704) 357-0036
Product(s) Covered By Program:
Risperda®
Other Program Information:
Reimbursement specialists will determine eligibility based upon medical criteria and financial resources. Janssen requests that physicians not charge patients beyond insurance coverage for professional services. The Risperdal Reimbursement Support Program is designed to answer physicians' and patients' questions and solve problems related to Risperdal reimbursement as efficiently and quickly as possible.

Knoll Pharmaceutical Company

Contact:
Knoll Indigent Patient Program
Knoll Pharmaceutical Company
3000 Continental Drive, North
Mount Olive, New Jersey 07828-1234
Attn: Telemarketing
Product(s) Covered By Program
Isoptin ® SR, Mavik, Rythmol®, Collagenase Santyl, Synthroid® Tablets, Tarka
Other Program Information:
Physician must submit documentation proving patient's indigence to the company. A maximum of three month's supply will be supplied on any one request.

Lederle Laboratories

NAME OF PROGRAM
Lederle PARTNERS IN PATIENT CARE™ Assistance
Program
(see Wyeth-Ayerst Laboratories Indigent Patient Program)

Eli Lilly And Company

Contact:
Lilly Cares Program Administrator
Eli Lilly and Company
P. O. Box 25768
Alexandria, Virginia 22313
(800) 545-6962
Product(s) Covered By Program:
Most Lilly prescription products and insulins (except
controlled substances) are covered by this program. Gemzar®
is covered under a separate program.
Other Program Information:
Patients must be U.S. residents. Eligibility is determined on a
case-by-case basis based upon patients inability to pay and
lack of third-party drug payment assistance. Medications will
be provided directly to the physician for dispensing to the
patient. Application forms will be provided to the physician to
complete and return. Subsequent requests requires another
prescription and restatement of medical and financial need.

NAME OF PROGRAM
Gemzar® Patient Assistance Program
Contact:
Gemzar ® Reimbursement Hotline
(888) 4-GEMZAR (888-443-6927)
Product Covered By Program: Gemzar®
Other Program Information:
Applications for the program are available by calling the
Gemzar Hotline. Applicants will be approved on the basis
their low income and of their not having medical insurance
and being ineligible for any programs with a drug benefit
including Medicare and Medicaid and third-party coverage.

The Liposome Company, Inc.

Contact:
Financial Assistance Program for ABELCET®
The Liposome Company, Inc.
One Research Way
Princeton, New Jersey 08540-6619
(800) 335-5476
Product Covered By Program: Abelcet®
Other Program Information:
Eligibility for this program is based upon the patient's
financial need and the lack of coverage for any third-party
reimbursement program. The company will determine
eligibility based upon medical and financial information
supplied by the hospital or physician.. Application forms must
be completed and signed by a physician.

Merck & Company, Inc.

Contact:
The Merck Patient Assistance Program
Health care professionals with prescribing privileges may call:
(800) 994-2111
Product(s) Covered By Program:
Most Merck products are covered. Requests for vaccines and
injectables are not accepted with the exception of requests for
anti-cancer injectable products.
Other Program Information:
The Merck Patient Assistance Program is designed to provide
temporary assistance to patients who truly are unable to
afford prescription medications and who have no access to any
insurance coverage. Eligibility is determined on a case-by-case
basis upon receipt of a completed application signed by both
the physician and the patient and accompanied by a
prescription. Once the application is approved a three month
supply of medication will be sent to the physician for
distribution to the patient.

NAME OF PROGRAM
SUPPORT™
Reimbursement Support and Patient
Assistance Services for Crixivan®
Contact: Health care professionals or patients may call (800)
850-3430
Product Covered By Program: Crixivan®

Novartis Pharmaceuticals

Contact:
Novartis Pharmaceuticals
Patient Assistance Program
P. O. Box 52052
Phoenix, Arizona 85072-9170
(800) 257-3273
Product(s) Covered By Program:
Certain single source and/or life-sustaining products.
Controlled substances are not included.
Other Program Information:
The Patient Assistance Program provides temporary
assistance to patients who are experiencing financial hardship
and who have no prescription drug insurance. Patient must
complete the application along with their physician and
return it for evaluation.

Ortho Biotech, Inc.

Contact:
The Ortho Biotech FAP™ Program
1800 Robert Fulton Drive, Suite 300
Reston, Virginia 20191-4346
(800) 553-3851
Product(s) Covered By Program:
Procrit® for non-dialysis use, Leustatin® Injection
Other Program Information:
A reimbursement specialist will determine eligibility for a
patient who meets specific medical criteria and who lack the
financial resources and third-party insurance necessary to
obtain treatment. Ortho Biotech requests that physicians not
charge FAP patients for professional services.

Ortho Dermatological

Contact:
Ortho-McNeil Patient Assistance Program
1800 Robert Fulton Drive, Suite 300
Reston, Virginia 20191-4346
(800) 797-7737
Product(s) Covered By Program:
Prescription products prescribed according to approved

labeled indications and dosage regimens.
Other Program Information:
To be eligible for this program patient should not be eligible
for other sources of drug coverage. They should also have
applied for and been denied for coverage under public sector
programs. Patient's income level should be below poverty level
and retail purchase would cause hardship. Health care
practitioner should request an application form.

Ortho-McNeil Pharmaceutical, Inc.

Contact:
Ortho-McNeil Patient Assistance Program
1800 Robert Fulton Drive, Suite 300
Reston, Virginia 20191-4346
(800) 797-7737
Product(s) Covered By Program:
Prescription products prescribed according to approved
labeled indications and dosage regimens.
Other Program Information:
The program is for indigent patients who lack other sources of
drug coverage including having applied for and been denied
assistance from public sector programs.

Parke-Davis

Division of Warner-Lambert Company
Contact:
The Parke-Davis Patient Assistance Program
P. O. Box 1058
Somerville, New Jersey 08876
(908) 725-1247
Product(s) Covered By Program:
Accupril, Cognex, Dilantin, Loestrin, Neurontin, Rezulin, and
Zarontin
Other Program Information:
The physician should request an application from their sales
representative. Patient must be deemed financially eligible
based on company guidelines and the physician's certification
and patient's lack of insurance coverage. Up to a three month
supply of medication will be supplied to the physician for
dispensing.

NAME OF PROGRAM
The Lipitor Patient Assistance Program
P. O. Box 1058
Somerville, New Jersey 08876
(908) 218-0120
Product Covered By Program: Lipitor
Other Program Information:
To be eligible for this program, the patient must not be eligible
for other sources of drug coverage and must be deemed
financially eligible based on company guidelines and physician
certification. Physician should request an application from
their Parke-Davis or Pfizer sales representative.

Pasteurmerieux Connaught

NAME OF PROGRAM
Indigent Patient Program
Contact:
Customer Account Management
Pasteur Merieux Connaught
Route 611, PO Box 187
Swiftwater, Pennsylvania 18370-0187
(800) 822-2463
Product(s) Covered By Program:
Imovax® Rabies, rabies vaccine; Imogam ® Rabies-HT, rabies
immune globulin (human); TheraCys ® BCG live intravesical
(Note: Imovax ® and Imogam® Rabies-HT are provided on a
post-exposure basis)
Other Program Information:
Patient must be identified as indigent, uninsured and
ineligible for Medicare or Medicaid. Physician must waive all
fees and certify that the product will not be sold, traded or
used for any other purpose than to treat the patient. Physician
needs to specify the quantity of Imogam® Rabies need for
patient (in mL) as well as the number of doses of Imovax®
Rabies needed.

Pfizer, Inc.

Contact:
Pfizer Prescription Assistance
PO Box 25457
Alexandria, Virginia 22313-5457

(800) 646-4455
Product(s) Covered By Program:
Most Pfizer outpatient products with chronic indications are covered by this program. Diflucan® and Zithromax® are covered by a separate program.
Other Program Information:
Any patient that a physician is treating as indigent is eligible. Patients must have incomes below $12,000 (single) or $15,000 (family). Patient must not be eligible for third-party or Medicaid reimbursement for medications. No copayment or cost-sharing is required by the patient.
Specific forms are not required. The physician must write on his/her letterhead to Pfizer stating that the patient meets the income criteria and is uninsured for prescription drugs. A prescription for the needed medication must also be enclosed. It may take up to 4 weeks to receive the product.

NAME OF PROGRAM
Diflucan® and Zithromax® Patient Assistance Program
(800) 869-9979
Product(s) Covered By Program:
Difucan® and Zithromax®
Other Program Information:
Patient must not have insurance or other third-party coverage including Medicaid and must not be eligible for a state's AIDS drug assistance program. Patient must have an income of less than $25,000 a year without dependents or less than $40,000 a year with dependents.
Physician should call the Program and explain the patient's situation to the Patient Assistance Specialist. The specialist will then send a short qualifying form that requests insurance status, income information and the amount of Diflucan® or Zithromax® the patient will need. Upon receipt of the completed form, the specialist will make the determination of eligibility the same day it is received.

NAME OF PROGRAM
Sharing the Care
Pfizer Inc.
235 E. 42nd Street
New York, New York 10017-5755
(800) 984-1500
Product(s) Covered By Program:
Certain Pfizer single-source products

Eligibility
The program, a joint effort of Pfizer, the National Governors' Association, and the National Association of Community Health Centers, works solely through community, migrant, and homeless health centers that are funded under Section 330 of the Public Health Service Act and that have an in-house pharmacy. The program includes the participation of more than 340 health centers throughout the United States. To be eligible to participate in Sharing the Care, the patient must be registered at a participating health center, must not be covered by any private insurance or public assistance covering pharmaceuticals, must not be Medicaid-enrolled, and must have a family income that is equal to or below the federal poverty level.

NAME OF PROGRAM
Aricept® Patient Assistance Program
(See Eisai Inc.)

NAME OF PROGRAM
Lipitor Patient Assistance Program
(Please see Parke-Davis)

NAME OF PROGRAM
A Participant in the Arkansas Health Care Access Program
Contact:
Program Director
Arkansas Health Care Access Foundation
P. O. Box 56248
Little Rock, Arkansas 72215
(800) 950-8233, (501) 221-3033
Product(s) Covered By Program:
Most Pfizer prescription products are covered
Other Program Information:
Must be an Arkansas resident to qualify. Eligible individuals are certified by the Arkansas Local County Department of Human Services as being Arkansas residents below the poverty level who do not have third-party insurance overage for medications. No co-payments is required. Physician must waive his/her fee for the initial visit. This program does not apply to individuals during hospital inpatient stays.

NAME OF PROGRAM
A Participant in the Kentucky Health Care Access Program
Contact:
Program Director
Kentucky Health Care Access Foundation
12700 Shelbyville Road, Suite 1000
Louisville, Kentucky 40243
(800) 633-8100, (502) 244-4214
(502) 244-4209 (fax)
Product(s) Covered By Program
Most Pfizer prescription products are covered
Other Program Information:
Must be a Kentucky resident to qualify. Patient must be
certified by the Kentucky Cabinet for Human Resources as
Kentuckians below the federal poverty standards without
third-party health insurance coverage. No copayment is
required from the patient.

NAME OF PROGRAM
A Participant in Commun-I-Care
Contact:
Ms. Parker Sparrow, Director
Commun-I-Care
PO Box 12054
Columbia, South Carolina 29211
(800) 763-0059, (803) 779-4875
(803) 254-0320 (fax)
Product(s) Covered By Program
Most Pfizer prescription products are covered
Other Program Information:
Eligible individuals must be South Carolina residents.
Patients are first certified by Commun-I-Care as below the
federal poverty line and not covered by any government
entitlement programs. No copayment is required from the
patient. Physician must waive his/her fee.

Pharmacia & Upjohn, Inc.

Contact:
Rx MAP Prescription Medication Assistance Program
P. O. Box 29043
Phoenix, Arizona 85038
(800) 242-7014

Product(s) Covered By Program:
Numerous products
Other Program Information:
Eligibility is based on federal poverty level and no prescription drug coverage. All inquiries should be go to RxMAP at 1-800-242-7014.

Proctor & Gamble Pharmaceuticals, Inc.

Contact:
Proctor & Gamble Pharmaceuticals, Inc.
P. O. Box 231
Norwich, New York 13815
Attn: Customer Service Department
(800) 448-4878
Product(s) Covered By Program:
Alora, Asacol, Dantrium Capsules, Didronel, Helidac, Macrodantin, Macrobid
Other Program Information:
The company relies on the physician's assessment of need to determine need. To qualify, patients should not have insurance coverage for prescription medicines or Medicaid reimbursement. The program is intended for patients who fall below the federal poverty level and have no other means of health care coverage.
The amount of product supplied depends on the diagnosis and need but generally one month's supply is provided for chronic medication. Refills require a new prescription and application form from the physician. Medication is sent to the physician who provides it to the patient.

Rhone-Poulen Rorer, Inc.

Contact:
Medical Affairs/Patient Assistance Program
Rhone - Poulenc Rorer Inc.
P. O. Box 5094, 500 Arcola Road
Mailstop #4C29
Collegeville, Pennsylvania 19426-0998
(610) 454-8110, (610) 454-2102 (fax)
Product(s) Covered By Program:
All products are included, with some limitations
Other Program Information:
A patient is eligible for this program if there is a medical and

financial need for assistance as identified by the physician, social agent or agency and if the effort to obtain assistance from all third-parties has been exhausted. Application forms are obtained from the company and completed by the physician and sent to the company along with a prescription. Medication will be sent to the physician for dispensing.

Roche Laboratories, Inc.

A Division of Hoffmann-La Roche Inc.
Contact:
Roche Medical Needs Program
Roche Laboratories, Inc.
340 Kingsland Street
Nutley, New Jersey 07110
(800) 285-4484
Product(s) Covered By Program:
Roche product line with some exceptions
Other Program Information:
This program is designed for patients who are unable to afford to purchase the medication and who have no third-party medication coverage. It is for individual outpatients and is offered through physicians. It is not intended for clinics, hospitals or other institutions.
Applications are provided only to licensed practitioners and a new application must be completed for refills. Up to a 3 month supply of the medication will be supplied directly to the physician within two to three weeks of acceptance to the program.

NAME OF PROGRAM
Roche Medical Needs Program for CellCept®, Cytovene®, and Cytovene® -IV
Contact:
Roche Transplant Reimbursement Hotline
(800) 772-5790
Product(s) Covered By Program:
CellCept® , Cytovene®; Cytovene ®-IV; Cytovene products for use with transplant patients

NAME OF PROGRAM
Roche Medical Needs Program for Fortovase™; Invirase®;

Cytovene®; Cytovene®-IV, and HIVID®
Contact:
Roche HIV Therapy Assistance Program
(800) 282-7780
Product(s) Covered By Program
Fortovase™; Invirase®; Cytovene®
Cytovene ® -IV, and HIVID®; Cytovene products for use with
HIV/AIDS patients

NAME OF PROGRAM
Roche Medical Needs Program for Roferon® -A, Vesanoid®,
and Fluorouracil Injection
Contact:
Oncoline™/Hepline™ Reimbursement Hotline
(800) 443-6676 (press 2 or 3)
Product(s) Covered By Program
Roferon® -A, Vesanoid®, and Fluorouracil Injection

Roxane Laboratories, Inc.

Contact:
Nexus Healthcare Patient Assistance Program
4161 Arlingate Plaza
Columbus, Ohio 43228
(800) 274-8651
Product(s) Covered By Program:
Duraclon; Marinol®; Oramorph SR® Tablets; Roxanol™ ;
Roxicodone Tablets; Roxicodone Intensol™; Viramune®
Other Program Information:
Medication will be provided free of charge through the
patient's pharmacist, provided the patient is uninsured and
meets annual income requirements.
The physician should call the toll-free number to discuss their
patient's eligibility with a program representative.

Sandoz Pharmaceuticals Corporation

(See Novartis Pharmaceuticals).

Sanofi Pharmaceuticals

Contact:
Sanofi Pharmaceuticals
Needy Patient Program
c/o Product Information Department
90 Park Avenue
New York, New York 10016
(800) 446-6267
Product(s) Covered By Program
Aralen®, Breonesin®, Danocrine®, Drisdol®, Hytakerol®,
Mytelase®, NegGram®, pHisoHex® , Plaquenil® ,
Primaquine®, Skelid® Photofrin®, Primacor®.
Other Program Information:
Eligibility determined on financial need on a case-by-case
basis. Physician can obtain an application from the Sanofi
Pharmaceuticals Product Information Department. Once the
application is approved by the company, a three month supply
of the medication will be sent directly to the physician in
roughly four to six weeks. Each physician is allowed to enroll
six patients per year.

Schering Laboratories/Key Pharmaceuticals

NAME OF PROGRAM
Commitment to Care
Contact:
For Intron A/Eulexin call: (800) 521-7157
For Other Products:
Schering Laboratories/Key Pharmaceuticals
Patient Assistance Program
PO Box 52122
Phoenix, Arizona 85072
(800) 656-9485
Product(s) Covered By Program:
Most Schering/Key prescription drugs
Other Program Information:
This program is designed to help patients who are truly in
need - who are not eligible for private or public insurance
reimbursement and cannot afford treatment.
Physician and patient complete an application form which will
be reviewed on a case-by-case basis.

Searle

Contact:
Administrator
Searle Patients in Need® Foundation
5200 Old Orchard Road
Skokie, Illinois 60077
(800) 542-2526
Fax: (1-847) 470-6633
or Local Searle Sales Representative
Product(s) Covered By Program:
Antihypertensives: Aldactazide®, Aldactone®, Calan® SR
sustained-release, Kerl one® Antihypertensive/Anti-Anginal/
Antiarrhythmic: Calan®, Covera-HS™
Antiarrhythmics: Norpace®, Norpace® CR extended-release
Prevention of NSAID-induced gastric ulcers: Cytotec®
Other Program Information:
The physician is the sole determinant of a patient's eligibility
for this program based on the patient's medical and financial
need. Searle provides guidelines for physicians to consider but
they are not requirements. Searle does not review
documentation for eligibility.
The guidelines suggest that: patient has a medical need for
the Searle Patients In Need® medication; does not qualify for
third-party medication coverage and that the patient's income
falls below a level suggested by Searle.
Once approved Searle will send the physician certificates for
free medications. The physician gives the certificate to the
patient who takes the prescription and certificate to a
pharmacy of their choosing. The pharmacy supplies the
medication free of charge and is then reimbursed by Searle.

Serono Laboratories, Inc.

NAME OF PROGRAM
Patient Assistance Programs
Contact:
Executive Director, Corporate Communications
Serono Laboratories, Inc.
100 Longwater Circle
Norwell, Massachusetts 02061
(617) 982-9000, (617) 982-1369 (fax)
Product(s) Covered By Program:

Saizen® for injection for treatment of pediatric growth
hormone deficiency
Serostim™ for treatment of AIDS

NAME OF PROGRAM
Serono Laboratories' Helping Hands Program
Contact:
Helping Hands Program
Serono Laboratories, Inc.
100 Longwater Circle
Norwell, Massachusetts 02061
(617) 982-9000 ext. 5522,
(617) 982-1369 (fax)
Product(s) Covered By Program:
Fertinex™, Gonal-F for treatment of infertility

Sigma-Tau Pharmaceuticals, Inc.

NAME OF PROGRAM
NORD/Sigma-Tau Carnitor®
Drug Assistance (CDA) Program
c/o NORD
P. O. Box 8923
New Fairfield, Connecticut 06812-8923
(800) 999-NORD
Product(s) Covered By Program:
Carnitor®
Other Program Information:
Usually a patient over the age of 18 may submit his/her own
application. If the patient is a minor his/her parent or
guardian must submit the application.
To be eligible, patient must be a resident of U.S. with a legal
prescription for Carnitor®. They must show that they have
financial need above and beyond any third-party insurance or
family resources.

SmithKline Beecham
Pharmaceuticals

Contact:
SB Access to Care Program
SmithKline Beecham

One Franklin Plaza-FP1320
Philadelphia, Pennsylvania 19101
(800) 546-0420
Product(s) Covered By Program:
Most SmithKline Beecham outpatient prescription products
are covered. Controlled substances and vaccines are not.
Kytril, Hycamtin and Paxil are covered under separate Access
to Care programs. (See listings below.)
Other Program Information:
To be eligible, patient's annual household income must be less
than $25,000. They must not have medical insurance or
coverage under any private of government program that
covers prescriptions. Physician must submit the application on
an original (not photocopied) SB Access To Care form supplied
by the company. The physician and patient must certify that
the program guidelines are being observed. Medication will be
sent to the physician for dispensing.

NAME OF PROGRAM
The Oncology Access to Care Hotline
(800) 699-3806
Product(s) Covered By Program: Kytril and Hycamtin

NAME OF PROGRAM
Access to Care Paxil Certificate Program
Contact: (800) 729-4544
Product(s) Covered By Program: Paxil®

Solvay Pharmaceuticals, Inc.
NAME OF PROGRAM
Patient Assistance Program
Solvay Pharmaceuticals, Inc.
c/o Phoenix Marketing Group
One Phoenix Drive
Lincoln Park, New Jersey 07035
(800) 788-9277
Product(s) Covered By Program:
Creon® 5, 10 or 20 Minimicrospheres™ Delayed-Release
Capsules; Dexone™ tablets; Estrata B®; Estratest® &
Estratest® HS Tablets; Lithobid® Slow- Release Tablets;
Lithonate®; Lithotabs®; Luvox® Tablets; Orasone™ Tablets;
Amantadine HCl Capsules; Advanced Formula Zenate®
Prenatal Multivitamin/ Mineral Supplement Tablets.
Other Program Information:

The patient's eligibility is determined in consultation with the physician and is based on the patient's inability to pay, lack of insurance and ineligibility for Medicaid. The physician is encouraged to waive their fee.

The physician must apply on behalf of the patient by submitting completing a request form obtained by call Solvay's Patient Assistance Program Message Center at 1-800-788-9277.

3M Pharmaceuticals

NAME OF PROGRAM
Indigent Patient Pharmaceutical Program
Contact:
Medical Services Department
275-2E-13, 3M Center
PO Box 33275
St. Paul, Minnesota 55133-3275
(800) 328-0255, (612) 733-6068 (fax)
Product(s) Covered By Program:
Most drug products sold by 3M Pharmaceuticals in the U.S.
Other Program Information:
Patients whose financial and insurance circumstances prevent them from obtaining 3M Pharmaceuticals drug products considered necessary by their physicians. Consideration is on a case-by-case basis

.

Wyeth-Ayerst Laboratories

Contact:
The Norplant Foundation
P. O. Box 25223
Alexandria, VA 22314
(703) 706-5933
Product Covered By Program: The Norplant® five-year contraceptive system
Eligibility
Determined on a case-by-case basis and limited to individuals who cannot afford the product and who are ineligible for coverage under private and public sector programs .
Other Program Information:
Eligibility is on a case-by-case basis and is limited to individuals who cannot afford the product and who are ineligible for coverage under private and public sector programs.

NAME OF PROGRAM
Wyeth-Ayerst Laboratories Indigent Patient Program
555 E. Lancaster Avenue
St. Davids, Pennsylvania 19087
Product(s) Covered By Program:
Various products (not including schedule II, III, or IV
products)
Eligibility
Limited to individuals, on a case-by-case basis, who have been
identified by their physicians as "indigent," meaning: low or no
income or not covered by any third-party agency
Other Program Information:
A three-month supply of specific products is provided directly to
the physician for dispensing to the patient. The patient's
signature is required on the application form.

Zeneca Pharmaceuticals

Contact:
Patient Assistance Program
Zeneca Pharmaceuticals Foundation
P. O. Box 15197
Wilmington, Delaware 19850-5197
(800) 424-3727
Product(s) Covered By Program:
Accolate®; Arimidex®; Casodex®; Kadian™; Noladex®;
Seroque®; Sorbitrate®; Sular™; Tenoretic®; Tenormin®;
Zestri®; Zestoretic®; Zolandex®; Zomig™
Other Program Information:
Eligibility is determined by the Foundation based on income
level/assets and absence of outpatient private insurance,
third-party coverage or participation in a public program.
Application forms may be obtained from Zeneca
Pharmaceuticals Foundation at the toll-free phone number
above.

Free Legal Services

Free Legal Help

If you have a legal problem and can't afford to pay a small fortune for an attorney, you can now get free legal assistance thanks to funding from the U.S. Government. To help you get the kind of legal help you need but can not afford, Congress has given close to 300 million dollars to The Legal Services Corporation. They in turn provide funds for 262 local Legal Services offices throughout the U.S. to give you legal assistance. The funding is used to help over 4 million low-income individuals in civil cases. To find out about the free Legal Services in your area check the listings below or contact Legal Services Corporation directly.

LEGAL SERVICES CORPORATION
750 FIRST ST., N.E.
WASHINGTON, DC 20002
(202) 336-8800

You can also get the information you need about local Legal Services programs in your area by visiting their Internet site at:
www.lsc.gov

In addition to the legal services funded by the federal government, there are hundreds of what are called 'pro bono' (in other words ... 'free') programs which are staffed by attorneys who volunteer their time and services to insure that you get the legal representation you deserve. The following is a listing of these programs. Simply call the program closest to your home for legal assistance.

Alabama
Alabama State Bar Volunteer Lawyers Program
415 Dexter Ave.
Montgomery, AL 36105
Phone: 334-269-1515

Legal Services Corporation of Alabama
500 Bell Building
207 Montgomery St.
Montgomery, AL 36104-3534
(334) 264-1471

Legal Services of North-Central Alabama
2000-C Vernon St.
P.O. Box 2465
Huntsville, AL 35804-2465
(205) 536-9645

Legal Services of Metro Birmingham
1820 Seventh Ave., North
P.O. Box 11765
Birmingham, AL 35202-1765
(205) 328-3540

Alaska
Alaska Legal Services Corporation
1016 West Sixth Ave., Suite 200
Anchorage, AK 99501-6206
(907) 276-6282

Alaska Pro Bono Program
1016 W. 6th Ave.
Suite 200
Anchorage, AK 99501
Phone: 901-272-9431

Arizona
Pinal & Gila Counties Legal Aid Society
343 West Central Ave.
Coolidge, AZ 85228
(520) 723-5326

Community Legal Services
305 South Second Ave.
P.O. Box 21538
Phoenix, AZ 85036-1538
(602) 258-3434 x 230

Papago Legal Services
Main St. & Education St.
P.O. Box 246
Sells, AZ 85634-0246
(520) 383-2420

Southern Arizona Legal Aid
64 East Broadway Boulevard
Tucson, AZ 85701-1720
(520) 623-9465

DNA-People's Legal Services
Route 12, Highway 264
P.O. Box 306
Window Rock, AZ 86515-0306
(520) 871-4151

Affordable Housing Law Program
Arizona Commnunity Service Legal Assistance
111 W. Monroe, Ste. 1800
Phoenix, AZ 85003
Phone: 602-340-7372

Disability Claim Service
Disability Advocacy Project
1314 N. 3rd St., Suite 116
Phoenix, AZ 85004-1749
Phone: 602-256-9673

Arkansas
Arkansas Volunteer Lawyers for the Elderly
2020 W. 3rd St., Suite 620
Little Rock, AR 72201
Phone: 501-376-9263

Ozark Legal Services
26 East Center St.
Fayetteville, AR 72701
(501) 442-0600

Legal Services of Northeast Arkansas
202 Walnut St.
Newport, AR 72112
(870) 523-9892

Western Arkansas Legal Services
100 North Sixth St., Suite 107
Fort Smith, AR 72901-2197
(501) 785-5211

East Arkansas Legal Services
500 East Broadway
P.O. Box 1149
West Memphis, AR 72303-1149
(870) 732-6370

Center for Arkansas Legal Services
209 West Capitol Ave., Suite 36
Little Rock, AR 72201-3678
(501) 376-3423

California
California Indian Legal Services
510 16th St., Suite 301
Oakland, CA 94612-1500
(510) 835-0284

Greater Bakersfield Legal Assistance
615 California Ave.
Bakersfield, CA 93304
(805) 325-5943

Central California Legal Services
2014 Tulare St., Suite 600
Fresno, CA 93721
(209) 441-1611

Legal Aid Foundation of Long Beach
Security Pacific Bank Building
110 Pine Ave., Suite 420
Long Beach, CA 90802-4421
(562) 435-3501

Legal Aid Foundation of Los Angeles
1102 South Crenshaw Boulevard
Los Angeles, CA 90019
(213) 801-7990

Legal Aid Society of Alameda County
510 16th St., Suite 560
Oakland, CA 94612
(510) 451-9261

Channel Counties Legal Services Association
132 South A St.
P.O. Box 1228
Oxnard, CA 93032-1228
(805) 487-6531

San Fernando Valley Neighborhood Legal Services
13327 Van Nuys Boulevard
Pacoima, CA 91331-3099
(818) 834-7509

Legal Services Program for Pasadena and San Gabriel-Pomona Valley
243 East Mission Boulevard
Pomona, CA 91766
(909) 620-5547

Legal Aid Society of San Mateo County
298 Fuller St.
Redwood City, CA 94063
(415) 365-8411

Contra Costa Legal Services Foundation
1017 MacDonald Ave.
P.O. Box 2289
Richmond, CA 94802-2289
(510) 233-9954

Inland Counties Legal Services
1120 Palmyrita Ave., Suite 210
Riverside, CA 92507
(909) 683-5841 x429

Legal Services of Northern California Inc.
517 12th St.
Sacramento, CA 95814
(916) 551-2150

Legal Aid Society of San Diego
110 South Euclid Ave.
San Diego, CA 92114
(619) 262-5557 x320

California Rural Legal Assistance
631 Howard St., Suite 300
San Francisco, CA 94105-3907
(415) 777-2752

San Francisco Neighborhood Legal Assistance Foundation
225 Bush St., 7th Floor
San Francisco, CA 94104
(415) 982-1300

Legal Aid of Marin
30 North San Pedro Rd., Suite 245
San Rafael, CA 94903
(415) 492-0230

Community Legal Services
2 West Santa Clara St., 8th Floor
P.O. Box 1840
San José, CA 95109-1840
(408) 283-3844

Legal Aid Society of Orange County
902 North Main St.
Santa Ana, CA 92701
(714) 571-5233

Legal Aid Society of the Central Coast
21 Carr St.
Watsonville, CA 95076
(408) 724-2253

Redwood Legal Assistance
123 Third St.
P.O. Box 1017
Eureka, CA 95502
(707) 445-0866

The State Bar of California
Office of Legal Services
555 Franklin St.
San Francisco, CA 94102

Disability Rights Education and Defense Fund
2212 Sixth St.
Berkeley, CA 94710
Phone: 510-644-2555

Colorado

Pikes Peak/Arkansas River Legal Aid
617 South Nevada Ave.
Colorado Springs, CO 80903-4089
(719) 471-0380

Colorado Rural Legal Services
655 Broadway, Suite 450
Denver, CO 80203
(303) 534-5702

Legal Aid Society of Metropolitan Denver
1905 Sherman St., Suite 400
Denver, CO 80203-1181
(303) 866-9399

Colorado Bar Association Pro Bono Project
1900 Grant St., 9th Floor
Denver, CO 80203
Phone: 303-860-1115

Connecticut

Statewide Legal Services of Connecticut
425 Main St.
Middletown, CT 06457
Phone: 860-344-8096 ext. 3003

Connecticut Bar Association Law
Works for People
101 Corporate Place
Rocky Hill, CT 06067-1894
Phone: 800-722-8811

AIDS Legal Network for Connecticut (ALN)
80 Jefferson St.
Hartford, CT 06106
Phone: 860-541-5000

Delaware
Legal Services Corporation of Delaware
100 West 10th St., Suite 203
Wilmington, DE 19801
(302) 575-0408

Delaware Volunteer Legal Services
Widener University School of Law,
Concord Pike
P.O. Box 7306
Wilmington, DE 19803
Phone: 302-478-8680

District of Columbia
Neighborhood Legal Services Program of the District of Columbia
701 Fourth St., N.W.
Washington, DC 20001
(202) 682-2720

American Association of Retired Persons
601 E St., N.W.
Building A, 4th Floor
Washington, DC 20049
Phone: 202-434-2120

Archdiocesan Legal Network
Catholic Charities of Washington, D.C.
1221 Massachusetts Ave., N.W.
Washington, DC 20005
Phone: 202-628-4265

Asylum & Refugee Rights Law Project
of Washington Lawyers' Committee for Civil Rights
1300 19th St., NW, Suite 500
Washington, DC 20005
Phone: 202-835-0031

DC Bar Public Services Activities Corporation
1250 H St., NW
Sixth Floor
Washington, DC 20005-3908
Phone: 202-737-4700 ext. 290

Florida
Central Florida Legal Services
128-A Orange Ave.
Daytona Beach, FL 32114-4310
(904) 255-6573

Legal Aid Society of Broward County
609 S.W. Firth Ave.
Fort Lauderdale, FL 33301
(954) 764-8957 x223

Florida Rural Legal Services
963 East Memorial Boulevard
P.O. Box 24688
Lakeland, FL 33802-4688
(941) 688-7376

Jacksonville Area Legal Aid
126 West Adams St.
Jacksonville, FL 32202-3849
(904) 356-8371

Legal Services of Greater Miami
3000 Biscayne Boulevard
Miami, FL 33137
(305) 576-0080 x501

Legal Services of North Florida
2119 Delta Boulevard
Tallahassee, FL 32303-4209
(904) 385-9007

Greater Orlando Area Legal Services
1036 West Amelia St.
Orlando, FL 32805
(407) 841-7777

Bay Area Legal Services
Riverbrook Professional Center, 2nd Floor
829 West Dr. Martin Luther King Jr. Boulevard
Tampa, FL 33603
(813) 232-1222 x137

Withlacoochee Area Legal Services
20 South Magnolia Ave.
Ocala, FL 32671-2037
(352) 629-0105

Three Rivers Legal Services
111 Southwest First St.
Gainesville, FL 32601
(352) 372-0519

Northwest Florida Legal Services
24 West Government St., Suite 205
P.O. Box 1551
Pensacola, FL 32597-1551
(850) 432-1750

Gulfcoast Legal Services
641 First St. South
St. Petersburg, FL 33701-5003
(813) 821-0726

Florida Association for Community Action
901 Northwest 8th Ave.
Suite A-2
Gainesville, FL 32601
Phone: 352-378-6517

Georgia
Atlanta Legal Aid Society
151 Spring St., N.W.
Atlanta, GA 30303-2097
(404) 614-3990

Georgia Legal Services Program
1100 Spring St., Suite 200-A
Atlanta, GA 30309-2848
(404) 206-5175

Guam
Guam Legal Services Corporation
113 Bradley Place
Agana, GU 96910
011-671-477-9811

The Pro Bono Project of the State Bar of Georgia
The Hurt Building
50 Hurt Plaza
Atlanta, GA 30303
Phone: 404-527-8762

Hawaii
Native Hawaiian Legal Corporation
1164 Bishop St., Suite 1205
Honolulu, HI 96813-2826
(808) 521-2302

Legal Aid Society of Hawaii
1108 Nuuanu Ave.
P.O. Box 37375
Honolulu, HI 96837-0375
(808) 536-4302

Hawaii Lawyers Care
1040 Richards St.
Suite 301
Honolulu, HI 96813
Phone: 808-528-7046

Idaho
Idaho Legal Aid Services
Contract Program
310 North Fifth St.
P.O. Box 913
Boise, ID 83701
Phone: 208-336-8980

Idaho Volunteer Lawyers Program
P.O. Box 895
Boise, ID 83701-0895
Phone: 208-334-4510

Illinois

Cook County Legal Assistance Foundation
1146 Westgate, Suite LL3
Oak Park, IL 60301-1055
(708) 524-2600

Legal Assistance Foundation of Chicago
111 West Jackson Boulevard, 3rd Floor
Chicago, IL 60604-3502
(312) 341-1070

Land of Lincoln Legal Assistance Foundation
2420 Bloomer Drive
Alton, IL 62002-4809
(618) 462-0036 x13

975 North Main St.
Rockford, IL 61103-7064
(815) 965-2134

West Central Illinois Legal Assistance
1614 East Knox St.
P.O. Box 1232
Galesburgh, IL 61402-1232
(309) 343-2141

Illinois Pro Bono Center
C-U Depot
116 N. Chestnut, Suite 220
Champaign, IL 61820
Phone: 217-359-6811

Lawyers for the Creative Arts
213 W. Institute Place
Suite 411
Chicago, IL 60610-3125
Phone: 312-944-2787

Indiana

Legal Services of Maumee Valley
203 West Wayne St., Suite 410
Fort Wayne, IN 46802
(219) 422-8070

Legal Services of Northwest Indiana
504 North Broadway, Suite 301
Gary, IN 46402-1921
(219) 886-3161

Legal Services Organization of Indiana
Market Square Center, Suite 1640
151 North Delaware St.
Indianapolis, IN 46204-2517
(317) 631-9410

Legal Services Program of Northern Indiana
105 East Jefferson Boulevard, Suite 600
South Bend, IN 46601-1915
(219) 234-8121

Iowa

Legal Services Corporation of Iowa
1111 Ninth St., Suite 230
Des Moines, IA 50314-2527
(515) 243-2151

Legal Aid Society of Polk County
Human Service Campus
1111 Ninth St., Suite 380
Des Moines, IA 50314-2527
(515) 282-8375

Iowa State Bar Association
Volunteer Lawyers Project
521 E. Locust
Suite 302
Des Moines, IA 50309
Phone: 515-244-8617

Kansas
Kansas Bar Foundation
1200 Harrison
Topeka, KS 66612
Phone: 913-234-5696

Kentucky
Access to Justice Foundation
209 E. High St.
Lexington, KY 40508
Phone: 606-255-9913

Louisiana
Louisiana Bar Association
Access to Justice Foundation
601 St. Charles Ave.
New Orleans, LA 70130
Phone: 504-566-1600

Eighth Coast Guard District Legal Office
Room 1311 Hale Boggs Federal Building
501 Magazine St.
New Orleans, LA 70130
Phone: 504-589-6188

Maine
Maine Volunteer Lawyers Project
66 Federal St.
Portland, ME 04101
Phone: 207-828-2300

Maryland
Advocates for Children & Youth
School House Legal Services
34 Market Place, Suite 500
Baltimore, MD 21202
Phone: 410-547-9200

Massachusetts
American Civil Liberties Union of Massachusetts
99 Chauncy St.
Boston, MA 02111
Phone: 617-482-3170

Michigan
Legal Services of Southeastern Michigan
420 North Fourth Ave.
Ann Arbor, MI 48104-1197
(734) 665-6181

Legal Services Organization of Southcentral Michigan
70 East Michigan Ave., 2nd Floor
Battle Creek, MI 49017
(616) 965-3951

Wayne County Neighborhood Legal Services
3400 Cadillac Tower Building, Ste 1
Detroit, MI 48226
(313) 962-0466

Legal Services of Eastern Michigan
547 South Saginaw St.
Flint, MI 48502
(810) 234-2621

Legal Aid of Central Michigan
300 North Washington Square, Suite 311
Lansing, MI 48933-1223
(517) 485-5418 x235

Lakeshore Legal Services
Robert A. Verkuilen Building
21885 Dunham Road, Suite 4
Clinton Township, MI 48036
(810) 469-5185

Oakland Livingston Legal Aid
35 West Huron St., 5th Floor
Pontiac, MI 48342-2125
(248) 456-8888

Berrien County Legal Services Bureau
901 Port St.
P.O. Box E
St. Joseph, MI 49085-0904
(616) 983-6363

Legal Services of Northern Michigan
446 East Mitchell St.
Petoskey, MI 49770
(616) 347-8115

Legal Aid of Western Michigan
Cornerstone Building, Suite 400
89 Ionia Ave., N.W.
Grand Rapids, MI 49503
(616) 774-0672

Legal Aid Bureau of Southwestern Michigan
308 Kalamazoo County Administration Building
201 West Kalamazoo Ave.
Kalamazoo, MI 49007-3777

Michigan Indian Legal Services
160 East State St., Suite 102
Traverse City, MI 49684-2572
(616) 947-0122

State Bar of Michigan
Access to Justice
306 Townsend St.
Lansing, MI 48933-2083
Phone: 517-372-9030 ext. 6317

Micronesia
Micronesian Legal Services Corporation
P.O. Box 269
Saipan, MP 96950-0269
011-670-234-6471

Minnesota
Legal Aid Service of Northeastern Minnesota
302 Ordean Building
424 West Superior St.
Duluth, MN 55802
(218) 726-4800

Judicare of Anoka County
1201 89th Ave., N.E., Suite 310
Blaine, MN 55434
(612) 783-4970

Central Minnesota Legal Services
430 First Ave. North, Suite 359
Minneapolis, MN 55401-1780
(612) 332-8151

Legal Services of Northwest Minnesota Corporation
403 Center Ave., Suite 403
P.O. Box 714
Moorhead, MN 56561-0714
(218) 233-8585

Southern Minnesota Regional Legal Services
700 Minnesota Building
46 East Fourth St.
St. Paul, MN 55101-1112
(612) 228-9823

Anishinabe Legal Services
411 First St., N.W.
P.O. Box 157
Cass Lake, MN 56633-0157
(218) 335-2223

Minnesota Volunteer Attorney Program
Minnesota State Bar Association
Minnesota Law Center
514 Nicollet Mall, Suite 300
Minneapolis, MN 55402
Phone: 612-673-6331

Mississippi
Central Mississippi Legal Services
414 South State St., 3rd Floor
P.O. Box 951
Jackson, MS 39205-0951
(601) 948-6752

North Mississippi Rural Legal Services
2134 West Jackson Ave.
P.O. Box 767
Oxford, MS 38655-0767
(601) 234-8731

South Mississippi Legal Services Corporation
202 Fountain Square Building
P.O. Box 1386
Biloxi, MS 39533-1386
(228) 374-4160

East Mississippi Legal Services Corporation
2305 Fifth St., 2nd Floor
P.O. Box 1931
Meridian, MS 39302
(601) 693-5470

Southeast Mississippi Legal Services Corporation
111 East Front St.
P.O. Drawer 1728
Hattiesburg, MS 39403-1728
(601) 545-2950

Southwest Mississippi Legal Services Corporation
221 Main St.
P.O. Box 1242
McComb, MS 39649-1242
(601) 684-0578

Mississippi Volunteer Lawyers Project
P.O. Box 2168
Jackson, MS 39225-2168
Phone: 601-948-4476

Missouri
Southwest Missouri Legal Services
116 North Main St.
P.O. Box 349
Charleston, MO 63834-0309
(573) 683-3783

Meramec Area Legal Aid Corporation
1412 Highway 72 East
P.O. Box 135
Rolla, MO 65401-0135
(573) 341-3655

Legal Aid of Western Missouri
Lathrop Building
1005 Grand Ave., Suite 600
Kansas City, MO 64106-2216
(816) 474-6750

Legal Services of Eastern Missouri
4232 Forest Park Ave.
St. Louis, MO 63108
(314) 534-4200

Mid-Missouri Legal Services Corporation
205 East Forest Ave.
Columbia, MO 65201
(573) 442-0116

Legal Aid of Southwest Missouri
Woodruff Building
333 Park Central East, Suite 426
Springfield, MO 65806-2227
(417) 862-1100

Paralegal Farm Project
P.O. Box 1086
St. Joseph, MO 64502-1086
Phone: 816-364-2325

Montana
Montana Legal Services Association
801 North Last Chance Gulch
Helena, MT 59601
(406) 442-9830

State Bar of Montana Pro Bono Project
2442 1st Ave. No.
Billings, MT 59101
Phone: 406-252-6351

Nebraska
Legal Services of Southeast Nebraska
Terminal Building, Suite 825
941 O St.
Lincoln, NE 68508
(402) 435-2161

Legal Aid Society
500 South 18th St., 3rd Floor
Omaha, NE 68102-2588
(402) 348-1060

Western Nebraska Legal Services
1423 First Ave.
P.O. Box 1365
Scottsbluff, NE 69363-1365
(308) 632-4734

Nebraska State Bar Association
Volunteer Lawyers Project
635 S. 14th St., Ste. 200
Lincoln, NE 68501
Phone: 402-475-7091

Nevada
Nevada Legal Services
701 East Bridger Ave., Suite 101
Las Vegas, NV 89101
(702) 386-1070

New Hampshire
New Hampshire Legal Services
33 North Main St., 2nd Floor
P.O. Box 4147
Concord, NH 03302-4147
(603) 224-5723

The Pro Bono Referral of the New Hampshire Bar Association
112 Pleasant St.
Concord, NH 03301
Phone: 603-224-6942

New Jersey
Cape-Atlantic Legal Services
One So. South Carolina Ave.
Atlantic City, NJ 08401
(609) 348-4200

Warren County Legal Services
91 Front St.
P.O. Box 65
Belvidere, NJ 07823-0065
(908) 475-2010

Camden Regional Legal Services
745 Market St.
Camden, NJ 08102-1117
(609) 964-2010 x233

Union County Legal Services Corporation
60 Prince St.
Elizabeth, NJ 07208
(908) 354-4340

Hunterdon County Legal Service Corporation
82 Park Ave.
Flemington, NJ 08822-1170
(908) 782-7979

Bergen County Legal Services
47 Essex St.
Hackensack, NJ 07601
(201) 487-2166

Hudson County Legal Services Corporation
574 Newark Ave.
Jersey City, NJ 07306-2377
(201) 792-6363

Essex-Newark Legal Services Project
106 Halsey St.
Newark, NJ 07102
(973) 624-4500

Middlesex County Legal Services Corporation
78 New St., 3rd Floor
New Brunswick, NJ 08901-2584
(732) 249-7600

Passaic County Legal Aid Society
175 Market St., 4th Floor
Paterson, NJ 07505
(973) 345-7171

Somerset-Sussex Legal Services Corporation
78 Grove St.
Somerville, NJ 08876
(908) 231-0840

Ocean-Monmouth Legal Services
9 Robbins St., Suite 2A
Toms River, NJ 08753
(732) 341-2727

Legal Aid Society of Mercer County
16-18 West Lafayette St.
Trenton, NJ 08608-2088
(609) 695-6249

Legal Aid Society of Morris County
30 Schuyler Place, 2nd Floor
P.O. Box 900
Morristown, NJ 07963-0900
(973) 285-6911

New Mexico
Legal Aid Society of Albuquerque
Springer Square Building
121 Tijeras Ave., N.E., Suite 3100
Albuquerque, NM 87102
(505) 243-7871

Southern New Mexico Legal Services
300 North Downtown Mall
Las Cruces, NM 88001-1216
(505) 541-4800

Northern New Mexico Legal Services
805 Early St., Building F
P.O. Box 5175
Santa Fe, NM 87502-5175
(505) 982-2504

Indian Pueblo Legal Services
7 Eagle Road, Santa Ana Pueblo
P.O. Box 817
Bernalillo, NM 87004-0817
(505) 867-3391

Lawyers Care Pro Bono Project
State Bar of New Mexico
Special Projects
5121 Masthead NE

Albuquerque, NM 87109
Phone: 505-797-1640

New York
Legal Aid Society of Northeastern New York
55 Columbia St.
Albany, NY 12207
(518) 462-1672 x304

Legal Aid for Broome and Chenango
30 Fayette St.
P.O. Box 2011
Binghamton, NY 13902-2011
(607) 723-7966

Neighborhood Legal Services
Ellicott Square Building, Room 495
295 Main St.
Buffalo, NY 14203-2473
(716) 847-0650

Chautauqua County Legal Services
7 West Third St., 2nd Floor
Jamestown, NY 14701-5103
(716) 483-2116

Chemung County Neighborhood Legal Services
318 Madison Ave.
Elmire, NY 14901-2889
(607) 734-1647

Nassau/Suffolk Law Services Committee
One Helen Keller Way, 5th Floor
Hempstead, NY 11550
(516) 292-8100

Legal Aid Society of Rockland County
2 Congers Road
New City, NY 10956-0314
(914) 634-3627

Legal Services for New York City
350 Broadway, 6th Floor
New York, NY 10013-9998
(212) 431-7200

Niagara County Legal Aid Society
775 Third St.
P.O. Box 844
Niagara Falls, NY 14302-0844
(716) 284-8831

Monroe County Legal Assistance Corporation
80 St. Paul St., Suite 700
Rochester, NY 14604-1350
(716) 325-2520

Legal Services of Central New York
472 South Salina St., Suite 300
Syracuse, NY 13202
(315) 475-3127

Legal Aid Society of Mid-New York
255 Genesee St., 2nd Floor
Utica, NY 13501-3405
(315) 732-2131

Westchester/Putnam Legal Services
4 Cromwell Place
White Plains, NY 10601
(914) 949-1305

North County Legal Services
100 Court St.
P.O. Box 989
Plattsburgh, NY 12901-0989
(518) 563-4022

Southern Tier Legal Services
104 East Steuben St.
Bath, NY 14810
(607) 776-4126

Asian American Legal Defense and Education Fund (AALDEF)
99 Hudson St., 12th Floor
New York, NY 10013
Phone: 212-966-5932

Covenant House
Legal Services Office
460 West 41st St., Suite 715
New York, NY 10036

American Civil Liberties Union
125 Broad St., 18th Fl.
New York, NY 10036
Phone: 212-549-2500

Department of Pro Bono Affairs
One Elk St.
Albany, NY 12207
Phone: 518-487-5641

The Door's Legal Services Center
121 6th Ave.
New York, NY 10013
Phone: 212-941-9090 ext. 233

Prisoners' Legal Services of New York
105 Chambers St.
New York, NY 10007
Phone: 212-513-7373

**United States Court of Appeals for the
Second Circuit Pro Bono Panel**
United States Courthouse
40 Centre St.
New York, NY 10007
Phone: 212-857-8800

Volunteer Lawyers for the Arts
1 E. 53rd St., 6th Flr.
New York, NY 10022
Phone: 212-319-2787

North Carolina
Legal Services of North Carolina
224 South Dawson St.
P.O. Box 26087
Raleigh, NC 27611-6087
(919) 856-2564

Legal Services of Southern Piedmont
1431 Elizabeth Ave.
Charlotte, NC 28204
(704) 376-1600

North Central Legal Assistance Program
301 West Main St., 5th Floor
P.O. Box 2101
Durham, NC 27702-2101
(919) 688-6396

Legal Aid Society of Northwest North Carolina
Patten Building
216 West Fourth St.
Winston-Salem, NC 27101-2824
(336) 725-9166

North Carolina Bar Foundation
Pro Bono Project
8000 Weston Parkway
Cary, NC 27513
Phone: 919-677-0561

Land Loss Prevention Project
P.O. Box 179
Durham, NC 27702
Phone: 919-682-5969

North Dakota
Legal Assistance of North Dakota
1025 Third St. North
P.O. Box 1893
Bismarck, ND 58502-1893
(701) 222-2110

North Dakota Legal Services
Main St.
P.O. Box 217
New Town, ND 58763-0217
(701) 627-4719

North Dakota State Bar Association LRS
515 1/2 E. Broadway, Suite 101
Bismarck, ND 58501
Phone: 701/255-1404

Ohio
Western Region Legal Services
265 South Main St., 3rd Floor
Akron, OH 44308-1223
(330) 535-4191

Stark County Legal Aid Society
306 Market Ave. North, Suite 730
Canton, OH 44702-1423

Legal Aid Society of Cincinnati
901 Elm St.
Cincinnati, OH 45202-1016
(513) 241-9400

The Legal Aid Society of Cleveland
1223 West Sixth St., 4th Floor
Cleveland, OH 44113-1301
(216) 687-1900

The Legal Aid Society of Columbus
40 West Gay St.
Columbus, OH 43215-2896
(614) 224-8374

Ohio State Legal Services
861 North High St.
Columbus, OH 43215-1427
(614) 299-2114

Legal Aid Society of Dayton
33 West First St., Suite 500
Dayton, OH 45402-3031
(937) 228-8088

Legal Aid Society of Lorain County
382 West Broad St.
Elyria, OH 44035
(440) 323-8240

Butler-Warren Legal Assistance Association
Society Bank Building, Suite 501
6 South Second St.
Hamilton, OH 45011-2808
(513) 894-7664

Allen County-Blackhoof Area Legal Services Association
311 Building, Suite 307
311 East Market St.
Lima, OH 45801-4565
(419) 224-9070

Advocates for Basic Legal Equality
Spitzer Building
520 Madison Ave., Suite 740
Toledo, OH 43604-1305
(419) 255-0814

The Toledo Legal Aid Society
One Stranahan Square, Suite 342
Toledo, OH 43604-1459
(419) 244-8345

Wooster-Wayne Legal Aid Society
121 West North St.
Suite 100
Wooster, OH 44691
(330) 264-9454

Northeast Ohio Legal Services
Metropolitan Tower, 7th Floor
11 Federal Plaza Central
Youngstown, OH 44503-1589
(330) 744-3196

Rural Legal Aid Society of West Central Ohio
31 East High St.
Springfield, OH 45502-1234
(937) 325-2809

Ohio Legal Assistance Foundation
42 East Gay St.
Suite 900
Columbus, OH 43215-2914
Phone: 614-752-8919

Oklahoma
Oklahoma Indian Legal Services
Founders Tower, Suite 610
5900 Mosteller Drive

Oklahoma City, OK 73112
(415) 840-5255

Legal Services of Eastern Oklahoma
115 West Third St., Suite 701
P.O. Box 8110
Tulsa, OK 74101-8110
(918) 584-3211

Legal Aid of Western Oklahoma
2901 Classen Blvd., Suite 112
110 Cameron Building
Oklahoma City, OK 73106
Phone: 405-521-1302

Oregon
Oregon Legal Services Corporation
700 S.W. Taylor St., Suite 310
Portland, OR 97205
(503) 224-4094

Lane County Legal Aid Service
376 East 11th Ave.
Eugene, OR 97401-3246
(541) 342-6056

Multnomah County Legal Aid Service
United Carriage Building
700 S.W. Taylor St., Suite 300
Portland, OR 97205
(503) 224-4086

Marion-Polk Legal Aid Service
1655 State St.
Salem, OR 97301-4258
(503) 581-5265

Oregon State Bar Foundation
Referral and Information Services
6200 SW Meadows Road
Lake Oswego, OR 97035
Phone: 503-620-0222, x323

Pennsylvania
Philadelphia Legal Assistance Center
1424 Chestnut Street, 2nd Floor
Philadelphia, PA 19102
(215) 981-3800

Legal Services
432 South Washington St.
Gettysburg, PA 17325
(717) 334-7623

Delaware County Legal Assistance Association
410 Welsh St.
Chester, PA 19013
(610) 874-8421

Bucks County Legal Aid Society
1290 New Rodgers Road
Box 809
Bristol, PA 19007
(215) 781-1111

Laurel Legal Services
306 South Pennsylvania Ave.
Greensburg, PA 15601-3066
(724) 836-2211

Southern Alleghenys Legal Aid
Suite 400, Franklin Center
225-227 Franklin St.
Johnstown, PA 15901-2524
(814) 536-8917

Central Pennsylvania Legal Services
213 North Front St., 3rd Floor
Harrisburg, PA 17101-1406
(717) 236-8932

Neighborhood Legal Services Association
928 Penn Ave.
Pittsburgh, PA 15222-3799
(412) 644-7450

Northern Pennsylvania Legal Services
12th Floor - SNB Plaza

108 North Washington Ave.
Scranton, PA 18503
(717) 342-0184

Keystone Legal Services
2054 East College Ave.
State College, PA 16801-7201
(814) 234-6231

Southwestern Pennsylvania Legal Aid Society
16 West Cherry Ave.
Washington, PA 15301
(724) 225-6170

Legal Aid of Chester County
112 West Gay St.
West Chester, PA 19380-2914
(610) 436-9150

Legal Services of Northeastern Pennsylvania,
Bicentennial Building, Suite 410
15 Public Square
Wilkes-Barre, PA 18701-1797
(717) 825-8567

Susqeuhanna Legal Services
329 Market St.
Williamsport, PA 17701-6306
(717) 323-8741

Northwestern Legal Services
Renaissance Centre, Suite 1200
1001 State St.
Erie, PA 16501-1833
(814) 452-6949

Lehigh Valley Legal Services
65 East Elizabeth Ave., Suite 903
Bethlehem, PA 18018
(610) 317-8757

Montgomery County Legal Aid Service
317 Swede St.
Norristown, PA 19401-4801
(610) 275-5400

Pennsylvania Bar Association
100 South St.

Harrisburg, PA 17108
Phone: 717-238-6807

Puerto Rico
Community Law Office
P.O. Box 8389
Fernández Juncos Station
San Juan, PR 00910
(787) 751-1600

Puerto Rico Legal Services
Ave. Ponce de Leon Num. 1859
Stop 26 Box 9134
Santurce, PR 00907-9134
(787) 728-9561

Rhode Island
Rhode Island Legal Services
56 Pine St., 4th Floor
Providence, RI 02903
(401) 274-2652

Legal Information & Referral Service for the Elderly Pro Bono Program
115 Cedar St.
Providence, RI 02903
Phone: 401-421-7758

South Carolina
Neighborhood Legal Assistance Program
438 King St.
Charleston, SC 29403-6283
(803) 722-0107

Palmetto Legal Services
2109 Bull St.
P.O. Box 2267
Columbia, SC 29202-2267
(803) 799-9668

Carolina Regional Legal Aid Services Corporation
279 West Evans St.
P.O. Box 479
Florence, SC 29503-0479
(803) 667-1896

Legal Services Agency of Western Carolina
1 Pendleton St.
Greenville, SC 29601
(864) 467-3248

Piedmont Legal Services
148 East Main St.
Spartanburg, SC 29306
(864) 582-0369

South Carolina Bar Pro Bono Program
P.O. Box 608
950 Taylor St.
Columbia, SC 29202-0608
Phone: 803-799-4015

South Dakota
Black Hills Legal Services
621 Sixth St., Suite 205
P.O. Box 1500
Rapid City, SD 57709-1500
(605) 342-7171

East River Legal Services
335 North Main Ave., Suite 300
Sioux Falls, SD 57102-0305
(605) 336-9230

Dakota Plains Legal Services
160 Second St.
P.O. Box 727
Mission, SD 57555-0727
(605) 856-4444

Southeast Tennessee Legal Services
414 McCallie Ave.
Chattanooga, TN 37402
(423) 756-4013

Legal Services of Upper East Tennessee
311 West Walnut St.
P.O. Drawer 360
Johnson City, TN 37605-0360
(423) 928-8311

Knoxville Legal Aid Society
502 South Gay St., Suite 404
Knoxville, TN 37902-1502
(423) 637-0484

Memphis Area Legal Services
Claridge House, 2nd Floor
109 North Main St.
Memphis, TN 38103-5013
(901) 523-8822

Legal Aid Society of Middle Tennessee
211 Union St., Suite 800
Nashville, TN 37201-1504
(615) 780-7123

Rural Legal Services of Tennessee
226 Broadway, Jackson Square
P.O. Box 5209
Oak Ridge, TN 37831-5209
(423) 483-8454

West Tennessee Legal Services
210 West Main St.
P.O. Box 2066
Jackson, TN 38302-2066
(901) 423-0616

Legal Services of South Central Tennessee
104 West Seventh St.
P.O. Box 1256
Columbia, TN 38402-1256
(931) 381-5533

Texas
Legal Aid of Central Texas
205 West Ninth St., Suite 200
Austin, TX 78701-2306
(512) 476-7244

Coastal Bend Legal Services
Pueblo Building
102 Pueblo St.
Corpus Christi, TX 78405
(512) 883-3667 x143

Legal Services of North Texas
1515 Main St.
Dallas, TX 75201-4803
(214) 748-1234

El Paso Legal Assistance Society
1220 North Stanton
El Paso, TX 79902
(915) 544-3022

West Texas Legal Services
600 East Weatherford St.
Fort Worth, TX 76102
(817) 877-0609

Gulf Coast Legal Foundation
1415 Fannin Ave., 3rd Floor
Houston, TX 77002
(713) 652-0077

Bexar County Legal Aid Association
434 South Main Ave., Suite 300
San Antonio, TX 78204
(210) 227-0111

Heart of Texas Legal Services Corporation
900 Austin Ave., 7th Floor
P.O. Box 527
Waco, TX 76703
(254) 756-7944

Texas Rural Legal Aid
259 South Texas Boulevard
Weslaco, TX 78596
(956) 968-6574

East Texas Legal Services
414 East Pillar St.
P.O. Box 631070
Nacogdoches, TX 75963-1070
(409) 560-1850

AIDS Legal Resource Project
Texas Human Rights Foundation
P.O. Box 1626
Austin, TX 78767
Phone: 512-479-8473

Next Lawfirm Pro Bono Project
140 E. Tyler St., Suite 150
Longview, TX 75601
Phone: 903-758-9123

Pro BAR
301 E. Madison Ave.
Harlingen, TX 78550-4907
Phone: 210-425-9231

Women's Advocacy Project
P.O. Box 833
Austin, TX 78767-0833
Phone: 512-476-5377

Utah
Utah Legal Aid Services
254 West 400 South, 2nd Floor
Salt Lake City, UT 84101
(801) 328-8891

Utah State Bar Association
Pro Bono Project
645 South 200 East
Salt Lake City, UT 84111
Phone: 801-531-9077

Vermont
Vermont Volunteer Lawyer's Project
Legal Services Law Line of Vermont
264 North Winooski Ave.
Burlington, VT 05401
Phone: 802-863-7153

Virgin Island
Legal Services of the Virgin Islands
3017 Orange Grove
Christiansted
St. Croix, VI 00820-4375
(340) 773-2626

Virginia
Legal Services of Northern Virginia
6400 Arlington Boulevard, Ste 630

Falls Church, VA 22042
(703) 534-4343

Rappahannock Legal Services
910 Princess Anne St., Suite 216
Fredericksburg, VA 22401
(540) 371-1105

Southwest Virginia Legal Aid Society
227 West Cherry St.
Marion, VA 24354
(540) 783-6576

Peninsula Legal Aid Center
2013 Cunningham Drive, Suite 336
P.O. Box 7502
Hampton, VA 23666
(757) 827-5078

Central Virginia Legal Aid Society
101 West Broad St., Suite 101
P.O. Box 12206
Richmond, VA 23241-2206
(804) 648-1012

Legal Aid Society of New River Valley
155 Arrowhead Trail
Christianburg, VA 24073
(540) 382-6157

Legal Aid Society of Roanoke Valley
416 Campbell Ave., S.W.
Roanoke, VA 24016-3627
(540) 344-2088

Tidewater Legal Aid Society
125 St. Paul's Boulevard, Suite 400
Norfolk, VA 23510
(757) 627-5423

Virginia Legal Aid Society
513 Church St.
P.O. Box 6058
Lynchburg, VA 24505-6058
(804) 528-4722

Southside Virginia Legal Services
10A Bollingbrook St.
Petersburg, VA 23803-4549

(804) 862-1100

Blue Ridge Legal Services
204 North High St.
P.O. Box 551
Harrisonburg, VA 22801-0551
(540) 433-1830

Client Centered Legal Services of Southwest Virginia
County Road 811 off Alternative Route 58
Castlewood, VA 24224-0147
(540) 762-5501

Piedmont Legal Services
416 East Main St., Suite 201
Charlottesville, VA 22902
(804) 296-8851

Virginia State Bar
Eighth & Main Building
707 E. Main St., Ste. 1500
Richmond, VA 23219
Phone: 804-775-0522

Washington
Northwest Justice Project
401 Second Ave. South, Suite 407
Seattle, WA 98104
(206) 464-1519

Washington State Bar Pro Bono Program
2101 Fourth Ave., 4th Flr.
Seattle, WA 98121-2330
Phone: 206-727-8282

West Virginia
West Virginia Legal Services Plan
922 Quarrier St., Suite 550
Charleston, WV 25301

Appalachian Research & Defense Fund
Private Bar Involvement Project
922 Quarrier St., Suite 500
Charleston, WV 25301
Phone: 304-344-9687

Pro Bono Referral Project
Legal Aid Society of Charlestown
922 Quarrier St., Suite 400
Charlestown, WV 25301
Phone: 304-343-4481
(304) 343-3013 x28

Wisconsin
Legal Action of Wisconsin
230 West Wells St., Room 800
Milwaukee, WI 53203-1866
(414) 278-7777

Wisconsin Judicare
300 Third St., Suite 210
P.O. Box 6100
Wausau, WI 54402-6100
(715) 842-1681

Legal Services of Northeastern Wisconsin
417 Pine St.
Green Bay, WI 54301-5101
(920) 432-4645

Western Wisconsin Legal Services
202 North Main
P.O. Box 101
Dodgeville, WI 53533-0101
(608) 935-2741

State Bar of Wisconsin
Delivery of Legal Services Program
402 W. Wilson St.
Madison, WI 53703
Phone: 608-250-6177

Wyoming
Wind River Legal Services
Highway 287
P.O. Box 247
Ft. Washakie, WY 82514-0247
(307) 332-6626

Nationwide Directory Of Consumer Protection Offices

Check Out A Company Before Doing Business With Them

It is always smart before doing business with any company you have questions about to check with your local Better Business Bureau. They will be able to tell you whether other consumers have reported any problems they have had with this company.

Usually you can find the address and phone number of the Bureau nearest you in your local phone book but some of the Better Business Bureaus are serviced by bureaus in adjoining states. To locate the bureau nearest you, you can also check with the U.S. National Headquarters listed below or use the zip code search or state directory at: **http://www.bbb.org/bureaus/index.html.**

UNITED STATES-NATIONAL HEADQUARTERS
Council of Better Business Bureaus
4200 WILSON BLVD., SUITE 800
ARLINGTON, VA 22203
703-276-0100
http://www.bbb.org

Don't Be The Victim Of Consumer Fraud

As a general rule, once it's clear that you are not going to get satisfaction directly from the company you are having a dispute with, the first place to call for help with a consumer problem is your local consumer protection office. It is their job to protect you, the consumer against unfair and illegal business practices.

Listed here are consumer protection offices throughout the country. If you have a complaint, check this directory for your state, city or county and call the office nearest you.

If you are having a problem with a business outside your state, however, contact the consumer office in the state in which you made the purchase.

When you call the consumer protection or Attorney General's office, simply ask to be connected to the person in charge of consumer complaints.

Alabama
Consumer Protection / 800-392-5658

Alaska
The Consumer Protection Section in the Office of the Attorney General has been closed. Consumers with complaints are being referred to the Better Business Bureaus in Anchorage and Fairbanks, small claims court, and private attorneys.

Arizona-State Offices
Phoenix Consumer Protection / 800-352-8431
Tucson Consumer Protection / 602-628-6504

Arizona-County Offices
Apache County / 602-337-4364
Cochise County / 602-432-9377
Coconino County / 602-779-6518
Gila County / 602-425-3231
Graham County / 602-428-3620
Greenlee County / 602-865-3842
La Paz County / 602-669-6118
Mohave County / 602-753-0719
Navajo County / 602-524-6161
Pima County / 602-740-5733
Pinal County / 602-868-5801
Santa Cruz County / 602-281-4966
Yavapai County / 602-771-3344
Yuma County / 602-329-2270

Arizona-City Office
Tucson Consumer Affairs / 602-791-4886

Arkansas-State Office
Consumer Protection / 501-682-2341

California-State Offices
California Consumer Affairs / 916-445-1254 (consumer information)
Attorney General's Office / 916-322-3360
California Bureau of Automotive Repair / 916-366-5100

California-County Offices
Alameda County / 415-530-8682
Contra Costa County / 415-646-4500
Fresno County / 209-488-3156
Kern County / 805-861-2421
Los Angeles County / 213-974-1452
Marin County / 415-499-6190
Consumer Protection / 415-499-6450
Mendocino County District / 707-463-4211
Monterey County / 408-755-5073
Napa County / 707-253-4059
Orange County / 714-541-7600
Orange County / 714-541-7600
Riverside County / 714-275-5400
Sacramento County / 916-440-6174
San Diego / 619-531-3507 (fraud complaint line)
San Francisco County / 415-552-6400 (public inquiries)
415-553-1814 (complaints)
San Joaquin County / 209-468-2419
San Luis Obispo County / 805-549-5800
San Mateo County / 415-363-4656
Santa Barbara County /805-568-2300
Santa Clara County / 408-299-7400
Santa Clara County / 408-299-4211
Santa Cruz County /408-425-2054
Solano County / 707-421-6860
Stanislaus County / 209-571-5550
Ventura County / 805-654-3110
Yolo County / 916-666-8424

California-City Offices
Los Angeles / 213-485-4515
Santa Monica / 213-458-8336

Colorado-State Offices
Consumer Protection Unit / 303-620-4500
Consumer and Food Specialist / 303-239-4114

Colorado-County Offices
Archuleta, LaPlata, and San Juan Counties / 303-247-8850
Boulder County / 303-441-3700
Denver County / 303-640-3555 (inquiries) / 303-640-3557 (complaints)
El Paso and Teller Counties / 719-520-6002
Pueblo County / 719-546-6030
Weld County / 303-356-4000 ext. 4735

Connecticut-State Offices
Department of Consumer Protection / 203-566-4999 / 800-538-2277 (CT only)
Antitrust/Consumer Protection / 203-566-5374 / 800-538-2277 (CT only)

Connecticut-City Office
Middletown / 203-344-3492

Delaware-State Offices
Division of Consumer Affairs / 800-443-2179
Office of Attorney General / 800-736-4000

District of Columbia
Consumer Affairs / 202-727-7000

Florida-State Offices
Division of Consumer Services / 904-488-2226 / 800-327-3382 (FL only)
Consumer Litigation Section / 904-488-9105
Office of the Attorney General / 305-985-4780

Florida-County Offices
Broward County / 305-357-6030
Metropolitan Dade County Consumer Protection / 305-375-4222
Dade County / 305-324-3030
Hillsborough County / 813-272-6750
Orange County / 407-836-2490
Palm Beach County / 407-355-3560
Palm Beach County / 407-355-2670
Pasco County / 813-847-8110
Pinellas County / 813-530-6200
Seminole County / 407-322-7534
Titusville Consumer Fraud Unit / 407-264-5230

Florida-City Offices
City of Jacksonville / 904-630-3667
Lauderhill / 305-321-2450
Tamarac / 305-722-5900

Georgia-State Office
Governors Office of Consumer Affairs / 404-651-8600 / 800-869-1123 (toll-free in GA only)

Hawaii-State Offices
Office of Consumer Protection / 808-586-2630
Hilo Office of Consumer Protection / 808-933-4433
Lihue Office of Consumer Protection / 808-241-3365
Honolulu Office of Consumer Protection / 808-586-2630

Idaho-State Office
Consumer Protection Unit / 208-334-2424 / 800-432-3545 (ID only)

Illinois-State Offices
Governors Office of Citizens Assistance / 217-782-0244 / 800-252-8666 (IL only)
Chicago Consumer Protection / 312-814-3580
Springfield Consumer Protection / 217-782-9011 / 800-252-8666 (IL only)
Chicago Department of Citizen Rights / 312-814-3289

Illinois-Regional Offices
Carbondale Regional Office / 618-457-3505
Champaign Regional Office / 217-333-7691 (voice/TDD)
East St. Louis Regional Office / 618-398-1006
Granite City Regional Office / 618-877-0404
Kankakee Regional Office / 815-935-8500
LaSalle Regional Office / 815-224-4861
Mount Vernon Regional Office / 618-242-8200 (voice/TDD)
Peoria Regional Office / 309-671-3191
Quincy Regional Office / 217-223-2221 (voice/TDD)
Rockford Regional Office / 815-987-7580
Rock Island Regional Office / 309-793-0950
Waukegan Regional Office / 708-336-2207
West Frankfort Regional Office / 618-937-6453
West Chicago Regional Office / 708-653-5060 (voice/TDD)

Illinois-County Offices
Cook County / 312-443-4600
Madison County / 618-692-6280
Rock Island County / 309-786-4451, ext. 229

Illinois-City Offices
Wheeling Township / 708-259-7730 (Wed. only)
Chicago Department of Consumer Services / 312-744-4090
Des Plaines Consumer Protection / 708-391-5363

Indiana-State Office
Consumer Protection / 317-232-6330 / 800-382-5516 (IN only)

Indiana-County Offices
Consumer Protection / 219-755-3720
Marion County / 317-236-3522
Vanderburgh County / 812-426-5150

Indiana-City Office
Gary Office of Consumer Affairs / 219-886-0145

Iowa-State Office
Consumer Protection / 515-281-5926

Kansas-State Office
Consumer Protection / 913-296-3751 / 800-432-2310 (KS only)

Kansas-County Offices
Johnson County / 913-782-5000
Sedgwick County / 316-268-7921
Shawnee County / 913-291-4330

Kansas-City Office
Topeka Consumer Protection / 913-295-3883

Kentucky-State Offices
Consumer Protection / 502-564-2200 / 800-432-9257 (KY only)
Louisville Consumer Protection / 502-588-3262 / 800-432-9257 (KY only)

Louisiana-State Office
Consumer Protection / 504-342-7373

Louisiana-County Office
Consumer Protection / 504-364-3644

Maine-State Offices
Consumer Credit Protection / 207-582-8718 / 800-332-8529
Office of the Attorney General / 207-289-3716

Maryland-State offices
Consumer Protection / 301-528-8662 / 800-969-5766
Motor Vehicle Administration / 301-768-7420
Consumer Affairs Specialist
Office of the Attorney General / 301-543-6620
Western Maryland / 301-791-4780

Maryland-County Offices
Hamard County / 301-313-7220
Montgomery County / 301-217-7373
Prince Georges County / 301-925-5100

Massachusetts-State Offices
Consumer Protection / 617-727-8400
Executive Office of Consumer Affairs / 617-727-7780
Western Massachusetts Consumer Protection / 413-784-1240

Massachusetts-County Offices
Franklin County / 413-774-5102
Hampshire County / 413-586-9225
Worcester County / 508-754-7420

Massachusetts-City Offices
Boston Mayor's Office of Consumer Affairs / 617-725-3320
Springfield Action Commission / 413-737-4376 (Hampton and Hampshire counties)

Michigan-State Offices
Consumer Protection / 517-373-1140
Michigan Consumers Council / 517-373-0947
Bureau of Automotive Regulation / 517-373-7858 / 800-292-4204 (Michigan only)

Michigan-County Offices
Bay County / 517-893-3594
Macomb County / 313-469-5350
Washtenaw County / 313-971-6054

Michigan-City Office
Detroit Department of Consumer Affairs / 313-224-3508

Minnesota-State Offices
Office of Consumer Services / 612-296-2331
Duluth Consumer Services / 218-723-4891

Minnesota-County Office
Hennepin County / 612-348-4528

Minnesota-City Office
Minneapolis Consumer Services / 612-348-2080

Mississippi -State Offices
Consumer Protection / 601-354-6018
Department of Agriculture & Commerce / 601-354-7063
Gulf Coast Regional Office / 601-436-6000

Missouri-State Offices
Office of the Attorney General / 314-751-3321 / 800-392-8222 (MO only)
Office of the Attorney General-Trade Offense Division / 314-751-3321 /
800-392-8222 ((toll-free in MO only)

Montana-State Office
Consumer Affairs / 406-444-4312 / 800-332-2272

Nebraska-State Office
Consumer Protection / 402-471-2682

Nebraska-County Office
Douglas County / 402-444-7040

Nevada-State Offices
Las Vegas Commissioner of Consumer Affairs / 702-486-7355 /
800-992-0900 ((toll-free in NV only)
Reno Consumer Affairs / 702-688-1800 / 800-992-0900 (Nevada only)

Nevada-County Office
Washoe County / 702-328-3456

New Hampshire-State Office
Consumer Protection / 603-271-3641

New Jersey-State Offices
Consumer Affairs / 932-648-4010 / 800-242-5846
Department of the Public Advocate / 609-292-7087 / 800-792-8600 (toll-
free in NJ only)
New Jersey Division of Law / 973-648-7579 / 800-242-5846

New Jersey-County Offices
Atlantic County / 609-345-6700
Bergen County / 201-646-2650
Burlington County / 609-265-5054
Camden County / 609-757-8397
Cape May County / 609-463-6475
Cumberland County / 609-453-2202
Essex County / 973-678-8071/8928
Gloucester County / 609-853-3349

Hudson County / 201-795-6295
Hunterdon County / 908-236-2249
Mercer County / 609-989-6671
Middlesex County / 732-324-4600
Monmouth County / 732-431-7900
Morris County / 973-285-6070
Parsippany Consumer Affairs / 973-263-7011
Perth Amboy / 732-826-0290, ext. 61
Plainfield Action Services / 908-753-3519
Secaucus Consumer Affairs / 201-330-2019
Union Township / 908-688-6763
Wayne Township / 973-694-1800
Weehawken Consumer Affairs / 201-319-6005
West New York Consumer Affairs / 201-861-2522

New Mexico-State Office
Consumer Protection / 505-827-6000 / 800-432-2070 (in New Mexico only)

New York-State Offices
New York State Consumer Protection / 518-474-8583
Bureau of Consumer Frauds & Protection / 518-474-5481
NY State Consumer Protection Board / 212-417-4908 (complaints) / 212-417-4482 (main office)
Bureau of Consumer Frauds & Protection / 212-341-2345

New York-Regional Offices
Binghamton Regional Office / 607-773-7877
Buffalo Regional Office / 716-847-7184
Plattsburgh Regional Office / 518-563-8012
Poughkeepsie Regional Office / 914-485-3920
Rochester Regional Office / 716-546-7430
Suffolk Regional Office / 516-231-2400
Syracuse Regional Office / 315-448-4848
Utica Regional Office / 315-793-2225

New York-County Offices
Broome County / 607-778-2168
Dutchess County / 914-471-6322
Eric County / 716-858-2424
Nassau County / 516-535-2600
Orange County / 914-294-5151
Orange County / 914-294-5471
Putnam County / 914-621-2317
Rockland County / 914-638-5282
Steuben County / 607-776-9631 (voice andTDD)
Suffolk County / 516-360-4600

Ulster County / 914-339-5680
Westchester County Fraud Bureau / 914-285-3303
Westchester Consumer Affairs / 914-285-2155

New York-City Offices
Babylon Consumer Protection Board / 516-422-7636
Town of Colonie Consumer Protection / 518-783-2790
Mt. Vernon Consumer Affairs / 914-665-2433
New York City Consumer Affairs / 212-487-4444
Bronx Consumer Affairs / 718-579-6766
Brooklyn Consumer Affairs / 718-636-7092
Queens Consumer Affairs / 718-261-2922
Staten Island Consumer Affairs / 718-390-5154
Oswego Consumer Affairs / 315-342-8150
Ramapo Consumer Protection / 914-357-5100
Schenectady Consumer Protection / 518-382-5061
White Plains Dept. of Weights & Measures / 914-422-6359
Yonkers Consumer Protection / 914-377-6807

North Carolina-State Office
Consumer Protection / 919-733-7741

North Dakota-State Offices
Office of the Attorney General / 800-472-2600 (toll-free in ND only)

North Dakota-County office
Quad County / 701-746-5431

Ohio-State Offices
Consumer Frauds and Crimes Section / 614-466-4986 (complaints) /
800-282-0515 ((toll-free in OH only)
Office of Consumers' Counsel / 614-466-9605 (voice/TDD) / 800-282-9448
((toll-free in OH only)

Ohio-County Offices
Franklin County / 614-462-3555
Lake County / 800-899-5253 (Ohio only)
Montgomery County / 513-225-5757
Portage County / 216-296-4593
Summit County / 216-379-2800

Ohio-City Offices
Cincinnati Office of Consumer Services / 513-352-3971
Youngstown Consumer Affairs / 216-742-8884

Oklahoma-State Offices
Attorney General / 405-521-4274
Department of Consumer Credit / 405-521-3653

Oregon-State Office
Financial Fraud / 503-378-4320

Pennsylvania-State Offices
Consumer Protection / 717-787-9707 / 800-441-2555 (PA only)
Consumer Advocate-(Utilities Only) / 717-783-5048
Pennsylvania Public Utility Commission / 717-787-4970 / 800-782-1110
((toll-free in PA only)

Pennsylvania- Branch Offices
Allentown Consumer Protection / 215-821-6690
Erie Consumer Protection / 814-871-4371
Harrisburg Consumer Protection / 717-787-7109 / 800-441-2555 (PA only)
Ebensburg Bureau of Consumer Protection / 814-949-7900
Philadelphia Consumer Protection / 215-560-2414 / 800-441-2555 (PA only)
Pittsburg Consumer Protection / 412-565-5394
Scranton Consumer Protection / 717-963-4913

Pennsylvania-County Offices
Beaver County / 412-728-7267
Bucks County / 215-348-7442
Chester County / 215-344-6150
Cumberland County / 717-240-6180
Delaware County / 215-891-4865
Montgomery County / 215-278-3565
Philadelphia District Attorney / 215-686-8750

Rhode Island-State Offices
Consumer Protection / 401-277-2104 / 800-852-7776 (RI only)
Rhode Island Consumers' Council / 401-277-2764

South Carolina-State Offices
Consumer Protection Office / 803-734-9452 / 800-922-1594 (in SC only)
State Ombudsman / 803-734-0457

South Dakota-State Office
Consumer Affairs / 605-773-4400

Tennessee-State Offices
Consumer Protection / 615-741-2672
Consumer Affairs / 615-741-4737 / 800-342-8385 ((toll-free in TN only)

Texas-State Offices
Dallas Consumer Protection / 214-742-8944
El Paso Consumer Protection / 915-772-9476
Houston Consumer Protection / 713-223-5886
Lubbock Consumer Protection / 806-747-5238
McAllen Consumer Protection / 512-682-4547
San Antonio Consumer Protection / 512-225-4191
Austin Consumer Protection / 512-322-4143

Texas-County Offices
Dallas County / 214-653-3820
Harris County / 713-221-5836

Texas-City Office
Dallas Dept. of Environmental & Health Services / 214-670-5216

Utah-State Offices
Consumer Protection / 801-530-6601
Assistant Attorney General for Consumer Affairs / 801-538-1331

Vermont-State Offices
Office of the Attorney General / 802-828-3171
Consumer Assurance / 802-828-2436

Virginia-State Offices
Richmond Branch of Consumer Affairs / 804-786-2042 / 800-552-9963 ((toll-free in VA only)
Northern Virginia Branch of Consumer Affairs / 703-532-1613

Virginia-County Offices
Arlington County / 703-358-3260
Fairfax County / 703-246-5949
Prince William County / 703-792-7370

Virginia-City Offices
Alexandria Citizens Assistance / 703-838-4350
Norfolk Consumer Affairs / 804-441-2821
Roanoke Consumer Protection / 703-981-2583
Virginia Beach Consumer Affairs / 757-426-5836

Washington-State Offices
Seattle Consumer Services / 206-464-6431 / 800-551-4636 (WA only)
Spokane Office of the Attorney General / 509-456-3123
Tacoma Office of the Attorney General / 206-593-2904

Washington-City Offices
Department of Weights and Measures / 206-259-8810
Seattle Prosecuting Attorney / 206-296-9010
Seattle Department of Licenses & Consumer Affairs / 206-684-8484

West Virginia-State Offices
Consumer Protection / 304-348-8986 / 800-368-8808 ((toll-free in WV only)
Division of Weights and Measures / 304-348-7890

West Virginia-City Office
Charleston Consumer Protection / 304-348-8172

Wisconsin-State Offices
Madison Consumer Protection / 608-266-9836 / 800-422-7129 (in WI only)
Altoona Consumer Protection / 715-839-3848 / 800-422-7128 (in WI only)
Green Bay Consumer Protection / 414-448-5111 / 800-422-7128 (in WI only)
Milwaukee Consumer Protection / 414-257-8956
Madison Department of Justice / 608-266-1952 / 800-362-8189
Milwaukee Department of Justice / 414-227-4948 / 800-362- 8189

Wisconsin-County offices
Marathon County / 715-847-5555
Milwaukee County / 414-278-4792
Racine County / 414-636-3125

Wyoming-State Office
Office of Attorney General / 307-777-7874

American Samoa
Consumer Protection / 011-684-633-4163/64

Puerto Rico
Secretary of Consumer Affairs / 809-721-0940
Department Of Justice / 809-721-2900

Virgin Islands
Commissioner & Consumer Affairs / 809-774-3130

Free & Low Cost Dental Programs

Throughout the U.S. professional dental care is available to senior citizens living on a limited budget at a reduced rate or even absolutely free depending upon their income and circumstances. This care is offered through a wide variety of programs including dental clinics, dental colleges, and through dentists who volunteer their time and service without charge or at a greatly reduced rate. You will get the finest professional dental care from licensed dentists with many years of experience.

To get free or low cost dental care, check the listing below for your state. Call the phone number listed for each of the organizations listed and explain that you are a senior citizen looking for a low cost dental program. In some instances you will be referred to an agency in your local area that will assist you in getting the dental care you need. If the organization you call does not have the particular kind of care you need, always ask them to refer you to another organization that does provide the care.

In addition to the listings below, be sure to check with your STATE'S OFFICE OF THE AGING (also listed in the back of this book). They often will have access to special programs not available anywhere else.

Alabama
Alabama Dental Association
836 Washington St.
Montgomery, AL 36104
334-265-1684
800-489-2532

University of Alabama
School of Dentistry
1919 Seventh Avenue, S.
Birmingham, AL 35294
205-934-2700

Alaska
Alaska Dental Society
3305 Arctic Blvd., Suite 102
Anchorage, AK 99503-4975
907-563-3009

Anchorage Neigthborhood Health Center
1217 East 10th Ave.
Anchorage, AZ 99501
907-257-4600

Senior Citizen Discounts
Anchorage Dental Society
3400 Spenard Rd., Suite 10
Anchorage, AK 99503
907-279-9144

Arizona
Arizona Dental Association
4131 N. 36th St.
Phoenix, AZ 85018
602-957-4777
800-866-2732

Department of Health Services
Office of Dental Health
1740 West Adams St.
Phoenix, AZ 85007
602-542-1866

Arkansas
Arkansas State Dental Association
2501 Crestwood Drive, Suite 205
North Little Rock, AR 72116
501-771-7650

California
Senior Dent Program
California Dental Association
P.O. Box 13749
1201 "K" Street
Sacramento, CA 95853-4749
916-443-0505
800-736-8702

Loma Linda University
School of Dentistry
11092 Anderson St.
Loma Linda, CA 92350
909-824-4675

University of California at Los Angeles
School of Dentistry
10833 LeConte Ave.
Los Angeles, CA 90095-1668
310-206-3904

University of Southern California
School of Dentistry Rm. 203
University Park, MC 0641
Los Angeles, CA 90089-0641
213-740-2800

University of California
School of Dentistry
513 Parnassus Ave., S-630
San Francisco, CA 94143
415-476-1891

University of the Pacific
School of Dentistry
2155 Webster Street
San Francisco, CA 94115
415-929-6400

Colorado
Colorado Dental Association
3690 S. Yosemite, Suite 100
Denver, CO 80237
303-740-6900
800-343-3010
Ask for Senior Discount referrals

State Health Dept.
Oral Health Department
4300 Cherry Creek Dr. South
Denver, CO 80246
303-692-2360

University of Colorado Medical
School of Dentistry
4200 East 9th Ave., Box A095
Denver, CO 80262
303-270-8751

Connecticut
Connecticut State Dental Association
62 Russ Street
Hartford, CT 06106
860-278-5550

The University of Connecticut
School of Dental Medicine
263 Farmington Avenue
Farmington, CT 06032
203-679-3400

Delaware
Delaware State Dental Society
1925 Lovering Ave.
Wilmington, DE 19806
302-654-4335

Division of Public Health
Department of Dentistry
501 W. 14th Street
Wilmington, DE 19801
302-428-4850

Nemours Health Clinic
1801 Rockland Rd
Wilmington, DE 19803
800-292-9538
302-651-4400

Ministry of Caring Dental Program
1410 N. Claymont St
Wilmington, DE 19802
302-594-9476

District Of Columbia
District of Columbia Dental Society
502 C Street N.E.
Washington, DC 20002
202-547-7613

Howard University
College of Dentistry
600 "W" Street, N.W.
Washingon, DC 20059
202-806-0100

Florida
Florida Dental Association
1111 E. Tennessee St.
Tallahassee, FL 32308
904-681-3629 / 800-877-9922

Department of Health & Rehabilitative Services
Public Health Dental Program
1317 Winewood Blvd
Tallahassee, FL 32399
850-487-1845
Ask for referral to a clinic near you

Nova Southeastern University
College of Dental Medicine
3200 S. University Drive
Fort Lauderdale, FL 33328
954-262-7500

University of Florida
College of Dentistry
P.O. Box 100405
Gainesville, FL 32610-0405
904-392-4261

Georgia
Georgia Dental Association
2801 Buford Highway, Suite T-60
Atlanta, GA 30329
404-636-7553
800-432-4357

West End Medical Center
868 York Ave
Atlanta, GA 30310
404-752-1443

Ben Massell Dental Clinic
18 7th St., NE
Atlanta, GA 30308
404-881-1858

Southeast Health Center
1039 Ridge Ave.
Atlanta, GA 30315
404-688-1350 ext 305

Medical College of Georgia
School of Dentistry
1459 Laney Walker Blvd.
Augusta, GA 30912-0200
706-721-2696

Hawaii
Hawaii Dental Association
1345 S. Beretania St. Ste. 301
Honolulu, HI 96814
808-593-7956

Department of Health
Dental Health Division
1700 Lanakila Ave. Room 202
Honolulu, HI 96817
808-832-5710

Idaho
Idaho State Dental Association
1220 W. Hays St.
Boise, ID 83702
208-343-7543
800-932-8153
Ask for a referral to your local
Community Health Center

Senior Care Program
Boise City/Ada County
3010 W. State St. Suite 120
Boise, ID 83703
208-345-7783

Illinois
Illinois State Dental Society
P.O. Box 376
Springfield, IL 62705
217-525-1406
800-475-4737

Southern Illinois University
School of Dentistry Medical Bldg 273
2800 College Avenue - Room 2300
Alton, IL 62002
618-474-7000

University of Illinois at Chicago
College of Dentistry
801 South Paulina Street
Chicago, IL 60612
312-996-7558

Northwestern University
Dental School
240 East Huron Street
Chicago, IL 60611
312-908-5950

Indiana
**Senior Smile Dental Care
Program**
Indiana Dental Association
401 W. Michigan Street
Indianapolis, IN 46206
317-634-2610
800-562-5646

Indiana University
School of Dentistry
1121 West Michigan Street
Indianaplis, IN 46202
317-274-3547

Iowa
Iowa Dental Association
505 5th Ave. #333
Des Moines, IA 50309
515-282-7250
800-828-2181

**The University of Iowa
College of Dentistry**
Dental Building
Iowa City, IA 52242
319-335-7499

Kansas
Senior Access Program
Kansas Dental Association
5200 SW Huntoon St.
Topeka, KS 66604
800-432-3583

Kentucky
Kentucky Dental Association
1940 Princeton Drive
Louisville, KY 40205
502-459-5373
800-292-1855

**Jefferson County Dental
Park Duval Community Health
Facility**
1817 South 34th St.
Louisville, KY 40211
502-774-4401

University of Kentucky
College of Dentistry
800 Rose Street - Medical Ctr.
Lexington, KY 40536-0084
606-323-6525

University of Louisville
School of Dentistry
Health Sciences Center

Louisville, KY 40292
502-852-5096

Louisiana
Louisiana Dental Association
7833 Office Park Blvd.
Baton Rouge, LA 70809
504-926-1986

Louisiana State University
School of Dentistry
1100 Florida Ave., Bldg. 101
New Orleans, LA 70119
504-947-9961

Maine
Senior Dent Program
Maine Dental Association
P.O. Box 215
Manchester, ME 04351
800-369-8217

Maryland
Maryland State Dental
Association
6450 Dobbin Road
Columbia, MD 21045
410-964-2880
800-766-2880

University of Maryland
Baltimore College of Dental Surgery
666 West Baltimore Street
Baltimore, MD 21201
410-706-5603

Massachusetts
Massachusetts Dental Society
83 Speen Street
Natick, MA 01760
508-651-7511
800-342-8747

Boston Univsity
School of Dental Medicine
100 East Newton Street
Boston, MA 02118
617-638-4671

Harvard School of Dental
Medicine
188 Longwood Avenue
Boston, MA 02115
617-432-1423

Tufts University
School of Dental Medicine
1 Kneeland Street
Boston, MA 02111
617-956-6547

Michigan
Michigan Dental Association
230 N. Washington Square #208
Lansing, MI 48933
517-372-9070
800-589-2632

The University of Michigan
School of Dentistry
1234 Dental Building
Ann Arbor, MI 48109-1078
734-763-6933

University of Detroit Mercy
School of Dentistry
8200 W. Outer Drive, PO Box 98
Detroit, MI 48219-0900
313-494-6600

Minnesota
Minnesota Dental Association
2236 Marshall Avenue
St. Paul, MN 55104
612-646-7454
800-950-3368

University of Minnesota
School of Dentistry
515 S.E. Delaware Street
Minneapolis, MN 55455
612-625-8400

In Minnesota also contact:
Neighborhood Health Care
Network
612-489-2273

Senior Link Line
1-800-333-2433
"First Call For Help"
612-224-1133

Mississippi
Mississippi Dental Association
2630 Ridgewood Road
Jackson, MS 39216
601-982-0442

The University of Mississippi
School of Dentistry - Med. Ctr.
2500 North State Street
Jackson, MS 39216-4505
601-984-6155

Missouri
Missouri Dental Association
230 W. McCarty Street
Jefferson City, MO 65102
573-634-3436
800-688-1907

University of Missouri
School of Dentistry
650 East 25th Street
Kansas City, MO 64108
816-235-2100

Montana
Montana Dental Association
P.O. Box 1154
Helena, MT 59624
406-443-2061 / 800-257-4988

Donated Dental Services
PO Box 1154
Helena, MT 59624
406-449-9670

Cooperative Health Dental Clinic
1930 Ninth Ave.
Helena, MT 59601
406-443-2584

Nebraska
Senior Dent Program
Nebraska Dental Association
3120 "O" Street
Lincoln, NE 68510
402-476-1704
800-234-3120

University of Nebraska Medical Ctr.
College of Dentistry
40th & Holdrege Street
Lincoln, NE 68583-0740
402-472-1333

Creighton University
School of Dentistry
2500 California Street
Omaha, NE 68178
402-280-2865

Nevada
Nevada Dental Association
6889 W. Charleston Blvd. #B
Las Vegas, NV 89117
702-255-4211
800-962-6710

New Hampshire
New Hampshire Dental Society
P.O. Box 2229
Concord, NH 03302
603-225-5961
800-244-5961

New Jersey
New Jersey Dental Association
One Dental Plaza
North Brunswick, NJ 08902-6020
732-821-9400

University of Medicine & Dentistry
New Jersey Dental School
110 Bergen Street
Newark, NJ 07103-2425
201-982-4300

New Mexico
New Mexico Dental Association
3736 Eubank Blvd. N.E. Suite C-1
Albuquerque, NM 87111
505-294-1368

New York
Dental Society of the State of New York
7 Elk Street
Albany, NY 12207
518-465-0044
800-255-2100

State University of New York
School of Dental Medicine
325 Squire Hall
Buffalo, NY 14214
716-829-2720

Columbia University
School of Dental & Oral Surgery
640 West 168th Street
New York, NY 10032
212-305-5665

New York University
College of Dentistry
345 E. 24th Street
New York, NY 10010
212-998-9800

State University of New York
School of Dental Medicine
South Campus
Stony Brook, NY 11794-8700
516-632-8974

North Carolina
North Carolina Dental Society
P.O. Box 4099
Cary, NC 27519
919-677-1396

University of North Carolina
School of Dentistry
104 Brauer Hall, 211 H
Chapel Hill, NC 27599-7450
919-966-1161

North Dakota
North Dakota Dental Association
Box 1332
Bismarck, ND 58502
800-795-8870

Ohio
Oral Health Access Coordinator
Bureau of Oral Health Services
246 North High St.
Columbus, OH 43266-0118
614-466-4180
In Ohio: 1-888-765-6789
Provides access to over 90 dental programs throughout the state

Ohio Dental Association
1370 Dublin Road
Columbus, OH 43215
800-MY-SMILE 1-800-69-76453)
or Options Program: 1-888-765-6789

Case Western Reserve Univ.
School of Dentistry
2123 Abington Road
Cleveland, OH 44106
216-368-3200

Ohio State University
College of Dentistry
305 West 12th Avenue
Columbus, OH 43210
614-292-2751

Oklahoma
Senior Dent/Care-Dent Programs
Oklahoma Dental Association
629 West Interstate 44, Service Rd.
Oklahoma City, OK 73118
405-848-8873
800-876-8890

University of Oklahoma Health Science Center
College of Dentistry
P.O. Box 26901
Oklahoma City, OK 73190
405-271-6056

Oregon
Oregon Dental Association
17898 S.W. McEwan Rd.
Portland, OR 97224
503-620-3230 / 800-452-5628

Department of Health
Dental Health Division
Community Access Programs
800 NE Oregon St.
Portland, OR 97232
503-731-4098

Senior Smile Dental Service
Multnomah Dental Society
1618 SW First Ave.
Portland, OR 97201
503-223-4738

Donated Dental Services
CDRC
PO Box 574 Room 2205
Portland, OR 97207
503-248-3816

The Oregon Health Services
University
School of Dentistry
Sam Jackson Park
611 S.W. Campus Drive
Portland, OR 97201
503-494-8867

Pennsylvania
Pennsylvania Dental Association
P.O. Box 3341
Harrisburg, PA 17105
717-234-5941 / 800-692-7256

Dental Care For Senior Citizens
Access To Care Program
3501 North Front St.
Harrisburg, PA 17110
717-234-5941

Temple University
School of Dentistry
3223 North Broad Street
Philadelphia, PA 19140
215-707-2900

University of Pennsylvania
School of Dental Medicine
4001 West Spruce Street
Philadelphia, PA 19104
215-898-8961

University of Pittsburgh
School of Dental Medicine
3501 Terrace Street
Pittsburgh, PA 15261
412-648-8760

Puerto Rico
Colegio de Cirujanos Dentistas
Avenida Domenech #200
Hato Rey, PR 00918
787-764-1969

University of Puerto Rico
School of Dentistry
G.P.O. Box 5067
San Juan, PR 00936
787-555-1212

Rhode Island
Rhode Island Dental Association
200 Centerville Place
Warwick, RI 02886
401-732-6833

Department of Public Health
Oral Health Division
3 Capital Hill
Providence, RI 02908
401-222-2588

South Carolina
Senior Care Dental Program
South Carolina Dental
Association
120 Stonemark Lane
Columbia, SC 29210
803-750-2277
800-327-2598

Medical University of South
Carolina
College of Dental Medicine
171 Ashley Avenue

Charleston, SC 29425
803-792-2611

South Dakota
South Dakota Dental Association
330 South Poplar
Pierre, SD 57501
605-224-9133

Tennessee
Tennessee Dental Association
2104 Sunset Place
Nashville, TN 37212
615-383-8962

Tennessee Department of Dentistry
Cordell Hull
425 Fifth Ave. North
Nashville, TN 37247
615-532-5073

University of Tennessee
College of Dentistry
875 Union Avenue
Memphis, TN 38163
901-448-6257

Meharry Medical College
School of Dentistry
1005 Dr. D.B. Todd Blvd.
Nashville, TN 37208
615-327-6669

Texas
Texas Dental Association
P.O. Box 3358
Austin, TX 78764
512-443-3675

Texas A&M University System
Baylor College of Dentistry
3302 Gaston Ave.
Dallas, TX 75266-0677
214-828-8100

The University of Texas
Health Science Center

Dental Branch
6516 John Freeman Avenue
Houston, TX 77030
713-792-4056

The University of Texas
Health Science -Dental School
7703 Floyd Curl Drive
San Antonio, TX 78284-7914
210-567-3222

Utah
Department of Health
Dental Health Division
1365 West 1000 North
Salt Lake City, UT 84116
801-328-5756

Utah Dental Association
1151 E. 3900 S., Suite B160
Salt Lake City, UT 84124
800-662-6500

Vermont
Island Pond Health Center
Dental Program
PO Box 425
Island Pond, VT 05846
802-723-4300

Vermont State Dental Society
100 Dorset Street Suite 12
South Burlington, VT 05403
802-864-0115

Virginia
Virginia Dental Association
P.O. Box 6906
Richmond, VA 23230
804-358-4927 / 800-552-3886

Health Department
Dental Division
1500 E. Main
Richmond, VA 23219
804-786-3556

Virginia Commonwealth Univ.
MCV-School of Dentistry
P.O. Box 566
Richmond, VA 23298
804-828-9095

Washington
Elderly and Disabled
Washington State Dental Assn.
2033 6th Ave., Suite 333
Seattle, WA 98121
206-448-1914
800-448-3368

University of Washington
School of Dentistry
Health Science Blvd. SC-62
Seattle, WA 98195
206-543-5830

West Virginia
West Virginia Dental Association
2003 Quarrier Street
Charleston, WV 25311
304-344-5246

West Virginia University
School of Dentistry
The Medical Center
P.O. Box 9400
Morgantown, WV 26506-9400
304-598-4810

Wisconsin
Wisconsin Dental Association
111 E. Wisconsin Avenue, Ste 1300
Milwaukee, WI 53202
414-276-4520
800-364-7646

Dane County Public Health Division
Dental Health Program
1202 Northport Drive
Madison, WI 53704
608-242-6510

Marquette University
School of Dentistry
604 North 16th Street
Milwaukee, WI 53233
414-288-6500

Wyoming
Wyoming Dental Association
P. O. Box #1123
Cheyenne, WY 82003
307-634-5878
800-244-0779

State Health Department
Dental Division
Hathaway Building, 4th Floor
Cheyenne, WY 82002
307-777-7945

Job Training Programs For Seniors

The government offers excellent programs aimed at helping seniors get back into the workforce. Listed below are the state offices you can contact for information about training programs in your area. When you call, ask about the *Senior Community Service Employment Program* (called Title V) and also *Job Training Partnership Act Programs* (JTPA). They offer job training, help with job searches and resume writing and more. They also offer financial assistance to companies who hire graduates of these programs.

Alabama Commission On Aging / 334-242-5743
      Department of Economic & Community Affairs / 334-242-5300
Alaska Older Alaskans Commissions / 907-465-3250
      Department of Community & Regional Affairs / 907-465-5545
Arizona Department of Economic Security / 602-542-4446
Arkansas Division of Aging & Adult Services / 501-682-2441
      Department of Labor - JTPA / 501-371-4487
California Department of Aging / 916-323-0217
      Employment Development - JPTA / 916-654-7110
Colorado Department of Labor & Employment / 303-620-4200
Connecticut Social Services/Elderly Services Division / 860-424-5274
Delaware Services For Aging & Adults w/ Disabilities / 302-577-4660
District Of Columbia Office On Aging / 202-724-7073
      Department of Employment Services / 202-724-7073
Florida Department of Elder Affairs / 800-96-ELDER
Georgia Department of Human Services / 404-657-5330
Hawaii Office On Aging / 808-586-0100
      Honolulu Community Action Program / 808-586-8813
Idaho Commission On Aging / 208-334-3833
Illinois Department On Aging / 1-800-252-8966
      Department of Commerce & Community Affairs / 217-782-7500
Indiana Disability/Rehabilitation & Aging Services / 317-232-7000
Iowa Department of Elder Affairs / 512-282-5187
Kansas Department of Aging / 913-296-4986
Kentucky Social Services/Aging Services Division / 502-564-6930
      JTPA Coordinator / 502-564-5360
Louisiana Office of Elderly Affairs / 504-342-7100
Maine Bureau of Elder Services / 207-624-5335
      Bureau of Employment Services (JPTA) / 207-624-6390
Maryland Office On Aging / 1-800-AGE-DIAL
Massachusetts Office Of Elder Affairs / 1-800-882-2003
Michigan Office of Services To The Aging / 517-373-8230
      Michigan Job Commission (JTPA) / 517-373-9808

Minnesota Board On Aging / 1-800-882-6262
Mississippi Division of Aging & Adult Services / 1-800-948-3090
Missouri Department Of Aging / 573-751-3082
    Division of Job Development (JPTA) / 1-800-877-8698
Montana Green Thumb Program / 406-761-4821
    Montana JTPA / 406-444-1309
Nebraska Department On Aging / 402-471-2307
Nevada AARP / 702-648-3356
    Nevada Business Services (JPTA) / 702-647-4929
New Hampshire AARP / 1-800-652-8808
    Job Training Council (JPTA) / 1-800-772-7001
New Jersey Division of Senior Affairs / 609-292-4833
    New Jersey Department Of Labor (JPTA) / 609-292-5005
New Mexico State Agency On Aging / 1-800-432-2080
    State Department of Labor (JPTA) / 505-827-6827
New York State Office For The Aging / 1-800-342-9871
North Carolina Division Of Aging / 919-733-3983
    DivisionOf Employment & Training JPTA) / 919-733-6383
North Dakota Aging Services Division (JPTA) / 701-328-8910
    Green Thumb / 701-258-8879
Ohio Department of Aging / 614-466-5500
    Employment Services (JPTA) / 614-466-3817
Oklahoma Aging Services Division / 405-521-2327
Oregon Department of Human Resources Seniors Div. / 503-945-6413
    JTPA Office / 503-373-1995
Pennsylvania Department of Aging / 717-783-1550
    Department of Labor & Industry (JTPA) / 717-783-0142
Rhode Island Department of Elderly Affairs / 401-222-2858
South Carolina Office On Aging / 803-253-6177
    JTPA Office / 803-737-2660
South Dakota Adult Services & Aging Division / 605-332-7991
Tennessee Commission On Aging / 615-741-2056
    Department of Labor - JTPA Office / 615-741-1031
Texas Senior Texans Employment Program / 254-776-7002
    Texas Workforce Commission (JTPA) / 512-936-0345
Utah Division Of Aging Services / 801-538-3910
    Economic Development & Training (JTPA) / 801-468-3246
Vermont Department Of Aging & Disabilities / 802-241-2400
    Vermont Training & Development / 802-524-3200
Virginia Department For The Aging / 804-662-9333
Washington Job Development & Training / 360-786-5586
West Virginia Bureau Of Senior Services / 304-558-3317
    JTPA Employment Services / 304-558-2664
Wisconsin Department of Workforce Development / 608-266-6886
Wyoming Senior Citizens Office / 307-635-1245

Colleges With Special Programs For Seniors

If you've been thinking how great it would be to go back to college either to finish your education or to get it started again, there is something very important you should know. There are colleges throughout the U.S. that offer special free or very low cost tuition programs for seniors. Many colleges let you take the courses for full college credit. Others you take just for the fun of it. But one thing's for sure...you can't beat the price!

The listings below are by no means complete. Because of the increase in the 55 plus age group, more and more colleges are adding courses and special programs for seniors. If there is a particular college in your town that you might want to attend, call them and ask if they have any programs for seniors.

Alabama

Glasden State Community College
Admissions
PO Box 227
Gadsden, AL 35902-0227
Call: 1-205-549-8201
The minimum age is 60 and you must be a state resident
Tuition: free
There will be fees for books , parking, etc. Check with the registrar.
Courses can be taken for credit if you have a high school diploma, or a GED diploma

Jefferson State Community College
Admissions
2601 Carson Rd.
Birmingham, AL 35215-3098
Call: 1-205-853-1200
The minimum age is 60 and you must be a state resident
Tuition: $6 per credit hour.
Courses can be taken for credit

Alaska
University of Alaska Southeast
Admissions
11120 Glacier Hwy
Juneau, AK 99801
Call: 1-907-465-6457
Web site: www.jun.alaska.edu
E-mail: jyuas@acad1.alaska.edu
The minimum age is 60 and you must be a state resident
Tuition is waived, but you must sign up for class the first day it is offered. There are additional fees for student government and books
You can take unlimited classes for credit provided there is space.

Arkansas
Arkansas State University
Admissions
PO Box 1630
State University, AR 72467-1630
Call: 1-800-382-3030
Web site: www.astate.edu
E-mail:
admissions@chickasaw.astate.edu
The minimum age is 60 and you must be a state resident
The tuition is free and courses can be taken for credit
Basic fees depend on the amount of credit hours taken.

Arkansas State University
Beebe Branch
PO Drawer H
Beebe, AR 72012
Call: 1-501-882-6452
The minimum age is 60
The tuition is free, and courses can be taken for credit
There are basic fees for books, parking, etc.

California
California State University at Chico
First&Normal Streets
Chico, CA 95929
Call: 1-800-542-4426
Web site: www.csuchico.edu
E-mail: info@
oavax.csuchico.edu
The minimum age is 60 and you must be a state resident
They have a program for seniors aged 60+ for credit, open to all state residents
You pay $93.00 per semester
Fees for books and activities are extra.
They also have Elder College where students audit only. This is $45.00 per semester. Both programs are based on space available.

Colorado
Adams State College
Alamosa , CO 81102
Call: 1-719-589-7712
The minimum age is 65 and you must be a state resident. Classes can be taken with the permission of the professor. No credit is given.

University of Colorado, Boulder
Regent Administrative Center, Room 125
Campus Box 6
Boulder, CO 80309
Call: 1-303-492-6301
Web site: www.colorado.edu
E-mail: apply@colorado.edu
The minimum age is 55 and the tuition is free. No classes for credit.

University of Colorado at Denver
PO Box 173364
Campus Box 146
Denver, CO 80217-3364
Call: 1-303-556-2400

The minimum age is 60, and you must be a state resident, and part of a senior citizen program. No grade is given and tuition is free
Web site: www.cudenver.edu
E-mail:
admissions@castle.cudenuer.edu

Connecticut
University of Connecticut, Storrs
2131 Hillside Road, U-88
Storrs, CT 06269
Call:1-860-486-3137
Web Site: www.uconn.edu
E-mail:
beahusky@uconnvm.uconn.edu
The minimum age is 62 and you must be a state resident and the fees are waived. The tuition is $15.00 per semester and courses can be taken for non-academic credit.

University of Hartford Adult Services
200 Bloomfield Ave.
West Hartford, CT 06117-0395
Call: 1-860-768-4457
Web site:
www.hartford.edu/uofhwelcome.html
E-mail:
admission@uhavax.hartford.edu
The minimum age 65 and you must be a state resident. You can audit one course free. Fees for books, activities, etc.

Delaware
Delaware Technical and Community College: Southern Campus
PO Box 610
Georgetown, DE 19947
Call: 1-302-856-5400
The minimum age is 60. They have an Adult Plus program with special interest courses. The tuition is free

District of Columbia
American University
c/o Institute for Learning Retirement
4400 Massachusetts Ave
Washington, DC 20016
Call: 1-202-885-6000
Web site: www.american.edu
E-mail: afa@american.edu
They offer non-credit -low cost classes for retired people.
 Seniors can take up to 3 classes per semester for $175.00

Florida
Florida Institute of Technology
150 W. University Blvd.
Melbourne, FL 32901
Call: 1-800-888-4348
Web site: www.fit.edu
E-mail: admissions@fit.edu
The minimum age is 65 and you can take a limited number of courses for free tuition.

Georgia
Augusta State University
2500 Walton Way
Augusta, GA 30910
Call: 1-706-737-1632
Web site: www. aug.edu
E-mail: lyoung@aug.edu
Seniors 62 and older can take courses free providing there is space available.
To study for credit you must apply and be accepted as a regular student .

Piedmont College
PO Box 10
Demorest, GA 30535
Call:1-800-277-7020
Web site: www.piedmont.edu
E-mail:
jem.clement@gateway.piedmont.edu
Seniors can attend classes at discounted prices. They can also register to audit a class as a guest.

Hawaii
University of Hawaii at Manoa
2600 Campus Rd.
Honolulu, HI 96822
Call: 1-808956-8975
Web site: www.hawaii.edu/
welcome/manoa.html
Seniors can take courses free with the permission of the professor for no credit.

Idaho
Boise State University
1910 University Dr.
Boise, ID 83725
Call: 1-800-824-7017
Web site: www.idbsu.edu
E-mail - Admissions:
mwheelcrobsu.edu
The minimum age is 60 and you must be a state resident There is a $20.00 Registration fee and they can take the classes for credit The cost is $5.00 per credit.

College of Southern Idaho
Admissions PO Box 315 Falls Ave.
Twin Falls , ID 83303-1238
Call:1-208-733-9554
The minimum age is 60 and you must be a state resident. You can get a Gold Card from their Office On Aging to take classes for free. There is a fee for books, activities, and supplies. They also have a special program for seniors over 60 called "Getting Fit."

Illinois
Belleville Area College
2500 Carlyle Ave.
Belleville, IL 62221
Call: 1-618-235-2700
The minimum age is 60 and you must be a state resident. Seniors pay $38.50 per credit hour for credit courses.

If you earn less than $14,000.00 you can apply for free tuition.

Indiana
Ball State University
2000 University Ave.
Muncie, IN 47306
Call: 1-765-285-8300
They only have an Elderhostel program. It's worth checking out.

University of Southern Indiana
8600 University Blvd.
Evansville, IN 47712
Call: 1-812-464-1765
Web site: www.usi.edu
The minimum age is 65 and you must be a state resident. You can take one class per semester for $5.00

Indiana University-Purdue
Office of Admissions
University Fort Wayne
2101 East Coliseum Blvd.
Fort Wayne, IN 46805
Call: 1-219-481-6812
Web site: www.iupui.edu
E-mail: Apply@SES.1upui.edu
The minimim age is 60 and you must be a state resident who is not employed full time. You can take courses at 1/2 off the regular State resident fee. You must register during the final regustration (providing there is room). The couses can be taken for credit.
The only cost is for books.

Iowa
Iowa Western Community College Business
923 East Washington St.
Clarinda, IA 51632
Call:1-712-542-5117
The minimum age is 55 and you must be a state resident. You can

attend classes for credit at a reduced tuition. The reduced rate would be equal to 1/3 of the regular hourly rate, and you are allowed three credit hours per semester.

Kansas
Baker University
PO Box 65
Baldwin City, KS66006
Call: 1-800-873-4282
Web site: www.bakeru.edu
AdmissionsE-mail:
jjohnson@harvey.bakeru.edu
The minimum age is 55 and you must be a state resident. You can take one course at a time for credit in the Arts and Sciences. All fees are waived except course supplies.

Bethany College
421 N. First
Lindsborg, KS 67456
Call: 1-800-826-2281
Web-site: www.bethanylib.edu
They offer a summer Elderhostel program for seniors.

Kentucky
Kentucky State University
400 East Main Street
Frankfort, KY 40601
Call: 1-800-325-1716
Web site: www.kysu.edu
Admissions E-mail:
idyson@gwmail.kysu.edu
The minimum age is 65 and you must be a state resident. Seniors can take courses for credit and all tuition and fees are waived.

Midway College
512 E. Stephens St
Midway, KY 40347
Web site: www.Midway.edu
Call: 1-800-755-0031
Web site: www.Midway.edu

The Lewis and Ann Piper Scholarship Program allows seniors age 60 plus (must be a state resident) to take academic courses with all fees waived including textbooks.
Women can take courses for credit or audit. Men through the Career Development School. You can take courses for audit or credit.

University of Kentucky
658 South Limestone
Ligon House
Lexington, KY 40506-0042
Call: 1-606-257-2000
Website www.uky.edu
The Donovan Scholars program offers seniors age 65 who are state residents free tuition for credit or non-credit. There are fees for books and supplies.

Louisiana
Louisiana State University at Alexandria
8100 Highway 71 South
Alexandria , LA 71302-9633
Call:1-318-473-6423
The minimum age for seniors is 65 and you must be a state resident. The tuition is waived. You pay for books, application fee and supplies. You can take courses for credit or audit the class.

Louisiana State University at Baton Rouge
Room 110 Thomas Boyd Hall
Baton Rough, LA 70803
Call: 1-504-388-1175
!-504-388-1175
The minimum age for seniors is 65 and you must be a state resident. The tuition is waived, you pay for books, application fee and supplies.

Maine
University of Maine-Augusta
46 University Drive
Augusta, ME 04330
Call: 1-207-621-3000
Web site: www.uma.maine.edu
Admissions E-mail:
umaar@maine.maine.edu
The minimum age for seniors is 65 and you must be a state resident. The tuition is waived. Books and supplies are extra.

University of Maine-Fort Kent
25 Pleasant St.
Fort Kent, ME 04743
Call: 1-888-879-8635
Web site:www.umfk.maine.edu
Admissions E-mail:
llmfkadm@maine.maine.edu
The minimum age for seniors is 65 and you must be a state resident. You can apply for a tuition waiver (must show financial need) and can take any course for credit or audit.

Maryland
St. Mary's College of Maryland
St. Mary's City, MD 20686
Call: 1-800-492-7181
Web site: www.smcm.edu
Admissions E-mail:
admissions@honors.smcm.edu
The minimum age for seniors is 60. You can take classes for credit or non credit. The tuition is waived. You pay for books, supplies, and parking.

Western Maryland College
2 College Hill
Westminster, MD 21157
Call: 1-800-638-5005
Web site: www.wmdc.edu
Admissions E-mail:
admissions@ns1.wmc.car.md.us
The minimum age for seniors is 65 and a you must be a state resident.

You pay $25.00 per class and can attend for credit or non-credit.

Massachusetts
Boston University
Evergreen Program
808 Commonwealth Ave.
Boston, MA 92215
Call: 1-617-353-9852
The minimum age for seniors is 60 and tuition is $20.00 per course but not for credit.

Michigan
Central Michigan University
Admissions Dept.
105 Warriner Hall
Mount Pleasant, MI 48859
Call: 1-517-774-3261
The minimum age is 60 and you must be a state resident. Tuition is free subject to available space.) No credit for the courses. There is a fee for books and supplies.

Spring Arbor College
106 E. Main
Spring Arbor, MI 49283
Call: 1-800-968-0011
Web site: www.arbor.edu
Admissions E-mail:
admissions@admin.arbor.edu
The minimum age is 65. The tuition is $25.00 per credit hour. You can take up to 7 hours in any semester. To audit, you pay $20.00 per credit.

Minnesota
Riverland Community College
1600 Eighth Ave., NW
Austin, MN 55912
Call: 1-507-433-0600
The minimum age is 62 and the cost is $9.35 per credit. You can take courses for credit.

Minnesota Universities-Twin Cities
150 Williamson Hall
231 Pillsbury Dr., SE
Minneapolis, MN 55455
Call: 612-625-5333
The minimum age is 62 and you must be a state resident. The tuition is $6.00 per credit hour, and you can take the course for credit.

Mississippi
Delta State University
Admissions Office
Cleveland, MS 38733
Call: 601-846-4018
The minimum age for seniors is 60, and you must be a state resident. The tuition is $10.00 for 1 course up to 3 credit hours; up to 15 credits @ 10.00 per 3 credits.

Mississippi Gulf Coast Community College:
Jackson County Campus Business Services
PO Box 100
Gautier, MS 39553
Call: 228-497-9602
The minimum age is 50 and you must be a state resident. They have a program for $50.00 a year where courses are given for non-credit, also with lunches and a trip once a month. You also can sign up free for regular courses for credit and pay only for books and activity fees.

Missouri
Crowder College
601 La Clede Ave.
Neosho, MO 64850
Call: 417-451-3223
The minimum age is 60, and you must be a state resident in the district. Tuition is free and courses can be taken for credit.

Missouri Western State College
4525 Downs Dr.
St. Joseph, MO 64507
Call: 816-271-4200
The minimum age is 60 and you must be a state resident. You can take courses for credit or non-credit at a 10% discounted price.

Montana
Montana Tech of the University of Montana
1300 West Park Street
Butte, MT 59701
Call: 406-496-4178
1-800-445-8324
Web site: www.mtech,edu
Admissions E-mail:
admissions@mtvms2.mtech.edu
The minimum age is 62 and you must be a state resident. The tuition id $59.10 for 3 credit hours; $285.00 for 12 credit hours.

University of Montana
Missoula, MT 59812
Call: 406-243-6266
Web site: www.umt.edu
Admissions E-mail:
admiss@selway.umt.edu
The minimum age is 65, and you must be a state resident. They have the Golden College plan for seniors where you attend college for credit or non-credit for greatly reduced tuition. (You pay about 20%).

Nebraska
McCook Community College
1205 East Third Street
McCook, NE 69001
Call: 308-345-6303
The minimum age is 60 and you must be a state resident. The tuition is waived and courses are given for non-credit.

Mid-Plains Community College
601 State Farm Rd.
Morth Platte, NE 69101
Call: 308-532-8740
The minimum age is 60 and you must be a state resident. The tuition is free and the only cost to you would be books, activity fees and supplies.

Nevada
University of Nevada: Las Vegas
4505 S. Maryland Parkway
Las Vegas, NV 89154
Call: 895-3394 (continuing Ed)
Web site: www.univ.edu
The minimum age is 62, and you must be a state resident for at least one year, to take courses for credit.

Western Nevada Community College
2201 West College Pkwy.
Carson City, NV 89703
Call: 702-887-3138
The minimum age is 62, and you must be a state resident. The tuition is free and you can take courses for credit. Your only cost is books and lab fees.

New Hampshire
New Hampshire Technical College: Manchester
1066 Front Street
Manchester, NH 03102
Call: 603-668-6706
The minimum age is 65, and you must be a state resident. The tuition is 50% of the cost, and you can take courses for credit.

University of New Hampshire at Manchester
220 Hackett Hill Rd.
Manchester, NH 03102
Call: 603-668-0700
The minimum age is 65, and you must be a state resident. The tuition is free and you can take up to 2 courses per semester (subject to available space). The only cost would be a registration fee, books and supplies. You can take courses for credit or non-credit.

New Jersey
Bloomfield College
467 Franklin Street
Bloomfield, NJ 07003
Call: 1-800-848-4555
Web Site: www.bloomfield.edu
Admissions E-mail:
admissions@bloomfield.edu
The minimum age is 62 and you must be a state resident. You pay a $25.00 registration fee and $15.00 for the course (subject to available space). You can take the course for credit and the college sets aside a day just for seniors to register,.

Fairleigh Dickinson University
1000 River Rd
Teaneck, NJ 07666
Call: 1-800-338-8803
Web site: www.fdu.edu
Admissions E-mail:
boyer@hrserv.fdu.edu
The minimum age is 62 and a you must be a resident. You can take any course with permission from the professor. You pay $100. per course.

New Mexico
New Mexico State University at Almogordo
Admissions
2400 N. Scenic Dr.
Almogordo, NM 88310
Call: 505-439-3720
The minimum age is 65, and you must be a state resident. The tuition is $8.00 per credit hour. The basic fees are $10.00, a one time

admission fee. Seniors can take courses for credit or non-credit.

New York
City University of New York
Hunter College
Admissions
695 Park Ave.
New York, NY 10021
Call: 212-772-4490
Web site: www.hunter.cuny.edu
The minimum age is 60 and you must be a state resident. A senior can audit any 2 classes for a fee of $70.00 per semester.

SUNY Purchase
735 Anderson Hill Road
Purchase, NY 10577
Call: (914) 251-6300
Web Site: www.purchase.edu
The minimum age is 62. Each semester there is one day seniors can register for classes. You pay $50.00 to audit classes, provided there is room in the class. The registration for seniors is usually after full-tuition paying students have registered for their classes.

Wells College
Route 90
Aurora, NY 13026
Call: 1-800- 052-9355
Web site: www.wells.edu
Seniors can audit any course for free provided there is room in the class.

North Carolina
High Point University
University Station
Montilieu Ave
High Point, NC 27262
Call: 1-800-345-6993
Web site: www.highpoint.edu
Seniors can audit classes for 1/2 price.

Appalachian State University
Boone,NC 28608
Call: 262-2120
Web site: www.appstate.edu
The minimum age is 65 and you must be a state resident. You can take courses free for crediit or non-credit. There are fees for books, supplies, activities.

North Dakota
North Dakota State University
PO Box 5454
Fargo, ND 58105
Call: 231-7981
Web site: www.ndsu.nodak.edu
They have a"Project 65" program, where seniors age 65+ can audit classes for free. Tuition and related fees are waived, however there is a $25.00 application fee.

Ohio
Lake Erie College
391 W. Washington Street
Painesville, OH 44077
Call: 1-800-533-4996
Web site: www.lakeerie.edu
Seniors can audit any course for free (no credit), provided there is room in the class.

Bowling Green State University
Dept of Continuing Education
McFall Center
40 College Park
Bowling Green, OH 43403
Call: 372-2086
They have a program for seniors called the "Sage Program", where seniors age 60 can take any courses free (subject to available space) paying only fees for books, supplies, labs. No credit is given.

Oklahoma
Oklahoma State University
104 Whitehurse
Stillwater, OK 74078
Call: 744-6858
Web site: www.okstate.edu
The minimum age for seniors is 65. You can audit any course for free (no credit).There is a fee for books and other supplies .

Oregon
University of Oregon
1217 University of Oregon
Eugene, OR 97403
Call: 1-800-232-3825
Web site: www.uoregon.edu
The minimum age for seniors is 62, and you can audit any class for free but not for credit.

Oregon Institute of Technology
3201 Campus Drive
Klamath Falls , OR 97601
Call: 1-800-422-2017
Web site: www.oit.edu
The minimum age for seniors is 65. You can take courses for free tuition. The classes can be for credit or non-credit. They also run an Elderhostel Program throughout the year.

Pennsylvania
University of Pennsylvania
3440 Market Street
Suite 100
Philadelphia, PA 19104
Call: 215-898-3526
The minimum age is 65 and they offer courses for seniors for a donation depending on the number of classes taken.

University of Pittsburgh-Bradford
Auxiliary Services
300 Campus Drive
Bradford, PA 16701
Call: 1-800-872-1787
Web site: www.upb.pitt.edu
Seniors are eligible to take non-credit courses for a discounted fee (call to check). They must be at least 65 and a state resident.

Rhode Island
Rhode Island College
600 Mt. Pleasant Ave.
Providence, RI 02908
Call: 401-456-8090
Seniors who are at least 60 and residents of the State, may enroll for free tuition in the 'Seniors Mean Test Program'. They must supply certain tax forms.

South Carolina
Clemson University
Business Office
105 Sikes Hall
Clemson, SC 29634-5307
Call: 864-656-5592
Web site: www.clemson.edu
The minimum age for seniors is 60 and you must be a state resident (age must be verified). They can audit or take any course (space available) for free tuition. Books and supplies are additional.

South Dakota
Dakota Wesleyan University
1200 W. University Avenue
Mitchell, SD 57301
Call: 1-800-333-8506
Web site: www.dwu.edu
Seniors age 62 or older can enroll in their Blue and White Club program which enables them to audit any classes (subject to available space) for free tuition.

Tennessee
Tennessee State University
3500 John Merritt Boulevard
Nashville, TN 37209
Call: 615- 963-5105
Web site: www.tnstate.edu
The minimum age for seniors is 65 and they must be residents of the State. They pay$75.00 for the semester.

Texas
University of Houston
Central Campus
Financial Services
Houston, TX 77204-2160
Call: 713-743-1096
The minimum age for seniors is 65 , and they must be a State resident. The tuition is free and they can take courses for no credit.

University of North Texas
PO Box 13797
Denton, TX 76203
Call: 817-565-2165
The minimum age for seniors is 65 and they can take classes for no credit , tuition free.

Utah
Brigham Young University
BYU Evening Classes
122 Harman Bldg.
Provo, UT 84602
Call: 801- 378-2872
Web site: www.byu.edu
The minimum age is 55, and they must be a State resident. The tuition is $10.00 per class and they can take any course but not for credit.

Utah State University
Registrar
Logan, UT 84322-1600
Call: 797-1128 (Summer program for seniors)
!-800- 606-4878
Web site: www.usu.edu
The minimum age is 62 and a resident of the State. The tuition is $10.00 per class, and no credit is given.

Vermont
Castleton State College
Business Office
Castleton, VT 05735
Call: 1-800-639-8521
Web site: www.csc.vsc.edu
Any senior 62 or older receiving retirement benefits can take any course for credit for $78.00 for 3 credits.

Virginia
Clinch Valley College of the University of Virginia
Admissions
College Ave.
Wise, VA 24293
Call: 1-888-282-9324
Web site: www.clinch.edu
Seniors age 60 plus, residents of Virginia (if taxable income does not exceed $10,000) can take courses for free. Any senior can audit or take non-credit courses for free.

College of William and Mary
Registrars Office
PO Box 8795
Williamsburg , VA 23187
Call: 257-221-2800
Web site: www.wm.edu
Any senior 60 years or older and a State resident can audit classes for non credit free. If they want to take classes for credit, the tuition will be waived for them according to their income.

Washington
University of Washington
Access Program
5001 25th Ave., NE
Seattle, WA 98195
Call:206-543-2320
Web site: www.wsu.edu
The minimium age for seniors is 60 and you must be a state resident. You can audit 1 or 2 classes, space permitting. You pay only a small registration fee and a small technology fee.

West Virginia
West Virginia State College
PO Box 1000
Institute, WV 25112
Call: 304-766-3221
Web site:
www.wvsc.wvnet.edu.wvsc.html
Seniors aged 60 or older can audit classes for non-credit for free tuition, providing space is available in the class.

Wisconsin
University of Wisconsin-Milwaukee
PO Box 413
Milwaukee, WI 53201
Call: 414-229-4481
Web site: www.uwm.edu
Anyone is able to audit classes for reduced tuition. Call for more information.

Wyoming
University of Wyoming
PO Box 3314, Old Main 321
Laramie, WY 82071
Call:307-766-5160
The minimum age for seniors is 65, and you must be a state resident. Courses can be taken for credit or non-credit and the tuition is free. There is a fee for books, supplies and computers.

Nursing Home Complaints

In each state there's someone with the strange sounding title of 'Long-Term Care Ombudsman' to investigate your nursing home complaints. This person acts on behalf of nursing home residents, and mediates disputes between nursing homes and residents or their families. Ombudsman are also ready to help if you need information on the nursing homes in your state, or if you have a complaint about a particular nursing home.

Alabama .... (334) 242-5743
Alaska .... (907) 563-6393
Arizona .... (602) 542-4446
Arkansas .... (501) 682-2441
California .... (916) 323-6681
Colorado .... (303) 722-0300
Connecticut .... (860) 424-5200
Delaware .... (302) 453-3820
Dist. of Columbia .... (202) 662-4933
Florida .... (904) 488-6190
Georgia .... (404) 657-5319
Hawaii .... (808) 586-0100
Idaho .... (208) 334-2220
Iowa .... (515) 281-5187
Illinois .... (217) 785-3143
Indiana .... (317) 232-7134
Kansas .... (913) 296-6539
Kentucky .... (502) 564-6930
Louisiana .... (504) 342-7100
Maine .... (207) 621-1079

Maryland .... (410) 767-1074

Massachusetts .... (617) 222-7457

Michigan .... (517) 336-6753

Minnesota .... (612) 296-0382

Mississippi ....(601) 359-4929 (ext.7)

Missouri .... (573) 751-3082

Montana .... (406) 444-7785

Nebraska .... (402) 471-2307

Nevada .... (702) 486-3545

New Hampshire .... (603) 271-4375

New Jersey (in-state only) .... (800) 791-8820

New Mexico .... (505) 827-7663

New York .... (518) 474-0108

North Carolina .... (919) 733-3983

North Dakota .... (701) 328-8910

Ohio .... (614) 644-7922

Oklahoma .... (405) 521-6734

Oregon .... (503) 378-6533

Pennsylvania .... (717) 733-7247

Rhode Island .... (401) 277-2858

South Carolina .... (803) 253-6177

South Dakota .... (605) 773-3656

Tennessee .... (615) 741-2056

Texas .... (800) 252 -2412

Utah .... (801) 539-3924

Vermont .... (802) 748 -8721

Virginia .... (804) 644-2923

Washington .... (206) 839 -6810

West Virginia .... (304) 558 -3317

Wisconsin .... (608) 266-8944

Wyoming .... (307) 322-5553

Puerto Rico .... (797) 721-9225

Free Help From Your State Government

The state governments of 49 of the 50 states have a phone number you can call if you are having problems or need the assistance of a state agency. For example, let's say you have a housing problem or a consumer complaint and don't know where to turn. By calling the phone number listed for your state, you will be referred directly to the state agency in your area that can help you solve the problem you are having.

Alabama	334-242-8000
Alaska	907-465-2111
Arizona	602-542-4900
Arkansas	501-682-3000
California .... Northern	916-322-9900
Southern	213-620-3030
Colorado	303-866-5000
In Colorado, call	800-332-1716
Connecticut	860-566-2211
Delaware	302-856-5011
DE Only	800-273-9500
Florida	850-488-1234
Georgia	404-656-2000
Hawaii	808-586-0222
Outer Islands Only	800-468-4644
Idaho	208-334-2411
Illinois	217-782-2000
Indiana	317-233-0800
In Indiana call	800-457-8283
Iowa	515-281-5011
Kansas	785-296-0111
Kentucky	502-564-3130
Louisiana	504-342-6600

Maine 207-582-9500

Maryland ....While state information number no longer exists, if directory assistance cannot help, call the Governor's office at:...410-974-3901

Massachusetts 617-727-7030

In Massachusetts only call 800-392-6090

Michigan 517-373-1837

Minnesota 612-296-6013

Mississippi 601-359-1000

Missouri 573-751-2000

Montana 406-444-2511

Nebraska 402-471-2311

Nevada 702-687-5000

New Hampshire 603-271-1110

New Jersey.. 609-292-2121

New Mexico 505-827-4011

New York 518-474-2121

North Carolina 919-733-1110

North Dakota 701-328-2000

Ohio 614-466-2000

Oklahoma 405-521-2011

Oregon ....State information number no longer exists. Must know the specific state office.

Pennsylvania 717-787-2121

Rhode Island 401-277-2000

South Carolina 803-734-1000

South Dakota 605-773-3011

Tennessee 615-741-3011

Texas 512-463-4630

Utah 801-538-3000

Vermont 802-828-1110

Virginia 804-786-0000

Washington 360-753-5000

In Washington only call 800-321-2808

West Virginia 304-558-3456

Wisconsin 608-266-2211

Wyoming 307-777-5910

U.S. Government Hotlines

Administration on Aging 202-401-4541

Federal Information Center (for all the U.S.) 800-688-9889

Food and Drug Administration 301-827-4420

Health Care Fraud Hot Line 800-447-8477

IRS – US Department of the Treasury Information Line 800-829-1040

    Forms Line 800-829-3676

    Tele-Tax Line 800-829-4477

Lawyers' Fund for Client Protection 518-474-8438

    New York State Only 800-442-3863

Legal Services Corporation 202-336-8800

Medicare Hot Line 800-638-6833
    TTY-TTD 800-820-1202

Social Security Administration Hot Line 800-772-1213
    TTY 800-325-0778

US Department of Veterans Affairs 800-827-1000

US Department of Housing & Urban Development/
    Public Affairs Offiice 202-708-1420

Nationwide Helplines

Alliance for Aging Research	202-293-2856
Alzheimer's Association	800-272-3900
Alzheimer's Disease Education and Referral Center	800-438-4380
American Association of Retired Persons (AARP)	800-424-3410
American Assoc. of Homes & Services for the Aging	202-783-2242
For publications call	800-508-9442
American Cancer Society Response Hot Line	800-227-2345
American Council for the Blind	800-424-8666
American Diabetes Association	800-342-2383
American Diabetes Foundation	800-232-3472
American Heart Association	800-242-8721
American Institute For Cancer Research	800-843-8114
American Lung Association	800-586-4872
Arthritis Foundation Information Line	800-283-7800
Bell Atlantic LifeLine Service	800-555-5000
Brookdale Center on Aging	800-647-8233
Cancer Care	800-813-4673
Cancer Information Service.	800-4-CANCER
Eldercare Locator	800-677-1116
Equal Employment Opportunity Commission	800-669-4000
Family Violence Information	800-537-2237
Gray Panthers	800-280-5362
Grief Recovery Institute	800-445-4808
Help for Incontinent People	800-252-3337
Hill-Burton Hot Line (if you need help with hospital costs)	800-492-0359
Leukemia Society of America	800-955-4572
Lighthouse Center for Vision and Aging	800-334-5497
Medicare Hotline	800-638-6833
National AIDS Hot Line	800-342-2437
National Alliance of Breast Cancer Organizations	888-806-2226

National Alliance for the Mentally Ill 800-950-6264

National Breast Cancer Coalition 202-296-7477

National Cancer Institute 800-422-6237

National Caregiving Foundation 800-930-1357

National Center on Elder Abuse 202-682-2470

National Citizens' Coalition for Nursing Home Reform 202-332-2275

National Clearinghouse for Alcohol & Drug Info. 800-729-6686

National Committee to Preserve Social Security & Medicare .. 202-822-9459

National Council of Senior Citizens 301-578-8800

National Diabetes Information Clearinghouse 301-654-3327

National Digestive Disease Clearinghouse 301-654-3810

National Eye Care Project Helpline 800-222-3937

National Health Information Center 800-336-4797

National Hospice Organization 800-658-8898

National Institute on Aging 800-222-2225

National Institute on Deafness & Other Communication
    Disorders Information Clearinghouse 800-241-1044

National Institute of Mental Health 800-421-4211

National Institute of Neurological & Stroke Disorders 800-352-9424

National Insurance Consumer Helpline 800-942-4242

National Kidney & Urological Disease Clearinghouse 301-654-4415

Parkinson's Disease Foundation 800-457-6676

Y-ME National Breast Cancer Organization 800-221-2141

The Best Free Things In America

Over the past 19 years, the authors, Linda & Bob Kalian, have uncovered over 6,000 of the very best things that are totally free for the asking. With over 900,000 copies sold, the book has clearly become what the Gannett Newspapers has called...*'The nation's leading guide to free stuff.'*

This book has a carload of free things for you no matter what your interests...computers, health, money sports, cars, cooking, self-improvement, religion, business, gardening, travel, pets - to mention a few...plus a ton of free things for the kids to send away for. Makes the perfect gift.

***The Best Free Things In America* - $8.95 + s&h**

Getting Your Book Published
by ROBERT W. BLY

"To see farther than your peers, you must stand on the shoulders of a giant."

Robert W. Bly is without a doubt one of America's foremost 'giants' when it comes to writing books and getting them published. Over the past 15 years he has written an average of 3 books a year and sold an incredible 95% of them to major New York publishing houses. Bly now shares his 'real world' experiences in this new important book, *Getting Your Book Published...Inside Secrets of A Successful Author.* In a thorough yet interesting style, Bly leads you through each of the essential steps from generating winning book ideas to finally selling the book to a publisher. Includes his actual book proposal and contract with his comments), listings of literary agents, publishers, ghost writers and much more. This book is an absolute must if you've ever dreamed of writing a book and getting it published.

GETTING YOUR BOOK PUBLISHED - $14.95 + s&h

Please add $2.00 shipping & handling for the first book and $1.00 for each additional book ordered.
Send all orders to:
ROBLIN PRESS   DEPT BSR-99   PO BOX 125   HARTSDALE, NY 10530